ASPECTS OF BARNSLEY
IV

Aspects of BARNSLEY

Discovering Local History – IV

Edited by
Brian Elliott

Wharncliffe Publishing Limited

First Published in 1996 by
Wharncliffe Publishing Limited

Copyright © Wharncliffe Publishing Limited 1996

For up-to-date information on other titles produced under the
Wharncliffe imprint, please telephone or write to:

>   **Wharncliffe Publishing Limited**
>   **FREEPOST**
>   **47 Church Street**
>   **Barnsley**
>   **South Yorkshire S70 2BR**
>   **Telephone (24 hours): 01226 - 734555**

ISBN: 1-871647-27-4

A CIP catalogue record of this book is available from the
British Library

Cover photograph: 'Wentworth Castle', from an
18th Century engraving

Printed in Great Britain by Redwood Books, Trowbridge,
Wiltshire

CONTENTS

INTRODUCTION

by Brian Elliott

There is something for everyone in the fourth volume of *Aspects of Barnsley* and it is very pleasing to welcome so many new contributors. This year the series has an international dimension with Philip Hansen and Geoffrey Tweedale's remarkable story - based on the surviving letters of Benjamin Illingworth - who, from humble beginnings in the hamlet of Snowdenhill in rural Hunshelf - became one of the most successful immigrants to nineteenth century America. Robert Illingworth, Benjamin's father, earned a hard living as a farm-hand and shepherd, growing a few crops around his small cottage. Sam Sykes's substantial study, 'Shepherds, Sheep and Gentlemen', provides us with a detailed insight into early nineteenth century moorland farming; and his authoritative research serves as an important contribution towards the recognition of a rare local breed of sheep, appropriately known as *Penistones*.

No *Aspects of Barnsley* would be complete without some reference to mining. The employment of children in mines was widespread during the early Victorian period as was demonstrated at the Husker Pit, Silkstone in July, 1838 when 26 boys and and girls aged between 6 and 16 were killed in a terrible disaster that not only highlighted dreadful working conditions but also contributed to a wider moral debate. The subsequent Children's Employment Commission, as is shown in a study by Melvyn and Joan Jones, involved considerable gathering of first-hand evidence from the Barnsley area. Geoffrey Hall's interest in mining is reflected in his tribute to Joseph Beaumont whose experience as a steward involved him in several notable pit disasters, paying the ultimate price at Pilley in 1847.

The construction of canal and railway was crucial to the economic development of coal mining regions. Roger Glister's article on the Barnsley Canal is an appropriate overview of the translation of an idea into a great engineering achievement. Trevor Lodge's detailed study of the South Yorkshire branch of the Midland Railway shows very clearly how an established company could respond to the immense potential of coalfield traffic and accordingly adapt and develop its resources. Harold Taylor's analysis of Barnsley in the 1860s provides us with an insight into the significant events - within their social and economic context - that culminated in the achievement of Borough status in 1869. Something of the pervading literary atmosphere of the period is captured by John Goodchild in his essay on local historian Joseph Wilkinson whilst Kate Taylor's interest in theatrical history is reflected in the first authoritative study of Barnsley's Wellington Street theatre. Our ancestors living in the1850s and 1860s also witnessed the beginnings of commercial photography, the subject of Brian Elliott's contribution.

Oral history and personal recollection has been a popular part of previous *Aspects* volumes. This year Phyllis Crossland provides us with a fascinating account - based on reminiscences of local people - of life in service at the largest country house in our area: Wentworth Castle. Joan Hartley's account of Mapplewell Bethel is based on the memories of previous congregations and, like Phyllis, her research has uncovered some excellent illustrations. Eileen Umpleby's evocative recollection of her grandmother's shop serves as a reminder of the lost world of the small 'corner' shop.

A lost Barnsley 'character expert' is the entertaining subject of Dr Jim Walker's contribution whilst Gerald Alliott explores the connection between a well-known Barnsley family and the construction of what was to become a national symbol of Britain: Big Ben.

The issue of this, the fourth volume, of *Aspects of Barnsley* means that over 60 articles on our town and district have been published by Wharncliffe Books Ltd. A fifth Barnsley volume has already been commissioned and the tremendous success of *Aspects of Rotherham* (1995) has resulted in a second and no doubt further volumes for that town. The Aspects Series will expand so as to include Doncaster, Sheffield and Leeds in 1997/98.

Researching and writing local history is an enjoyable but time-consuming activity especially when deadlines have to be met but my frequent requests have been answered by very enthusiastic and dedicated writers. The production of local books of such quality and value is a remarkable achievement for such a small publication team. My sincere thanks are therefore due to Alan Twiddle, Barbara Bramall, with grateful support from Managing Director Timothy Hewitt and all at Customer Care and Yorkshire Web. Barnsley Archives and Local Studies Library and John Goodchild's Local Study Centre continue to offer an excellent service for local history researchers; we are very fortunate at having their help.

Anyone interested in making a contribution to *Aspects of Barnsley 5* should, in the first instance, contact Brian Elliott c/o **Wharncliffe Publishing (Book Division) Limited, 47 Church Street, Barnsley S70 2AS** enclosing a brief description of the proposed work.

1. LIFE IN SERVICE AT WENTWORTH CASTLE

Phyllis Crossland

BARNSLEY'S NORTHERN COLLEGE at Stainborough is well-known, not only in the Barnsley area but also in the country at large, as a reputable establishment of Adult Education. Most of today's students who pass through the college are no doubt acquainted with the history of the building, generally known as *Wentworth Castle*, but what do they know of the people who lived and worked there in days gone by?

Looking today at the vast expanse of Wentworth Castle's ornate east wing and the splendid south front, the present college students may wonder perhaps about the many men and women who worked inside those walls before them and how different was the work they did. What kind of lives did they lead? And who were those people who looked after the gardens, the farm, the woodlands, and reared the pheasants for the annual shoots? Thanks to the existing records and to the memories of today's elderly people who had connections with Wentworth Castle, we are able to find answers to some of these questions.

During the nineteenth century the 'Upstairs Downstairs' way of life certainly prevailed at the stately mansion. In 1861 master of the house was Frederick Vernon-Wentworth, landed proprietor. The name of Vernon had been added to that of Wentworth after Harriet, sister to an Earl of Strafford, had married Harry Vernon in 1743. Frederick was Harriet's grandson. He had been born in Staffordshire, not unusual since the family had properties in places other than Stainborough. His wife, formerly Lady Augusta Bruce, had been born in Hamburg, but was noted in the record as a British subject. Only one daughter, Louisa, was living with them at that time, her place of birth being Middlesex. To cater for the needs of these three people and keep the house running to the high standard required was a substantial work force of servants. At their head was the housekeeper, 50 year old Amelia Kohler, a widow from Hamburg. Ann Yates, aged 35, was the cook from Kidderminster, Worcestershire. Two ladies' maids were Jane Wayland, 31, and

Elizabeth Ellis, 23. Jane had been born in Somerset and Elizabeth in Cornwall. Three housemaids were employed - Mary Beechill, a 24 year old widow from Braithwell, Yorkshire, Mary Goodwin, 38, born in Essex, and Mary Haveron, 27, born in Ireland. Fanny Phillips, 35, born in Essex, was the laundress. The two unmarried footmen were Edward Haveron, 27, and William Mabe, 24, born in Scarborough. Edward's birthplace was recorded as Scotland which would rule out the idea that he was the housemaid Mary's twin brother, unless a mistake was made by the census taker. The coachman in 1861 was William Mandry, 40 years old and married. Instead of his place of birth being recorded, the words 'refused information' are listed. We may ask what secrets did this coachman keep that he should not disclose his place of origin? Henry Fox, a 17 year old groom, was Middlesex born.

In addition to workers who actually lived in the big house there were many others living in houses, lodges, and cottages on the estate. Some of these were George Surtees, the Tankersley born land agent who occupied Garden House, and John Berry, farm agent living at Park Lodge. His place of birth was Linlithgowshire in Scotland. At Lowe Lodge were the Firth family who worked as agricultural labourers. Broom Royd Lodge was occupied by Owen Haveron, 54, his wife Elizabeth and daughter Hellen. He was a game watcher, born in Ireland. It is likely that he was father to the housemaid Mary and footman Edward. Another game watcher was Thomas Child, 34, born at Altofts, who lived in the Keepers House with his 7 year old daughter Jane.

It is obvious from the mid-nineteenth century records that the Vernon-Wentworths recruited their staff from places far afield from Stainborough. People born locally are not seen to have been employed. In fact, I have been told by 88 year old Mrs Whittaker, a Barnsley lady who worked on the Wentworth Castle farm, that in her young days tenants on the estate were not employed inside the house. They were only allowed to work on the farm, in the gardens, or at other outdoor work. The fact that some servants came from Scotland is probably due to the Vernon-Wentworths having an estate there called *Dall House* (Figure 1), at which they sometimes stayed, particularly during the grouse-shooting season.

It is not difficult to imagine what the work of all these servants involved in those days before the benefits of electricity. Cooking and washing for large numbers, cleaning vast areas of floors on one's hands and knees, carrying coal and water up long flights of stairs were all part of the daily round. Work on the farm meant long hours

Figure 1. Dall House, the Scottish residence of the Vernon-Wentworth family
Norah Wade

of heavy labour and exposure to cold when out in the fields in wintertime with horses. We are not to know whether these servants were contented with their lot at that time, or even if they lived peaceably together. In that age of wide class divisions between master and servant, and between the so-called higher and lower servants, men and women were supposed to know their place in the scheme of things and adhere to that place. For some young girls life in domestic service seemed preferable to work in a factory while those from poor families would probably be better fed at Wentworth Castle than in their own homes.

The 1871 census records for Wentworth Castle show an increase in the number of household servants from ten years previously, probably due to an increase in family members. Frederick Vernon-Wentworth, still head of the family, had been widowed during the previous decade but his son Thomas and daughter-in-law Lady Harriet were now in residence too. Also living in the house were their four children, Harriet, 9, Bruce, 8, Mary 6, and Frederick, 4. All the children except Mary had been born in Scotland while her place of birth was Silkstone. The staff now included two unmarried governesses - Jane Coleby, 36, born in Norfolk, and Louise Henry, 20, from France. Four young garden labourers were listed as Wilson

Tomlinson, 21, born at Worksop, William Coulson, 21, from Hessle, Thomas Leake, 26, from Wakefield, and Tom Leech, 20, born at Silkstone. The housekeeper was 45 years old Eliza Milton, an Exeter born woman. Ann Griffiths, a 47 year old widow from Ireland, served as cook. It would seem that the mistress, Lady Harriet Vernon-Wentworth, followed the fashion of many high society ladies by engaging a French lady's maid for herself as well as a French governess for her children. Her personal maid, born in France, was a 33 year old spinster, Eugénie Dubois. The school room maid, Mathilde Kriete, 18, came from Hanover. Three housemaids, all unmarried, were Anne Morris, 41, from Caernarvonshire, Sarah Collins, 21, born at Deptford, and Fanny Sellers, 20 from Wath. Jane Dobdie, the 19 year old kitchenmaid, was Scottish born, as was John Fraser, the butler, aged 55. A married couple, Charles and Elizabeth Sampson, served as cowman and dairywoman. Charles, 39, was from Pontefract and his wife, 36, from Lincolnshire. Samuel Harrison, the 22 year old groom, was from Lincolnshire too. John Wilkinson, 21, listed as a helper, was born at Worsbrough. Occupying dwellings outside the big house were members of outdoor staff. James Batley, 50, a gardener with his son George, 22, assistant gardener lived in Garden House. George Borthwick, 40, the head

Figure 2. Gamekeeper's Cottage in the park
Bertha Wigfield

gamekeeper was Scottish born and occupied a house in the park (Figure 2). Another gamekeeper named Joseph Silverwood, 28, lived at a lodge in the park.

We can see that a complete change of staff had taken place during the decade prior to 1871. This could have been due to sickness, marriage, servants growing too old to perform the duties expected of them, or perhaps obtaining better situations.

Similarly, a whole new lot of names is recorded in the census record ten year later. The 1881 list of Wentworth Castle's inhabitants is:

Name	Age	Status	Place of Birth
F C Vernon Wentworth	49	Landowner, Magistrate	London
Harriet	47		London
Harriet Vernon Wentworth	19	Young lady	Scotland
Bruce C V Wentworth	18	Scholar	Scotland
Mary J V Wentworth	16	Scholar	Silkstone
Muriel H V Wentworth	9	Scholar	Silkstone
William Dewar	34	Private Tutor	Scotland
Margaret Smith	32	1st Housemaid	Scotland
Fanny Unwin	20	2nd Housemaid	Derbyshire
Emma Bird	20	3rd Housemaid	Northampton
Caroline Smith	16	4th Housemaid	Yorks, Kippax
Agusta Riems	40	Cook	Belgium
Thomas Pennington	20	Footman	Yorks. Brough
Arthur Pulsford	22	Footman	Dorset, Lyme Regis
Lucy Cooper	18	Nursery maid	Rotherham
Mary Cooke	25	Kitchen maid	Northants
Georgina Parker	19	Scullery maid	Buckinghamshire
Charles Pilmer	19	Footman	Ferrybridge
Dina Ogley	57	Head nurse	Herts
Rosette Chevalier	37	Lady's maid	Switzerland
Emily Heggins	17	Lady's maid	Scotland
Charlotte Symonds	26	Head laundry maid	Alford, Lincs
Sarah Slater	27	2nd Laundry maid	Staffordshire
Elizabeth Marshall	20	3rd Laundry maid	Wiltshire
John Raithby	48	Coachman	Lincolnshire
Harry Raithby	26	Groom	Yorks, Hall
Hannah Raithby	45	Domestic Servant	Lincolnshire

Again the staff have been recruited from distant parts of Britain and from countries abroad.

In 1891 the Vernon-Wentworths were evidently staying at one of their other residences when the census was taken as they are not recorded at Wentworth Castle. The only servants listed at the big house at that time were Hannah Seymour, 39, housekeeper, Jane Parker, 33, laundrymaid, Emma Lane, 16, laundrymaid, Mary Kister 39, Ann Rogers 21, Dinah Fisher 19, housemaids. John Baker, 40, the butler, was named as a Boarder rather than a servant, as were George Woodgate 23, footman, and Edgar Balls, 23, oddman. No doubt most of the regular servants accompanied the family to their new destination. With the family elsewhere we may be tempted to imagine that these servants remaining at Stainborough had an easy time. This was probably not the case since it was the custom for a huge 'spring clean' to take place at such times. Indeed, one reason for the family's changing residences was to enable cleaning to be done without their having to be present to witness such upheaval. Floors without carpets, windows without curtains, ladders propped against walls being washed, and chimneys being swept were sights the mistress would not wish to see. It was the housekeeper's responsibility to ensure that the cleaning operations were carried out and everything returned to comfortable order before the family's return.

As in most large gentlemen's residences the same way of life both 'upstairs' and 'downstairs' continued at Stainborough from the nineteenth century until well into the twentieth. A Barnsley lady, Mrs Annie Whittaker was born on the Wentworth Estate in 1907 and spent all her early life there. At 88 she has clear memories of people and events when she was young:

> When I was about ten I worked in the Wilderness with Kathy Symonds during the holidays. She was the gamekeeper's daughter. The head gardener was Mr Thornton. We picked pods from the rhododendrons and azaleas and packed them round the bottom. If it was raining we had to work in the gardens, thinning the grapes and washing the plant pots. I always got that job because he said they were clean if I did them. We did potato-picking and potato-setting. Your mother had to make you a harding apron to tie over your clothes. They were made from empty flour sacks which she'd washed. When you planted the potatoes you put one in at your heel and one at your toe all the way along. We took our own lunch and ate it in the deer sheds. They had deer in the park then and Highland cattle (Figure 3).

Annie Whittaker was happy living on the Wentworth Estate in spite of having the cane a couple of times at school. One occasion was the outcome of a visit to a certain crab-apple tree with her friend Kathy Symonds and two other girls. Kathy's father, the gamekeeper, did not condone their behaviour and reported it to the schoolmaster who gave them all a caning. 'After that my father gave me a good hiding as well when I got home,' said Annie. So much for discipline in those days. The other caning resulted from Captain Wentworth's visiting

Figure 3. Highland Cattle can be seen in this fine photograph of Wentworth Castle by Warner Gothard c1895 *Elliott Collection*

the school to report the girls had been singing too near the front of his house. 'We'd been to the choir practice and were just doing a bit more singing on the way back. We were a long way from the house really,' Annie insisted. It appeared that though these misdemeanours had occurred out of school it was left to the schoolmaster to mete out punishment.

During the 1920s there was still a large number of workers employed at Wentworth Castle, the housekeeper being Mrs Smithson. Mr Walton was the butcher. All their own meat was killed on the premises. Ellen, the head laundry- maid was assisted by Edith and Phyllis Harper, two sisters, and other young workers. When the laundry was not in use brewing could take place as the water pipes between laundry and cellar had to suffice for both brewing and laundry work. There was no wringing-machine in the laundry in 1917. Mrs Whittaker remembered that Eric Walton's help had to be enlisted for the mangling process though Eric's job was actually in the blacksmith's shop. He filled a big wooden tub with pieces of iron and pulled it over the sheets to press out the water. The Castle had its own dairy in charge of Mr Crapper. Mr Senior was head joiner and Mr Bower the master mason. 'There'd been a Bower on the

Wentworth Estate since the Earl of Strafford's time', said Mrs Whittaker. One of the landworkers was Mr Cotterill whose son was a footman. Two more sons were also employed on the estate. The butler at that time was Mr Chambers and the chauffeur Mr Hepworth. One of the three housemaids, Eva Holmes, eventually became Annie Whittaker's sister-in-law. Eva's many duties included washing the stone stairs and burnishing all the fireplaces.

Annie reckoned that in her young days the household staff at Stainborough had an easier time than some who were in service at other places. This was because Captain Bruce Vernon-Wentworth (Figure 4) was the only family member living there. He remained a bachelor throughout his long life. As there was no lady of the house he did not give large dinner parties which would have involved more work for his servants. Though Annie lived on the Wentworth Estate she wasn't employed inside the house but worked in service at a similar residence in Silkstone.

Figure 4.   Captain BC Vernon - Wentworth, last of the family to own Wentworth Castle

Her wages at Noblethorpe were 2/6d (12.5p) a week. She obtained another post after a while in Kensington Road, Barnsley, working for a couple named Gregory. Her wages there were ten shillings (50p) a week. She was well-treated and stayed with them until her marriage in 1930. Annie's husband was a plumber working for Rushforth's in Barnsley. He put in the bathrooms at Wentworth Castle. Before then the maids had to take water upstairs to the bedrooms for hip-baths. They did not receive electricity and proper plumbing until 1930.

Annie remembers Captain Bruce Wentworth (Figure 5) as a shy sort of man who kept out of the way of his workers. This opinion was endorsed by Mr Edwin Price of Hood Green, whose maternal grandfather, Edwin Bower, had been a master mason on the estate following the tradition of many generations of that family before him (Figure 6).

Figure 5.   Captain Bruce Vernon-Wentworth, in later life *Edwin Price*

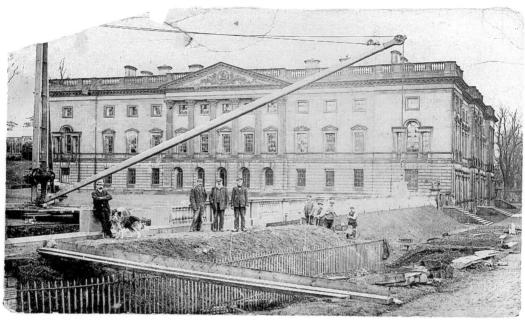

Figure 6. Erecting Pallisade around the lawn at the South front, photographed by Lamb in about 1905. Edwin Bower (Edwin Price's grandfather) is the centre figure of the three men. He was master mason. On the right is his son who worked with him but was killed in 1916 *Edwin Price*

According to Edwin, born in 1923, Captain Wentworth's two main interests were his rhododendrons and his pheasants. He didn't concern himself much with his estate workers. The Estate, however, was run like a business, the agent being Mr Petch. During the 1930s all the tradesmen at the Castle worked on Shed Lane. John Denton and Dick Taylor were in the saw mills, while across the path was the blacksmith's shop. Eric Walton took over as blacksmith after Jimmy Broadhead died. Eric had been his striker and when he got the blacksmith's job Edwin Price, then about fifteen, acted as Eric's striker. He says:

We shoed the horses and repaired the metal fence around Stainborough Park. There were deer in the park at that time. There were iron gates at the bottom, near the pub, also at Steeple Lodge and at the top of Hood Green. So the park was actually locked up. All the keys were brass and not everybody had one. If you did have a key you could consider yourself quite high up the ladder.

The farm was always a busy place. The bailiff was Jimmy Dawson, Jack Stagg from Norfolk was a horseman, and Robbie Dennis in charge of the cows. At pheasant shooting times a beast was killed in the farmyard to supply the extra meat required. A butcher called Carr came to Stainborough from Birdwell to do the slaughtering; at other times sheep were killed by Herbert Walton, a worker on the estate. Albert Baines, an old retired land worker, spent all his days chopping sticks in the old carriage-house. The farm had its own mill for grinding corn. There was always plenty of work to be done with the horses, cows and sheep to attend to and crops to be grown. Horses were used for the field work and the cows milked by hand.

Speaking of the head gardener, Edwin says:

> *Mr Thornton was tall and wore a bowler hat. Every morning he was out early on Haybarn Road and when it was 7.30 prompt he'd pop his head into the shed where the gardeners were sitting together talking. He would say quickly, 'Good morning, good morning', and that was the signal for the gardeners to get up and start work. Then he'd walk into the saddle shed to get the farm workers going by saying the same thing to them. After that he would visit the blacksmiths and stonemasons. Only when he saw everybody working did he go into his own place, perhaps to have a cup of tea. The workers always knew to get moving when he appeared. They were all anxious to keep their jobs even though they weren't very well paid.*

Before Edwin Price's time an incident had happened which was told to him later. It concerned a former bailiff by name of Just. Apparently Robbie Dennis the cowman was in the yard one day when he heard a shot. He went up the cornchamber steps from where he could look down onto Mr Just's garden. He saw that the bailiff had just shot a pheasant. This was reckoned to be a criminal offence. Robbie Dennis reported the incident to Mr Petch the estate agent and the bailiff was sacked next day.

There were many gamekeepers employed on the estate during the 1930s In the absence of telephones it was their custom to meet together at certain pre-arranged times at the Cinder Bridge in order to discuss work and exchange news. Since their work involved covering a wide area of land, this form of communication seemed appropriate.

As a lad one of Edwin's jobs was to carry coal into the laundry. He remembers:

There were great big copper pots six feet across with fires underneath. I had to light the fires for boiling the clothes. The sinks against the windows were all made of wood. There were eight or ten sinks. The ironing was done up above the garages. There were about twenty irons on a special stove for heating them. When the clothes were finished they were put into various baskets for taking back to the house. The head laundry-maid, Eleanor, was a tall, elegant woman with white hair. She'd given all her life to the service of Captain Wentworth and was one of those who always went to Scotland with him.

Captain Wentworth always went to *Dall House*, his Scottish estate, in August for the grouse-shooting, taking with him part of the household staff. Later in the year he returned to Stainborough for the pheasant-shooting. That was a time of great activity in the house. All the silver had to be cleaned in advance in preparation for the visiting gentry. On arrival these gentlemen would park their cars in front of the Castle and enter through the Hall, which Edwin described as 'very flash'. He says:

No one else was allowed to walk along the front of the house. The main hall was used only when the shoots took place. The gentry brought their own loaders with them; these were usually their head-gamekeepers. While the gentry went in at the front door the gamekeepers went in at the back. That's how it was. The keepers had a meal down in the servants' hall. Alf Senior the chief joiner helped in the servants' hall during this period because there was a lot of extra washing-up - plates piled a yard high. They got a good meal though and plenty of beer. It gave the game-keepers a good chance to talk together. One of the regular guests at the shoots was Lord Wharncliffe from nearby Wortley Hall who brought his head keeper, a man called Maidment, and Jimmy Lane, a loader. Mr Spencer-Stanhope from Cannon Hall, Cawthorne, was usually one of the shooters too. He was quite a small man, only 5ft2in. or 5ft3in. in height. Other gentlemen came from further afield and were accommodated at the Castle for the duration of the shooting which was a few weeks.

Beaters were recruited from outside the estate, often unemployed men from Gilroyd. On being engaged they were given tickets from the keepers. Besides being paid a few shillings the beaters received, on production of their tickets, a 'beater's lunch'. This was two slices of bread about an inch thick with plenty of meat between and wrapped in newspaper.

During the 1930s Captain Wentworth owned four vehicles. One was a black American *Packard* - enormous by English standards. There was a Fiat which did not have metal wheels but wooden spokes. It carried a spare rim and tyre on the back. If it punctured they changed the rim, not the tyre. Another vehicle was a sort of minibus, a very early *Austin* with a brass radiator in which you could see your face, and a big starting handle. This vehicle had to be run downhill to start it because if it was cranked it kicked. There was space for eight men inside, four at each side sitting facing each other. Edwin Price reckoned this must have been one of the earliest vehicles registered in Barnsley because the number was HE 5,6 or 7. He couldn't exactly recall which, but it was one of them. Captain Wentworth's other car was a little, canvas-topped *Landseer* which he used for running about in. His chauffeur had always to get it out and warm it up for him. All the cars were jacked up onto wooden blocks when not in use. They were as clean underneath as they were on top. The chauffeur, Harold Hepworth, was able to keep them in immaculate condition because that was his only job.

An enormous amount of coal was consumed at the Castle in those days. This was obtained from Wentworth Silkstone Colliery which was owned by the Vernon-Wentworths. The colliery ran tubs to a tip in Lowe Wood and the coal was fetched from there by two men, Johnnie Cotterill and Jack Stagg. They each had a cart with two horses. Coal was tipped into the carts then pulled up a rough, dirty track to the Castle to be tipped in a special place near the porter's hall. The men did this job day after day, most of their time being spent in fetching coal. Coal for the house had to be hand-picked. According to Edwin:

> *They wouldn't have any sort in there. It had to be all lumps. For the gardens anything would do. If you were an estate worker you got a free load of coal when you wanted it. You could have logs brought besides. The workers didn't get big wages but they had these little perks. They didn't pay much rent at all. My father was the only one I remember who paid enough to warrant him going to the rent dinners like the farmers. There were two dinners a year at the Strafford Arms. At the summer one they had beef and at Christmas it was pheasant.*

Mrs Nellie Dawson, a Hood Green lady (b 1916), lived at Lundwood during her early life. On leaving school she applied for a post as laundrymaid at Wentworth Castle, but soon discovered that her friend Margaret had been there before her and got the job. Consequently she went to work as a maid at Dodworth Hall.

Nellie came to live at Stainborough when she married her first husband, Cecil Webb. He was a young gamekeeper on the Wentworth Estate and had worked there since leaving school (Figure 7). They had a cottage at the bottom of the park. She remembers what a lot of work was involved to provide enough pheasants for the

Figure 7. Gamekeepers at Wentworth Castle in 1938. Cecil Webb is on the back row, extreme right *Nellie Dawson*

Figure 8.(*Above*) Gamekeepers with sitting hens, tiers of nest boxes in the background *Nellie Dawson*

Figure 9.(*Right*) Pheasant chicks in coops, but in the woods *Nellie Dawson*

winter shoots. In spring the gamekeepers visited farms over a wide area to buy broody hens for sitting on the pheasant eggs. They paid about 3/6d (17.5p) each hen. These birds were kept in tiers of nesting boxes, thirteen pheasant eggs to each box (Figure 8). They were tethered to the boxes, only being allowed out to feed and drink. While they were out the keeper would clean the boxes. After the pheasant chicks were hatched the hens were sold and the young birds put into coops (Figure 9). These were gradually moved nearer to the woods and the birds released into the trees. At this stage the keeper would whistle when he took their feed and they would all come flying down out of the trees to settle on the ground to eat. A barrel of water was kept for them in the field. When shooting eventually took place, spaniel dogs were employed to retrieve the dead birds from where they had fallen (Figure 10).

The gamekeepers were encouraged to produce as much game as possible to ensure good shoots. It was told to my husband, Charles Crossland, that one year the Captain was displeased because the number fell rather short of what he expected. He was reported as saying that if there weren't a thousand brace at the following year's first shoot, all the gamekeepers would be sacked. Needless to say, the required number was forthcoming. The keepers had always to be on the look-out for foxes and anything else which might harm the pheasants. They were paid for shooting predators when they produced the tails as proof, the rate being sixpence for a foxtail, threepence for a cat's and a penny for a rat's. The head gamekeeper

Figure 10. Spaniels retrieving pheasants after a shoot *Nellie Dawson*

Figure 11. Collecting pheasants' eggs. The young man is Cecil Webb, c1930
Nellie Dawson

during the late 'thirties' was Mr Spinks.

Cecil Webb (Figure 11) enjoyed his work as a gamekeeper but was called up when the Second World War broke out and was killed in Belgium. His widow Nellie was allowed to stay on at the cottage rent free and was given free coal and milk from the farm for her young son Peter.

Nellie Dawson speaks well of Captain Wentworth:

He was always kind to me. He was a gentleman - very tall, very thin, but never dressed smart.

Recounting her first impressions of him she tells how she actually mistook him for a tramp:

I hadn't been married long and went out one afternoon to gather sticks. As I was coming back to the cottage I saw this shabbily dressed man a bit further on. I was too scared to meet him so turned back and went home a longer way round, got inside and locked the door. When Cecil came home he asked what I was doing with the door locked so I explained about being scared of the strange man. I was very surprised to be told, 'Well, that's the man who gives you your daily bread'.

Cecil's wages were '3-7s-6d (£3.37½p) a fortnight with free house and coal.

Nellie thought their employer was very well respected. He was interested in the Stainborough cricket team and had been a good batsman himself in younger days. He also took interest in the school which, like the church, had been built by the Wentworths. At Whitsuntide he gave a party for the children when there would be games and dancing. Captain Wentworth thought a lot about his rhododendrons. He opened the grounds to the public on Whitsunday and Whitmonday when people came from far and wide to admire the flowers. Nellie sometimes worked amongst the rhododendrons.

Mrs Bertha Wigfield of Darton tells how her late husband's family had strong connections with Wentworth Castle. Her father-in-law, Arthur Wigfield, was a shepherd on the estate in the early years of the twentieth century. He married Emily, one of the laundrymaids who came to the Castle from an orphanage (Figure 12). Arthur and Emily had three sons and a daughter and lived in a small cottage in

the middle of the park. All the sons were employed on the estate. Les, who was Bertha's late husband, started work as a trainee gamekeeper but later moved to a similar job at Bretton Hall. From there he went to Harewood House in the employ of Lord Harewood and the Princess Royal. During shoots he served as personal loader to Lord Harewood. When war began Les joined the Military Police. Arthur's and Emily's second son, Tommy, spent all his working life on the estate farm. His loyal service was recognised when he was eventually made farm bailiff. He held this responsible position until Wentworth Castle became a college. On retirement he was allowed to live rent-free in an estate cottage until he died about two years ago, aged eighty-one. His younger brother, Harry worked in the Castle gardens from leaving school until he was called up for the war and served in a

Figure 12. Arthur and Emily Wigfield with their son, Les. They all worked at Wentworth Castle - Arthur as a shepherd, Emily in the laundry, and Les as a gamekeeper, c1912-13 *Bertha Wigfield*

Scottish regiment. Doris, the daughter, never worked at the Castle but went into service elsewhere.

Mr Roy Beet of Hoyland Common says his wife was a niece of Thomas Wigfield. He was known as 'Tommy' to everyone and a popular character in the area. At one time he had lived on Stainborough's Ratten Row. Roy says:

It was known locally as Rat Row and was comprised of two rows of small terraced houses, twelve in one row and six in the other. The houses were situated on the small back road from the top of Hood Green to Cranemoor but were pulled down many years ago.

When speaking of the Wigfield family, Roy thought that Emily, the former laundry-maid, lived to be quite old. She was not a very big woman but was a wiry sort of person with plenty of energy.

Another laundry-maid, Harriet Ellen Piper (Figure 13), began work at the Castle in 1909 at the age of nineteen and stayed there six years until she married. Her daughter, Mrs Gibbs of Dodworth, remembers her speaking of that time. She says:

Figure 13. Harriet Piper (in her long white apron), laundry maid. This photograph was taken when she worked at Keswick, before coming to Wentworth Castle. Notice the laundry basket *Mrs Gibbs*

There were twenty-four members of the indoor staff (Figure 14). Work in the laundry was very hard, particularly during shoot weeks

Figure 14. Maids and men in the Sunday best c1914. Ellena, the long-serving head laundrymaid is the elderly lady at the back (far left) of the group. Olive Bower (Centre, backrow) was kitchen maid at the time of the photo and later became cook at Noblethorpe Hall, Silkstone *Mrs Gibbs*

Figure 15. The Castle Folly *Bertha Wigfield*

because then they had the gentry's clothes to deal with as well. The shooters would often return wet - through, when their garments would be brought to the laundry to be cleaned and dried.

Despite the hard work, however, Harriet had told her daughter that it was a good life. The maids had usually to be indoors by half-past eight but were sometimes allowed to go to dances in the village. This meant they were out later of course and permission had first to be obtained from the housekeeper on these occasions. Harriet was one of the household staff who went up to Scotland each year for the grouse-shooting.

One of her recollections regarding Stainborough concerned the Folly (Figure 15) in the grounds. There were rooms in the Folly in her day where the ladies - Captain Wentworth's sisters - would sometimes sit to do their needlework. They would also take afternoon tea in there, being waited on by the butler and housemaids.

Mrs Norah Wade (née Manterfield) of Silkstone Common, was a member of the household staff during the 1930s, starting work at the age of fourteen. After being interviewed by Mrs White, the housekeeper, whom she described as 'a very nice person', Norah was appointed to the post of second cook. Besides herself and the head cook a scullery-maid was employed in the kitchen to prepare vegetables, wash-up and help generally. All the cooking was done on two enormous black, old fashioned ranges which consumed huge quantities of coal and needed constant stoking up. The kitchen staff provided most of the food needed for people in the Castle, their hardest work being at shooting times. 'Everything was home-made,' said Norah.

> *We baked all our own bread and pickled our own eggs from the farm. When they had shoots we roasted great joints of beef. We had to be up at half-past five to make up sandwiches for the beaters' lunches. We did manage a bit of rest in the afternoons but were busy again for dinner at eight o'clock. It was easier when Captain Wentworth was on his own.*

All the servants were well fed. They had a cooked meal at one o'clock and another in the evening. There was always plenty of food, with a jug of beer and glasses placed on the table in the servants' hall. The kitchen workers, however, did not eat in the servants' hall but stayed in the kitchen for meals. Norah's uniform was a blue dress with white cap and apron. Unlike the housemaids, the kitchen staff did not have to change for afternoons. Recalling the times when she travelled up to Perthshire with the Captain and other staff, she says:

> *We went about the beginning of May for the deer-stalking and then the grouse-shooting. We had to be up very early to make fresh scones for breakfast. The coal we used had to be sent up from the Strafford Colliery because what fuel there was up there wouldn't get the ovens hot.*

When the Stainborough party returned from Scotland in October, Norah was given four days holiday before the pheasant shooting began. This gave a brief respite before the onset of extra work that the visiting gentry would occasion. She also had a few days free before going to Scotland. Other off-duty time was a half-day each week and three weeks' holiday in the year. The servants during her time were very well treated. On Sundays they went to Stainborough Church where they had their own special pews. Captain Wentworth had his own pew too, which was up in the gallery.

Norah remembers an old man in his seventies working at the Castle. His name was Edgar. Generally known as the hall-boy, his duties included sweeping up, fetching coal, laying tables in the servants' hall and helping generally. He had worked on the place since boyhood and eventually died there.

The late Mrs Mary Hill of Penistone recorded her experiences as a domestic maid at Wentworth Castle for her history group's publication, *Times Remembered*. As a fifteen year-old she applied for a position as housemaid but, as that post was already filled, was offered a place as laundry-maid, on the understanding that if a housemaid's post became vacant she would be considered for it. At that time during the thirties there were only two laundry workers. Mary's superior was Miss Taylor, quite an elderly person with white hair which she wore in a bun at the top of her head. It seems certain that she was the Eleanor already mentioned.

The laundry was in a separate building across from the main house. It was comprised of two large rooms, one for washing and the other for drying. Ironing was done upstairs. The only times when the laundry-maids went into the main house were for daytime lunch and evening dinner. These meals were taken in the basement, the servants sitting on benches around a stone table covered with a white cloth. The butler served the meat and everyone helped themselves to vegetables from dishes placed on the table. The food was good, consisting of a main course, a sweet , and a drink of ale for those who wanted it.

Mary shared a bedroom with Miss Taylor. She remembered:

It was known as the Poppy Room, for some reason or other. It was quite large, with plenty of room for the two beds it contained. The beds were very comfortable. There was an iron frame-work for hanging curtains on but we didn't have the curtains and the frame rattled when we turned over in bed. In front of the fireplace was a small threadbare carpet given to the Captain's mother by Queen Victoria, so I was told.

The laundry workers rose at half-past six and made their way down a spiral staircase by candlelight. Mary admitted to feeling scared at first because she had heard that a part of the Castle might be haunted. Breakfast was eaten in the upper room of the laundry. They were allowed bacon and eggs, half a pound of butter per week, milk, bread, biscuits, and a large cake for their afternoon teas.

Describing her work at Stainborough, Mary said:

The work in the laundry began on a Saturday, when we went into the main house to collect the dirty washing. We had quite a load with bedding, table linen, towels, maids' uniforms, etc. The first thing we did was to put the clothes to soak in cold water, any extra stained ones had special treatment. Mostly these were the maids' uniforms; some had blacklead on their aprons. The ones from the kitchen staff were badly stained. We had to stoke a coal-fired boiler to get the water really hot. Large wooden tubs were attached to the wall in front of the windows in the washroom, into which were put the clothes and hot water. Then a wooden board about twelve inches wide was laid across the tub and we scrubbed the clothes on this, using a large piece of yellow soap cut from a long bar. It was very tiring work to get things clean. The white clothes had to be put into the boiler along with some grated soap and it was hard work lifting the hot clothes out of the boiler. We had to put them through a large wringer, then into the rinsing tub, then the blue tub, and those needing starching in the last tub.

Drying was done on racks suspended from the ceiling. It took two days to do the washing, then there was the mangling. Everything went through the mangle. We had to be careful for buttons on dresses etc. Ironing was done on large tables in the upper room, the irons being heated on a large coal-fired stove. The irons rested on a ridge each side of the stove, about six a side. Everything was ironed, sheets, towels, the lot. There had to be no creases in anything. Sheets were ironed flat, then folded loosely. Ironing took two to two and a half days particular attention had to be paid to the caps which the maids wore. They were starched very stiff and were ironed flat, then drawn into shape by a string.

At the end of the week we had to clean the laundry; everything that had been used had to be thoroughly brushed and cleaned, including the windows, steps and floors, everything ready for starting again on Saturday.

Mary spent her evenings sitting with Miss Taylor in the upper room of the laundry. Though there was a sitting room in the house for the maids to use, also a bathroom by this time, Miss Taylor was against their using these facilities. Mary passed her time during the evenings in reading and sewing. She remembered having to let down the hem of her uniform because Miss Taylor said it was too short. She had also to take a hip-bath in the room, which she didn't like at all. Her weekly wage was eight shillings and keep. There was one free afternoon a week when she had to be back by ten o'clock. Mary worked for only a few months at the Castle. When it seemed unlikely that the housemaid's post would become vacant she decided to leave. She then obtained work as a general daily help at a farm near her home.

When army lorries rolled into Stainborough Park at the beginning of the Second World War they signified the end of the old order. Rolled-up tents were dropped off the lorries every twenty yards or so and erected within the hour so that the park quickly appeared to be full of them. Wentworth Castle was taken over by the Military for the duration of the war. The Vernon-Wentworths' possessions had been taken from the house after being carefully marked. It was thought they went into storage with a view to their being returned after the war. As it happened, they never did return. The palatial building which had been home for generations of the Vernon-Wentworth family opened as a Teacher Training College in October 1948.

Captain Bruce Vernon-Wentworth, the last member of his family to live in the Castle, spent his last years in Scotland. He died there in 1951 at the age of eighty-nine. Beside his grave at Rannock in Perthshire is another with a similar cross. Some say it is the grave of a favourite sister but the locals reckon it is that of the Captain's favourite horse.

Now that those days of masters and maids, affluence and servitude, are gone from Wentworth Castle, only the records and memories remain. Do the Northern College students of today reflect sometimes on those people who were there before them? Do they think of their way of life which has now passed into history?

Acknowledgements

I express my gratitude to the many kind people who offered help when I was searching for material about Wentworth Castle. Some of them had little or no information themselves but took time and trouble to put me in touch with those who had. Help came from various parts of the Barnsley area and beyond, one lady writing to me from Scarborough! So, my thanks to:- Roy and Wendy Beet, John Hopkins Jnr, Annie Whittaker, John Wade, Muriel Pallett, Mrs Gibbs, Trevor Maxfield, Nellie Dawson, Bertha Wigfield, Lady Barbara Ricardo, Edwin Price, Maureen Pickering, Rita Poole, Norah Wade, and the late Mary Hill. I am particularly grateful for the photographs which some of them loaned. My thanks to the Editor of the *Barnsley Chronicle* - for publishing my letter requesting information, also to Barnsley Local Studies Library and Archives for access to records. Thanks also to Diane Thornton for word processing my original text and to Brian Elliott for encouraging me to undertake the research.

2. SOME MEMORIES OF MAPPLEWELL BETHEL

by Joan Hartley

ON SUNDAY NINTH OCTOBER 1955, at about six o'clock in the evening at Mapplewell Bethel, every seat in the box-like pews was filled, and chairs had to be brought in and placed on the broad steps of the two sloping aisles. The singing, as on other occasions, had been inspired as the service progressed. Now it was the last hymn: *The Day Thou Gavest, Lord, is Ended.* The notes faded away, the congregation stood for the blessing, then sat down, nobody moved and for more than a minute it was like a scene set in aspic. Then

Figure 1. Outside Mapplewell Bethel after the service, 9 October 1955. From left to right: Reg Pye, Cousin Cis, Uncle George Edwin, Cyril Mason, Graham Flynn and George Birkinshaw

reluctantly and as if in slow motion people stirred, sighed and surreptitious handkerchieves were applied to eyes which were overflowing and there was a clearing of masculine throats, for this was the very last service in the Chapel they all loved (Figure 1).

For many it was the only place of worship they had attended. They had been carried there as babes in arms clad in snowy white family christening gowns to be baptised; they had attended Sunday School from 'the primary' to 'the seniors'; they had met and married their partners there and in time had brought their own children to be christened; eventually they had arranged and attended the final rites of their loved ones there; and now all this would be gone. The pattern of their lives would be changed. The following Sunday they would no longer be going 'down't Ginnill' or Spark Lane to Bethel, but instead going up from the Four Lane Ends to Greenside, to be part of another church - Greenside Methodist, or as it was known locally 'The Prims' (Primitive Methodists), something of an unknown entity to Bethel members.

It says a great deal about the unitedness of the Bethel Society when only two members did not join Greenside. This feeling of unity had been going on for 150 years every since the founding fathers left the cottages in which they had been meeting for worship, because of expanding congregations, the Bethel Free Church was built. They called themselves Protestant Methodists as opposed to Wesleyans, from whom they had seceded, and the foundation stone was laid on 17 August 1829. The chapel was finished and opened on 16 December of that year. The congregation at that time was about two hundred.

Much has been written about Methodism in the village ever since Wesley's visit in 1761, when he preached there. It is not my purpose to write, or even re-write the history of Mapplewell Bethel. Other and more erudite local historians have done that. My 'memories' of Bethel are roughly from 1929 to its closure in 1955 and as memory is selective, this chapter may have not a little of the 'rose-coloured spectacles' air about it.

The centenary year in 1929 seems to have come and gone without any documents such as programmes or posters extant; however after some discussion with my cousin, Len Kilner, he believes that it was on this august occasion, when there was a lull in the proceedings, possibly after a faith tea, that he and another boy - Charles Walker - had an adventure. They went to investigate what looked like a cupboard door high in the wall of the large schoolroom, near to where an indoor coal-place and a book cupboard were. Not realising they had found one of the outlets to the hot air heating apparatus (put in, according to JR Wilkinson's brief history, between 1870 - 80). Crawling onwards and upwards they found themselves looking through the grating which was let into the steps of the eastern aisle of the upstairs chapel, where warmth percolated during cold weather. That they lived to tell the tale shows that the 'apparatus' fuelled first by coal, then coke, was not in operation that day. He does remember getting into very hot water for dirtying his best suit and for going where no one was supposed to go.

It occurred to me whilst writing about this incident that when my parents, George and Cissie Birkinshaw (Figure 2) were caretakers for some years my Dad lit the boiler fire on Saturday mornings and during the day walked from New Street via the Narrow Ginnill to stoke up; this last visit was just before supper (ie in the Yorkshire not the modern sense) and his remark would be before he set off 'I'm off to see to the apparatus' - never the boiler, but we knew what he meant.

Figure 2. George and Cissie Birkinshaw, caretakers of the Bethel in the 1930's

In any Methodist Chapel, anniversaries of various kinds loom large throughout the year. My earliest memory of a Sunday School Anniversary, was possibly in 1929, when I was placed on the lowest tier of the 'stage' amongst the little girls of the primary class. This 'stage' was built up in many tiers to a dizzy-making height at the Spark Lane side of the chapel near the choir. There were the usual solos and recitations from scholars of all ages - the older boys rarely performed. My mother was given a poem of two verses for me to learn. Miss Doris Harper (later

becoming Mrs Granville Eyre) the primary leader had chosen it and
I still remember the first verse:

What a busy world is this
Everything I view
Has a task it must not miss
Something it must do

instilling early perhaps the nonconformist work ethic? The
Anniversary was round about the third Sunday in June and I cannot
really remember a wet Sunday - the sun always shone then.
However, the hot Sunday produced a rash of coloured patches on the
backs of the varnished pews from the men's best navy suits and the
flowery dresses of mums, aunties and grannies.
Those in the know leaned back on their pink
hymn sheets when sermon time came and then
were literally 'stuck for words' for the last hymn.
The final hymns spoke about 'golden sunsets' or
'the last golden gleams in the west' - and so it
always seemed on those memorable third
Sundays in June, when little girls wore pretty
frilly dresses in pastel colours, little boys wore
short trousers and neatly ironed shirts and in the
congregation there bloomed veritable flower
gardens on the obligatory straw hats as though
each lady tried to 'out-trim' the other (Figure 3).

Later in the week I helped my parents to bring
back the pews to their original but rather sticky
shine, ready for the ordinary and less exciting
service -not less exciting if Herbert Silverwood
was planned to preach!

Anniversaries usually had the same format -
part sacred and part secular and took up most of
the week-end. On the Saturday evening there

Figure 3. 'Sunday Best', c.1932

would be a concert preceded by a 'faith' tea. For the uninitiated a
'faith' tea was one where members of the church brought whatever
home-baked goodies they made best - cakes, pastries, tea-cakes plain
and currant and fruit loaves.

Others promised best butter, sandwich fillings - boiled ham and
potted meat (from Birds?). I can still remember the taste of Mrs
Lilian Rimmington's iced French buns which were, to quote my
Dad, 'moreish'. The picture is still strong in my mind of the trestle
table spread with a white paper tablecloth, in what was 'The Young
Ladies' Classroom', and behind it, a row of middle-aged ladies,

aproned but still hatted, busily cutting and buttering and spreading and filling large white plates. These had 'Bethel Free Church' within a border stamped in black on the edge. This then was the 'faith' tea which everyone would be enjoying later.

As with the Feeding of the Five Thousand there were always left-overs. These were known as 'cut-up stuff' and were made into slightly greasy parcels from the white paper tablecloth. Eaten perhaps next day as a snack, their flavourings were rather mixed and one could find a potted meat sandwich tasting strongly of seed cake, or a glacé cherry nestling amongst the ham. It never mattered. This second bite of the cherry - literally - was always welcome.

Mapplewell's motto is supposed to be *Nails, Mules and Music*, but when I was young the mules had been supplanted first by horse-drawn drays, then lorries which took away the nails to the buyers. The nails I well remember and all the working nail shops in the village - now all gone. Music was made every Sunday and sometimes during the week at the many nonconformist chapels, singing classes and male-voice choirs (Figure 4). In the golden age before

Figure 4. Bethel Methodist Choir, 1914. Some known names: Freddy Peckett, Fred Walker, Arnold Brooke, Annie Birkinshaw, Ivy Brooke, Mr. Backhouse, Sam Birkinshaw, Charlie Wilson, Norman Shaw, Austin Goldthorpe, Lily Pye, Alice Backhouse, Alithea Walker, Esther Amanda Roberts, Mary Colley, Florrie Cross, Fred Hayes, Lilian Dearnley, William Waring

Figure 5. Bethel Operatic Society: *Cupid and the Ogre*, c.1935.
Back Row (L to R): JW Land, Hannah Birkinshaw, Linda Dyson, Stanley Whiteley, Mrs.Cross, Kath Micklethwaite, Ruby Winstanley, Horace Land (electrics).
Second Row (L to R): Marion Goldthorpe, Len Ives, Doris Harper, Evelyn Sanderson, Cyril Bamford.
Third Row (L to R): Doris Waring, Don Micklethwaite, Dorothy Heeley, Gran Eyre, Lorna Wilkinson, Clarence Ibberson, Alice Street, George Birkinshaw, Peggy Alderson, Gladys Roberts (wardrobe).
Front (L to R): Truelove(?), Alfie Lake, Ronnie Alderson, Freddie Boyle, Frances Goldthorpe, Len Fleetwood, Albert Truelove, Arthur Pearson, Harry Waller (?).
Flower Girls (Left): Winnie Waring, Freda Horsefield, Ruth Goldthorpe. (Right) Margaret Whiteley, Alithea Heeley, Doreen Micklethwaite, Sybil Pickering.

television, the chapel was the centre of our lives, not only for spiritual needs but also the secular. Music making went on which was not only *Messiah* or Stainer's *Crucifixion* or anthems for harvest, or those strange offerings called *A service of Song* beloved of Ladies' Bright Hours; at our concerts we heard *Tea for Two* from *No No Nanette, Dan Cupid had a Garden* from *Merrie England*, pieces from Gilbert and Sullivan and even 'comic songs'.

Bethel had a strong choir and dramatic tradition. I am told that *Pearl the Fisher Maid* was presented with great success. Hard on the heels of that production *The Gondoliers* was cast but never presented. When I was seven or eight years old a large and enthusiastic group, including my parents, produced what we would call in these days - a musical. This was *Cupid and the Ogre*(Figure 5). This three-act extravaganza was a very ambitious undertaking, but was successful. It was put on in *The Picture House*, Greenside, and played to large audiences and brought in a substantial sum for the New Building Fund. Later came *The Bandolero* (Figure 6), still ambitious in its way because the large group which peopled 'Cupid' had shrunk a great deal to more manageable proportions.

Bethel's musical life owed much to the calibre and dedication of

Figure 6. Bethel Choir: *The Bandalero*, c1948 *C.Shaw*

the choirmasters and organists. As a child in Sunday School I was
not a little afraid of the first choirmaster I can remember - Mr Austin
Goldthorpe - I was not alone in that feeling I am sure. I daresay his
bark was worse than his bite, but he both terrified and coaxed us into
doing our best for him on Sunday School Anniversary day. His
daughter, Frances Alice, was an accomplished organist. I remember
her as a lady with a pale, oval, rather sad face and thick hair plaited
into 'earphones' - rather Pre-Raphaelite in appearance. Sadly she
died when only a young woman, and her death devastated her
parents and was a great loss to Bethel. Various other organists came
and went, amongst them a youthful Harold Taylor before he went to
university. Then from Gawber came Annie Harrison (Figure 7), who
used to walk over the fields from her village to Bethel to practise.
Later her family moved into the village and joined the chapel. Annie
was fifteen when she became our organist and continued until she
went to Training College at Bingley when she was eighteen.

The choirmaster round this time and for many years to follow was

Figure 7. Choir Trip to Blackpool, c 1932.
Back Row (L to R): C.Ibberson, Alice Street, Winnie Waring, Marion Goldthorpe,
Annie Harrison, Peggy Whiteley, Fred Boyle, Sybil Pickering.
Middle Row (L to R): Simeon Street, Stanley Whiteley, Joyce Merton, Cissie
Birkinshaw, Freda Horsefield.
Front Row (L to R): Lorna Wilkinson, Louie Ibberson, Ernest Pickard, 'Sammy'
Lindley, Arthur Pearson

Mr Clarence Ibberson (Figure 8). His gentle, quiet and persuasive manner would have encouraged a corncrake to sing beautifully. He himself had a fine tenor voice and he was always in demand for solo work both in the choir and at the many concerts throughout the church year.

When Annie went to College, Margaret Rimmington took over. I am sure everyone at chapel remembers the 'Man from the Chronicle' arriving one Sunday to take photographs of Margaret at the organ. Nothing surprising in that? Well, she was only thirteen when she took the post - the youngest organist in the Barnsley West Circuit.

Both Annie and Margaret used their not inconsiderable talent for music in many ways and the music life at the chapel was greatly enriched. Anyone who heard them at Choir Anniversary services' playing duets on two pianos, particularly remember *Grieg's Piano Concerto in A Minor* (First Movement) and the very lively *Scherzo* by Litolf - a feast of music indeed.

So it was in mid-twentieth century there was a late flowering of music as exciting and fulfilling as I suppose it must have been when, in mid-nineteenth century 'Good un' Ledger, Johnnie, George and Tom Birkinshaw amongst them played a number of instruments - bassoon, cornet and euphonium. Francis (Frank) son of Johnnie played the organ, Sam son of Francis sang with the tenors and the last George, son of Sam, took his place with the basses. The tradition of music to the greater glory of God set down by the founding fathers was satisfied.

Figure 8. Clarence Ibberson, choirmaster, mid-1930s to 1940s

At all the chapels, towards Christmas saw much rehearsing going on mainly from the *Messiah*. We also learned new pieces from *The Oxford Book of Carols*. But the greatest 'buzz' which came with Christmas was the Conversazione - or 't' Conversass!' This was held on Boxing Day evening and woe betide any visitors who arrived unexpectedly. They were invited - or rather dragooned into joining the family at the annual and never-to-be-missed 'Conversass'. When entertainment in my early days consisted of 'the penny rush' at the local picture house (never called

Figure 9. *Cinderella*, produced by Doris Waring: Sunday School Concert on New Year's Day. Some known children: Heather Mason, Pat Whiteley, Avril Fleetwood, Christine Eyre, Gwen Sanderson, Philip Gill, Brian Clarke and David Cooper.

a cinema) and the occasional Christmas visit to the old Theatre Royal in Leeds to see a pantomime (and longing to be a Francis Laidler Sunbeam!) this home-grown Boxing Day event was a treat. Bethel was fortunate in having a group of people with the differing talents of writing comic satire, arranging music, singing and stand-up comedy. Some weeks before Christmas they got together and put together a whole evening of non-stop variety. Many young hopefuls were 'tried out' on this evening, talents were discovered which had been hidden; one such was Sybil Clarke (née Pickering) who went on to become a fine soprano and was much in demand for oratorio and other solo work. My favourite of hers was *A Birthday* - words by Christina Rossetti and a fiendishly difficult piano accompaniment. My father, George Birkinshaw, usually had the comic spot. Usually a quiet, mild tempered and patient man, he let his hair down (the bit he had) at t' conversass. He became a loud-mouthed quick-talking huckster selling Dr Somebody's 'Do it Now Drops', which would put hair on billiard balls and other miraculous cures. How the audience laughed! - but I curled up inside thinking they were laughing at him - they were - but as I learned later, they loved the material and the outrageous claims he was making. The variety show ended with an Abel Heywood's sketch. These were *de rigueur* in those days as a finale. The plots were contrived and impossible but the more incredible the ideas, the more the audience liked it. Our visitors, sometimes 'dragged unwillingly' always came back the following year for more of the same.

New Year brought with it the New Year's Eve party - rather more up-market with catered supper and good pencil and paper games and good prizes. This ran into the Watch Night Service and then the traditional Carol Singing with other chapels, round the lamp and telephone box which used to stand like an island in the middle of the Four Lane Ends - joined also by one or two rather inebriated persons! New Year's Day was Sunday School Prize-giving and concert - faith tea beforehand obligatory (Figure 9). Prizes were awarded on attendance and came in three categories - First, Second or Third. First prizes were always hoped for as more money was allocated to them and so a superior book would be the result. As one got older the choice of book could be one's own. Being an inveterate hoarder I have all my prizes in a bookcase, many of them well thumbed by successions of God-children. Another treasured possession is my *Lord Wharton's Bible*. Philip Lord Wharton died in 1696 and his will left provision for Bibles to be given to children who should commit to memory the 1st, 15th, 25th, 37th, 101st, 113th and 145th Psalms. Most of the scholars at Bethel received these Bibles, my Mother and Father in 1907 and myself and fellow scholars in 1938.

It seems that even from as long ago as 17 February 1902, various efforts were held to raise money for The New Building Fund. I can remember in the decade leading up to 1939 we worked for the same cause. Our dream too was a new chapel and Sunday School. There were mammoth bazaars where beforehand hundreds of pounds worth of tickets were sold for goods specially ordered. I still have a beautiful white damask tablecloth and napkins which come out every Christmas and other special occasions.

In the early 1900s the members chose Shrovetide for their money raising events which were also special occasions. This tradition was carried on for many years until closure. One year I remember well, the event took the form of a novelty head-dress parade. Philip Turton took first prize for the men as 'Knight of the Chamber'. I will leave you to guess what his beautifully trimmed headgear really was! Philip had married into the chapel and became a trustee, treasurer, choir member and actor in the Dramatic Society. He was a quiet man with a dry sense of humour. He was also a 'Desert Rat' in the North African Campaign gaining oak leaves twice for mentions in dispatches. Sad to say this quiet hero and man of courage died not very long ago.

Figure 10. Bethel Dramatic Society: *No Medals*, produced by Doris Waring. Cast shown here (L to R): Joan Birkinshaw, George Birkinshaw, Margaret Rimmington.

Figure 11. Bethel Dramatic Society: *Lace on Her Petticoat,* produced by Lorna Wilkinson. Cast (L to R, Back) 'Hamish' (Brian Ibberson,) 'Mrs Colquhoun (Winnie Turton), 'Faith' (Joan Birkinshaw), 'Granny' (Margaret Harrison), 'Mac' (Frank Harrison). Front (L to R): 'Alex' (Pat Longley) and 'Elspeth' *Marian Turton.*

Towards the end of the chapel's life, what most people remember is a flourishing Dramatic Society. We had a large group of playing and non-playing members, and even attracted at least one member from the Anglican Church and another from one of the other Methodist chapels in the village. The Society was really the brain-child of Lorna Wilkinson who was our main producer. Once a month there was a play reading with only one rehearsal and different producers. Some of the more hysterical things happened in play readings but the audience took it all in good part. Then there were two or three productions in season (Figure 10).

We had great fun at rehearsals and probably drove Lorna to distractions. In the winter when the pea and pie man came up Spark Lane shouting his wares, we stopped being WRNS or Admirals, detectives or murderers and rushed out with cups to be filled with mushy peas and then eaten with relish. Our performance, after a top-up of protein from the humble pulse, was just that little bit better - or so we said! The productions were always a great success thanks to our mentor, guide and producer, Lorna Wilkinson (Figure 11). One night in production week we knew that 'Thespis' from the *Barnsley Chronicle* would be coming to review the play for his

Figure 12. Bethel Football Team, c 1935.
Back Row (L to R): Alf Lake, Ron Alderson, Harry Waller, Cyril Bamford, Len Fleetwood, Mr.Boyle; Centre: Freddie Boyle; Front (LtoR): Horace Land, Fred Cross, Arnold Hanks, ----------- , Frank Wilkinson

column. His appearance spied through a gap in the curtains gave us an extra frisson and put us on our mettle.

As a church we owed much to Lorna Wilkinson. She held many offices in the running of things; she was a superb organiser of any new efforts which we had in hand; she was lively, intelligent, had a bubbly sense of humour and was no mean actress herself. She had a sweet and true singing voice - the song *Dream O' Day Jill* was a favourite of hers and ours.

One memorable play reading was *Hobson's Choice* with the late Ronald Eyre in the main role. He was masterly even then and of course went on to do great things in the London theatre scene as writer and director until his untimely death. It was a privilege for us all to work alongside him.

Lest anyone should think that the chapel's activities were confined to Church Services, entertainments and fund raising, we also had a thriving Sports Section. When I was very young there was a very successful cricket team and football team; later just the football team remained and although my father no longer played he kept up his interest and acted as honorary groundsman (Figure 12). Every year the football team got to the semi-final in the cup tie but never won the cup. They were of course disappointed but never down-hearted and the Football tea and concert was another highlight of the year.

Bethel was always known as the 'Endeavour Church'. The idea of forming a Christian Endeavour Society (known as C.E. for short) came from Mr J R Wilkinson in his young days. The idea took root and flourished. In the late 1920s there were enough members to form Junior, Intermediate and Senior Sections. The Junior C.E. was run very successfully by Mrs Doris Eyre (née Harper). Miss Harper had taught most of us in the 'Babies' class in the village infants' school and was loved by all. It was in Junior Endeavour that we learned how to organise a meeting; in our turns we chose the hymns from the *Endeavour Hymnal*, thought out and wrote the prayer, sang solos and duets, recited poems and listened to Mrs Eyre who gave the talk. The meetings always ended with the singing of the 'Mizpah' - *The Lord watch between me and thee.*

In the summer we sometimes went on rambles into the countryside, which was much quieter in those days, and held our meetings in the open air. In the winter we had a 'Floating Endeavour'. These meetings were very different from the general run of things; Juniors and Intermediates joined together and the evening was spent making useful objects for the men on merchant ships. I often wondered what those sailors thought of our offerings. There were, of course, little girls who were adept at sewing pieces of flannel to make needlecases, but I was not one of them. Some people knitted scarves and socks or wrote letters. The older boys seemed always to be doing something with fret-saws, but in that time of inequality between the sexes, saws were for boys and needles and cotton were for girls.

Perhaps you might say that Junior C.E. was a gentle form of brain-washing, but the main aim was to win young people for the church and train them for work in the various departments. There were of course successful evangelistic mission bands sent out from Bethel in the very early days; C.E. underlined the need for early training and the measure of its success can be seen in the number of local preachers Bethel sent to work in the Barnsley Circuit. At first these too were members of a mission band, then as they became more confident and more proficient they studied for the Local Preachers' Examination and eventually became fully accredited. C.E. had many loyal workers, but the two people I best remember were the

Figure 13. The Bethel Methodist Chapel, 1829-1955 *photographed in 1985 by Harold Taylor*

Eyres - Doris and her husband Granville. 'Gran' was Secretary for the Barnsley Union for many years and one year became President of the Union. They carried on the tradition of C.E. introduced a generation before, enriching the fabric of church life and fellowship.

When J R Wilkinson wrote his 'brief-history' in c1929 he said that '...the best is yet to be'. He could not have foreseen that with the outbreak of World War Two in 1939 all thoughts of building a new church had to be put on hold - although enough money had been raised, and a piece of land near the top of Darton Lane had been acquired. At the end of the war and shortly after when the service men came home, and my age group had been to college and had returned to take up teaching posts in the area, once again thoughts turned in one direction- the new church. But the Powers That Be said: 'No, Mapplewell is over-churched'. Indeed, Mapplewell had been 'over-churched' for years, but none of the five main Methodist

Churches had ever thought of it in that light. However, our building at Bethel was unsafe and so Trustees' Meetings were held to look at options. They put their findings to a full Church meeting and it was decided to seek amalgamation with the Greenside Methodist Church. Joint meetings were held and they welcomed our move. So the deed of amalgamation was drawn up, sealed and signed.

That the Church was not split showed that the influence of our Founding Fathers and many good men and women through more than a century had kept us together as an alive Society. Their names come down the generations to us: the Pye family, the Pecketts, the Birkinshaws, the Warings, the Wilkinsons, the Goldthorpes and others - a 'cloud of unseen witnesses' who by their spiritual fervour, loyalty and living example encouraged us, their heirs, to be a real and true 'United Church'; to leave behind the ailing bricks and mortar (Figure 13), however painful, and move on to make a new Society carrying the torch of faith thrown down to us by those stalwarts of Bethel's past.

Acknowledgements

C P Shaw - notes and personal memories; Mrs Doris Eyre - the Christian Endeavour and its work; Mrs Annie Rimmington - musical matters; Mrs Sybil Clarke - the choir; Mrs Winnie Turton - the Dramatic Society; Mr Len Kilner - Sunday School and general topics; Mr Doug Robinson - photographs; Mr Harold Taylor - photographs; Mrs Diane Thornton - word processing.

3. Joseph Wilkinson of Barnsley: Victorian Scholar and Journalist

by John Goodchild, M. Univ

A SCHOLARLY AND CREATIVE spirit flourished in Barnsley and its vicinity in the mid and later nineteenth century: poets, historians, prose writers, creative journalists, mostly men but with at least one woman among their number, and all keenly interested in politics, religion and philosophy, education and science. Interesting and interested people.

Among their number was Joseph Wilkinson, remembered nowadays for his historical books and his biographical one, but described during his own lifetime as very kindly, of an amiable disposition, and courteous. Could a man hope for any better opinion on the part of his contemporaries? In fact, his interests spread widely and actively through the affairs of Barnsley and its neighbourhood, and upon his death in 1906 the *Barnsley Chronicle* newspaper described him in a lengthy obituary notice as 'most highly esteemed'.

This present study is based upon some of his own voluminous collections of papers which have been purchased by the present writer, and upon a variety of further references from newspapers and other sources of his period: we find not only a 'nice man',

WORSBOROUGH:

ITS

HISTORICAL ASSOCIATIONS

AND

RURAL ATTRACTIONS.

BY

JOSEPH WILKINSON.

LONDON:
FARRINGTON & CO., 112, FLEET STREET.
BARNSLEY:—THOMAS LINGARD, "CHRONICLE" OFFICE.

WORTHIES, FAMILIES

AND

CELEBRITIES

OF

BARNSLEY AND THE DISTRICT

BY

JOSEPH WILKINSON.

London:
BEMROSE & SONS, 23, OLD BAILEY,
AND DERBY.

Figure 1. (*Above*) Title-page to the 453 page 'History of Worsborough', printed by Thomas Lingard of the Chronicle office, Barnsley, and published in 1872 by Farrington & Co of Fleet Street, London. Note the old Municipal Borough coat of arms. Wilkinson dedicated the book to F W T Vernon-Wentworth of Wentworth Castle and W H Martin-Edmunds of Worsbrough Hall

Figure 2. (*Right*) Title-page of Wilkinson's 'Worthies of Barnsley', printed by Bemrose in 1881. Dedicated to F W T Vernon-Wentworth 'as a small tribute to his worth, and in grateful acknowledgement of many favours received at his hands'. Some 351 subscribers are listed, accounting for 433 copies of the book

but one very busy and very able, and one whose books, especially his *History of Worsbrough* (Figure 1) and his *Worthies of Barnsley*, (Figure 2) are still in constant use today.

Wilkinson was born at Darton in 1830, son of a working gardener. He was indeed to inherit his father's horticultural interests, not only in the maintenance of his own garden, described as trim and well kept, but as an active committee member of the Barnsley Floral and Horticultural Society which had been established in 1838. After school, he worked for Hargreaves & Bailey, pawnbrokers, in Barnsley, and letters survive from when he was in his 'teens, when he was discussing philosophical and religious questions with an old school-fellow. He later became clerk and bookkeeper at the Beevor Bleach Works, but from his early twenties he took up journalism, initially part time, as Barnsley and district correspondent for the *Leeds Mercury*, the *Sheffield Independent* and other newspapers, while in 1852 the newly-established *Wakefield Express*, which in its prospectus as well as on its front page declared its inclusion of Barnsley within its area of concern, appointed Wilkinson as its Barnsley area correspondent at a salary of £10 per year and three free copies of the paper. It was in 1852 too that he was one of those responsible for the first Barnsley newspaper as such, the *Barnsley Telegraph & West Riding Advertiser*, and in that paper wrote articles on the history of Stainborough and Rockley, which work was ultimately published as a book in two successive editions in 1853 (Figure 3), by which time he had also become the author of *Village Rambles*.

The 1850s and 60s were an exciting time in Barnsley. Not only was the coal trade developing on a huge and quite new scale as a result of the opening of the new railways through and near the town, and the newly-mechanised linen industry still flourishing, but there was intellectual excitement in the area too. This took a variety of forms, but included the writing (and publishing) of verse, prose, local history, dialect, newspapers, and the consequent existence of a group - largely of younger men - keenly interested in such matters,

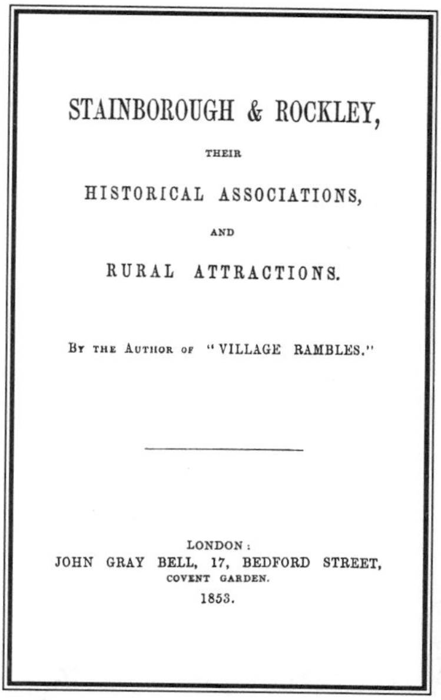

STAINBOROUGH & ROCKLEY,

THEIR

HISTORICAL ASSOCIATIONS,

AND

RURAL ATTRACTIONS.

BY THE AUTHOR OF "VILLAGE RAMBLES."

LONDON:
JOHN GRAY BELL, 17, BEDFORD STREET,
COVENT GARDEN.
1853.

Figure 3. Title-page and opening paragraph from Wilkinson's 'Stainborough & Rockley', printed in 1853 by Bell of London and dedicated to F W T Vernon-Wentworth. Subscribers numbered 175, reserving 625 copies of the 86+ page book. A second edition was published in 1853

numbers of whom met in Stainborough Club and Library: the present writer has one of its bound volumes of pamphlets. In this period, Rowland Jackson was to publish his *History of Barnsley* (1858), J H Burland was writing verse and local history, a biography of the local Joseph Locke was written by the editor of the *Barnsley Chronicle*, George Hanby the Staincross literateur was appearing in print - and others included Louisa A Horsfield of Blacker Hill, whose *Cottage Lyre* was published in 1861. The literary history of Barnsley at this period is seemingly extraordinary, and the Barnsley writers were in correspondence with at least one other such group. Joseph Wilkinson belonged to this loose Barnsley grouping.

In 1849 Wilkinson became the honorary secretary of the Barnsley Franklin Club, an organisation for the advancement of education and self-instruction. This had been established formally in the spring of 1843, when a group of working men left the Barnsley Mechanics' Institution (founded in 1837) after disputes with the middle class administrators of that organisation. The Franklin Club met in Market Street and had a wide range of activities - a library, lectures, classes, concerts, excursions - so that being its secretary was necessarily an active position. The Club joined the Yorkshire Union of Mechanics' Institutions, and achieved comment in the *People's Journal* and in the *Working-Man's Friend*, while branch Clubs were formed at Monk Bretton and Kexborough, and there were similar clubs in Doncaster and Halifax. The Mechanics' Institute was re-formed in 1848, but it was with the Franklins that the People's College at Sheffield formed an association; there was between the two Barnsley groups 'a strong feeling of caste', and the Franklins claimed 'the democratic element'. In fact, the Mechanics' was the body which was to survive, and it outlived too the denominational Church Institute, which collapsed in 1856. Curiously, in later years Wilkinson was a member of the Mechanics', then the only survivor in its field in the town.

As a journalist, Wilkinson's career blossomed to the extent that he was able to take up that profession full time. Numbers of letters from newspaper editors survive among his own papers, showing that he wrote for the *Manchester Examiner & Times*, *The Halifax Guardian*, *The Manchester Guardian*, the *Sheffield Telegraph*, the *Sheffield Free Press*, the *Leeds Times*, the *Leeds Mercury*, the *Wakefield Express* - and no doubt others too. *The Leeds Times* editor writes at the beginning of 1852 that Wilkinson's paragraphs are intelligently written, and are not so prolix as they were at the beginning of his engagement. Later he writes 'We are very well satisfied with your correspondence, but have to complain of your illegible writing.' Wilkinson was to find himself very busy as the local reporter following the appalling Lund Hill Colliery explosion in 1857, although he found one editor at least willing to argue over payment for the news, and to argue too that Wilkinson should get his report off (to Manchester) by an earlier train. *The Manchester Guardian* paid 1½d (0.625p) per line for what it described as 'extraordinary news', (murders, explosions, riots or other great catastrophes). At this time, reference is made to Wilkinson the journalist and 'the fairness of his reports, and his active business habits'. Wilkinson was also engaged in the formation of the *Barnsley Chronicle's* business in 1858, although he withdrew from active involvement with the publication within a few weeks.

In the early 1860s, a relative's death provided Wilkinson with sufficient to allow him to retire - still only in his early thirties, living in Dodworth Road in Barnsley. He increasingly devoted himself to historical scholarship, and was granted access to many gentlemen's private collections. His own library included numerous volumes of press cuttings, some of which are now in the Barnsley Local Studies Library. His work on the *History of Worsbrough* was published in the autumn of 1872, the larger part of it having appeared earlier in the columns of the *Barnsley Chronicle*: it was a model work of its period, bringing the story into then modern times - although one wishes today that more had been recorded of that period. In 1881 Wilkinson published his *Worthies of Barnsley and the District.* The book (of some 500 pages) concentrates upon the great and (perhaps) good, as a Victorian would have seen them (Figure 4). Wilkinson had however published numerous other biographical sketches in newspaper form,

Figure 4. Preface to Wilkinson's 'Worthies' book

STAINBOROUGH,

ITS HISTORICAL ASSOCIATIONS, &c.

THE neighbourhood of Barnsley abounds with picturesque beauty. In whatever direction we walk, scenery of a luxuriant and variegated richness unfolds itself. Its charming landscapes however, are not the only feature of attraction. It is dotted with many points of historic interest, of which Stainborough and Rockley, whether regarded as the residence of distinguished and ancient families, for their historical associations, or the grandeur of their rich scenic beauties, may claim pre-eminence.

and apparently intended there to be a successor volume of Worthies:
The writer has a volume of his rough notes for this purpose, and a
list is included in Wilkinson's obituary notice in the *Barnsley
Chronicle* of 10 March 1906. He had envisaged publishing the useful
diary of John Hobson of Dodworth Green between 1726 and 1735
as a volume, but it was incorporated, with his notes to it, in the first
volume of *Yorkshire Diaries and Autobiographies* published in 1877 by
the Surtees Society as its volume LXV.

Wilkinson took an active part in local affairs outside those which
might be described as literary. He was a sometime overseer of the
poor in Barnsley township, and for over twenty years an elected
Guardian for Worsbrough in the Barnsley Poor Law Union; he was
an elected member of both the Worsbrough Local Board and School
Board there, and a Pitt Charity trustee. He was his usual active and
efficient self as secretary to the fund raised upon the Swaithe Main
Colliery disaster of 1875, and became the treasurer to the West
Riding Miners' Permanent Relief Fund from its establishment in
1877 until his own death very nearly thirty years later - an onerous
task indeed.

He was that relatively unusual combination of his period, a
churchman and a Liberal - although his political interests were not
expressed in close association with politicians. Among his papers are
the printed reports of several Barnsley area organisations which show
him as a subscriber: to the Barnsley Ragged School, the Barnsley
Town Mission, the Church Missionary Society, the Barnsley
Benevolent Society (through his wife - all the subscribers were
females), the Church Pastoral Aid Society (Barnsley Branch).
Wilkinson's ecclesiastical allegiance was to St Mary's and St
George's churches, and it was in the graveyard of the latter that he
was to be buried; he left a widow, a son and two daughters.

Wilkinson died at his home, *The Hollies*, in Victoria Road, at the age
of seventy-five. His health had been failing for some time, but he had
attended to the affairs of the Permanent Relief Fund within a very
few days of his death, and was taken ill while walking in his garden.
His funeral was numerously attended, and in the snow. He was
described by his friend and obituarist Alexander Paterson as 'one of
the kindest and most unassuming of men'.

4. BARNSLEY, BECKETTS AND BIG BEN

by Gerald J Alliott

ONE MIGHT ASK 'What is the connection between *Big Ben* and Barnsley?' The answer lies within the family of Beckett. For more than two centuries its members were associated with all principal events, charities, relief of the poor, enquiries and the church. The family, said to come from humble beginnings, rose to become amongst the most wealthy in Yorkshire.

The Becketts, as can be seen by reference to their Pedigree (Figure 1), were resident in Elizabethan Barnsley and appear to have been of some status, having marriage links with the Ushers who were mercers (and later apothecaries). Becketts were soon involved in local business activities. Gervase (or Gervaise), for example, described himself as 'wiredrawer' in his will of 1716 but he was a master rather than an ordinary tradesman, sufficiently prosperous as to leave £620 to his widow and children, equivalent to tens of thousands of pounds today. Gervase, his eldest son, carried on with his father's wiredrawing business. A second son, John, after apparently modest beginnings became a very successful grocer and married the sister of the Quaker linen manufacturer William Wilson who was far from happy with the liaison. John had a substantial modern house built on Church Street (Figure 2) in keeping with his gentry status. Daniel, son number three, became a well-known apothecary and was generally regarded as the 'town doctor'. Thus by the middle and later decades of the eighteenth century the Becketts had established themselves as one of the most prosperous and therefore influential families of the small but changing market town of Barnsley.

Joseph Beckett inherited the family business but his interests in the town's developing linen industry were such that he was regarded as founding father of the trade. It was this Beckett who, in partnership with George Clark and then later with John Birks established Barnsley's first bank. On the day of his funeral, in 1840, shops stayed closed as a mark of respect and a marble monument was subsequently placed in the south chancel of St Mary's.

The Beckett Family

Only the principal line of descent is given.

1547 Agnes Beckett, widow, lived in a cottage owned by the Chantry of Our Lady in the Church of Barnsley. Died 18 January 1571

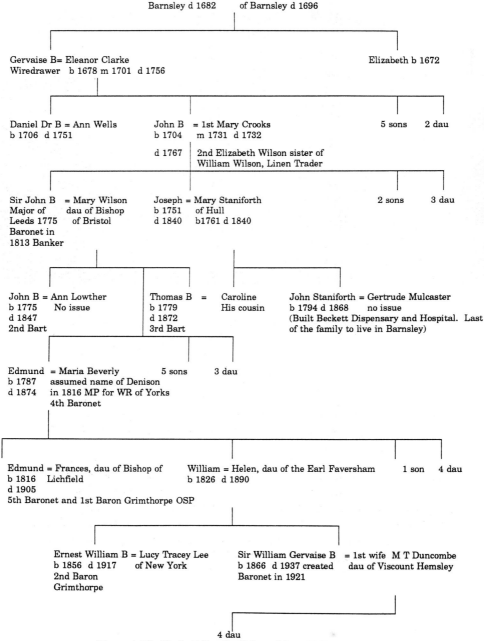

Figure 1: **The Beckett Family** (*Adapted from W E England*)

Figure 2. Copper Hall *Tasker Trust*

Joseph's son, John Staniforth (named after his grandmother who was from the Staniforths of Hull) died without issue in 1868 but was a great benefactor of Barnsley. It was J S Beckett who funded the building of the Beckett Dispensary (opened in 1865) and endowed it with £5,000 (Figure 3). Further support from the family enabled a twenty-bed surgical ward to be added at a time when colliery accidents were so common. Beckett's personal estate amounted to a very substantial £350,000. His bequests included gifts of £200 to Barnsley Ragged School, five pictures to the National Gallery and £600 to the National Lifeboat Institution.

The Beckett fortune continued to prosper in the Leeds branch of the family, Sir John Beckett, brother of Joseph, becoming Lord Mayor of the city in 1775 (and again in 1779). He was rewarded with the dignity of a Baronet for his opposition to the Luddite Riots. John, the second Baronet, was a lawyer and politician whilst his brother Thomas, who inherited the title, was a notable Leeds merchant,

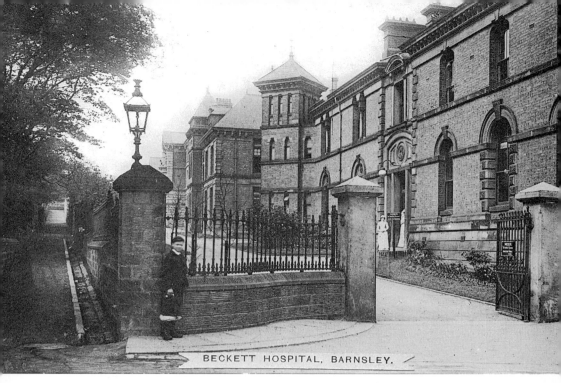

BECKETT HOSPITAL, BARNSLEY.

Figure 3. (above and below) Beckett Hospital: From an Edwardian Postcards
Elliott Collection

retiring to Somerby Park, Lincolnshire in 1861. The fourth Baronet, Edmund (b 1787) was a West Riding MP and in his inaugural speech

LAMBERT WARD, BECKETT HOSPITAL BARNSLEY

referred to his 'humble' Barnsley ancestors. He was to marry Maria, daughter of William Beverley of Beverley and great niece of Lady Denison, wife of Sir Thomas Denison, Judge of the Common Pleas. Edmund assumed the name of Denison by royal licence on inheriting the property of his great aunt and was generally known as E Beckett Denison until he succeeded to the Baronetcy as Sir Edmund Beckett, Bart. He resided at Carlton Hall, Newark where his eldest son, also Edmund, was born in 1816 but moved to Doncaster two years later and was prominent in the developing railway industry associated with the town. He died a very wealthy man.

Sir Edmund Beckett, Bart. (E.B. Denison), first Baron Grimthorpe and 'Big Ben'

In many respects Edmund Beckett, fifth Baronet (Figure 4) and cousin of John Staniforth Beckett, Barnsley's great benefactor, was the most controversial of this prestigious family but was a man of considerable distinction and achievement. Called to the Bar in 1841, a QC by 1854, leader of the Parliamentary Bar in 1860, he became Chancellor of the Province of York (1877-1900) but engaged in theological controversy, opposing the New Testament revision.

Sir Edmund designed several Yorkshire churches and although only an amateur architect wrote *A Book on Building, Civil and Ecclesiastical* (1876). He also had a fondness for mechanical objects,

Figure 4. Lord Grimthorpe (E B Denison) at the time of Big Ben
Courtesy of John Murray

inventing a lock, though it was never patented. He did, however, design clocks for the Great Exhibition of 1851, for St Paul's Cathedral (1893) and, as we shall see, the great clock for the Houses of Parliament (1859). Such was his prestige that he served as President of the Royal Horological Institute from 1868 until his death in 1905.

Edmund was very sarcastic and assertive but got results. He was a fighter and a virulent correspondent. His life centred around two celebrated public affairs, the designing and installing of Big Ben and the Westminster Clock and the restoration of St Alban's Cathedral. What follows is the story of his work with Big Ben the first, Big Ben the second and the Westminster Clock.

The Westminster Clock, (i) 1844-48

For almost ten years the architect Sir Charles Barry had been supervising the building of Westminster, designing it as he went along. Barry had won the commission in a competition, claiming that it would cost £750,000; it actually cost more than two million. He was later plagued by complaints about the costs. Barry did the bulk of the work and if anything went wrong had to take the blame, so everything was against him and for years had to struggle against expert lunacy. On top of this the Office of Works were always late in paying his commission and then underpaid him by two per cent.

The most experienced civil servant, if ordered to procure a splendid clock of this dimension, would give it some thought but Barry took the easy way out and at the end of March 1844 wrote to the Queen's clockmaker, Lewis Benjamin Vulliamy, about the clock. Vulliamy replied that he would want a hundred guineas for the commission and two hundred if he did not. Barry wrote to the Office of Works recommending acceptance of the offer and in two weeks the Board approved it.

E J Dent, a specialist in marine chronometers designed the first turret clock for the Royal Exchange. At the time he did not even have a factory and although the profession did not like the intruder, they had made no mechanical improvements for fifty years. On 14 November 1845 he enquired if he could be admitted as a candidate for supplying the large clock and such others as would be required for the new Houses of Parliament. He enclosed a testimonial from G B Airy the Astronomer Royal and one from William Tite, architect of the Royal Exchange. Dent undercut the competition by half to £1600 in order to establish himself in the Turret Clock trade. In May 1848 E Beckett Denison wrote to the First Commissioner stating that few people (out of the trade) had paid more attention to the subject of turret clocks than he had. He said that he had employed both Dent and Vulliamy to make church clocks for friends who had consulted him but had no hesitation in saying Dent's work was superior to that of Vulliamy's — so Dent had found another great champion. Barry knew nothing about clocks. Vulliamy knew about the sort of clock made in the 1790s. Dent knew more about chronometers than clocks and out of all this a great clock was expected. The Office of Works, in 1848, gave up and told Barry to get on with the tower but nothing happened for the next three years.

ii) 1851-54

Edmund Beckett Denison, by the end of the 1840s had made many experiments in Dent's workshops, written about clocks in the *Encyclopaedia Britannica* and in 1850 published *A Rudimentary Treatise on Clocks and Watchmaking*. As we have seen, he (with Dent) exhibited (and won an award) at the Great Exhibition of 1851. When the Office of Works again took up the question of the great clock it was to be E B Denison who was called upon for his expertise and Dent as manufacturer. Barry was informed that Dent's offer, now at £1800, was accepted.

Airy and Denison inspected the tower, in company with the architect, and discovered that the interior walls were so far advanced and too small for the clock to go in! The clock had to be redesigned and Denison never forgave Barry; Dent agreed to make the redesigned clock for an extra £100. Vulliamy's friends at the Company of Clockmakers of the City of London did not like to see this progress. They did not like Airy and Denison and were surprised that the clock was put in their hands in place of competition. It was worse than impudence when the Company dismissed Denison's claims as to the accuracy of the Great Exhibition Clock. So the arguments and obvious jealousy carried on with Vulliamy and the Commissioners. Vulliamy told them that Dent's clock would cost £3,500 by the time it was completed but as he was old and sick by now, the Commissioners turned a deaf ear.

Dent was taken ill and Denison, his unofficial partner and adviser persuaded him to make his stepson, Frederick, his successor. Frederick then wrote to the Commissioners and informed them he would carry on with the clock but delays in the building of the tower were holding things up. Dent's contract was now questioned but confirmed as good, after much argument. Vulliamy died in January 1854. In that year Barry was being awkward with Denison and would not say what alterations were being made to the tower. Denison, not satisfied with his own three-legged dead escapement, invented an alternative version. This masterpiece of applied mathematics was to be used in all good turret clocks from then onwards and it became customary to announce that all turret clocks had been 'designed by E B Denison', because they incorporated his improvements. The great clock (Figure 5), now in 1854, was completed at last, by Dent

Figure 5. The
Westminster Clock
Percy Fellows

and Denison: and the latter took great pride in the achievement after all the efforts that had been made to get rid of him.

Big Ben: Number 1, 1854-58

The making of the clock had been an untidy business but the bellmaking was to be, by comparison, a rough house. From 1854, when the clock was finished and negotiations on the bell started, the great clock was to lie about getting rusty for a few years until Barry pronounced his tower was ready.

The bell business was to progress at an alarming rate. In February 1855 the Office of Works asked Denison to prepare a specification for the bell which he did immediately, with the advice that Warner's tender should be acceptable if it was reasonable. It was accepted. A new Commissioner was appointed at the Office, Sir Benjamin Hall, who wanted to get on with things, so Denison was back attending the bell as if there had been no argument with his predecessor, Sir William Molesworth who had been given a more important position to avoid further confrontation.

On the morning of 6 August 1856 Warners cast the bell at Norton, near Stockton-onTees. The mould had been in preparation for six weeks and two furnaces capable of melting ten tons of metal had been built especially for the bell. It took an hour to pour the metal in and two and a half hours for fusion to take place. At the success of the casting three hearty cheers were given by the workmen and spectators.

The bell had inscribed on it:

> *Cast in the 20th year of the reign of Her Majesty Queen*
> *Victoria, and in the year of Our Lord 1856; from the design of*
> *Edmund Beckett Denison, Q.C.; Sir Benjamin Hall, Baronet,*
> *M.P., Chief Commissioner of Works.*

The bell was sounded for the first time on 22 August 1856. Denison was very happy. However, there were unpromising signs too. It was found to weigh fifteen tons one quarter and twenty two pounds which was a great deal more than it should have been.

In October the bell arrived at Maudsley's Wharf on the schooner *Wave* and was then conveyed to Palace Yard on a truck pulled by sixteen white horses (Figure 6). The crowd of spectators was so large

Figure 6. 'Big Ben' being hauled to Westminster *John Murray*

that police control was difficult. In the afternoon it was raised on a massive frame at the foot of the tower and then propped up with timbers to take the strain off the chains.

Everybody was delighted with the new bell and for the first time Denison got some sort of reward and Sir Benjamin Hall congratulated him on the way he had conducted the whole business. *The Times* also praised him, commenting that 'the new bell at Westminster will perform no inconsiderable part in this community of thought and feeling'. The Commons debated a whole afternoon on the name of the bell without coming to an agreement until a backbencher shouted out 'call it Big Ben'. This was received with amusement though not recorded in *Hansard* but the name was adopted.

In October 1857 'Big Ben' cracked. Everybody started blaming everybody else. Warners claimed the clappers were too heavy. Denison said the waist of the bell was too thick. It was agreed that a replacement was needed. Warners were asked to tender but their bid was regarded as too excessive and rejected, Mr Mears gaining the contract. In February 1858 the damaged bell was lowered to the ground and on 17 March a ball of iron weighing twenty-four hundred weights was dropped on it from a framework thirty feet up. The ball crashed down eighteen times and the pieces were carried off to Mears' Foundry.

Big Ben Number 2, 1859

The new bell was cast by Mears at his Whitechapel foundry. When cool it was struck by a small hammer; the sound spread out with a solemn boom, rich and deep. It weighed thirteen tons ten hundred weight and twelve pounds and Denison was satisfied. The work in getting it in place started in October which was no easy task. Barry's 320 foot tower had been built regardless of the bell shape. The lifting chain made specially for the job was 1600 feet long. The oak beam was twenty-five inches wide and nineteen inches thick, capable of holding a hundred tons. Eight men started winding the bell upwards on 12 October and after thirty-two hours it was at the floor of the clock chamber.

Once more there were differences between Denison and the Office of Works but by November it was sorted out and the bell was tried, not with the hammer but with a light clapper. The triumph was marred by the discovery that the collar and standards of the frame were not strong enough so Barry had to put things right.

By now the delays were beginning to annoy both Press and Parliament. The bell had been bolted up too tight and adjustments had to be made as instructed by Denison. In April, at last, the clock was being installed. *The Times* talked of blunders but did not mention that the clock had been ready some four years earlier. The total cost, according to Barry, was £22,075 but he put in expenses which were nothing to do with the clock or bell. Denison complained in no uncertain terms.

In the summer the bell was being heard every hour as far away as Richmond Park. Now that the clock and bell were in place, and working, it was hoped that Barry, Denison and the Office of Works could live happily ever after. This was not to be and the pessimists had not long to wait. The minute hands, some Barry-Pugin art-work, were too heavy for the clock mechanism. Barry wrote to *The Times* and every insult was thrown back.

On 7 September the quarter chimes rang out but three weeks later Denison received a letter of a further disaster. The Mears' bell had cracked and Dent's men, on examination, had found defects - holes filled with cement in the metal. In the first week of October *The Times* blamed Denison once more. Sir Edmund replied, saying that it was due to bad casting, the bell was porous and the holes filled up as a dentist fills teeth and the whole thing had been given a colour to hide the faults - in short it was a fraud. He said it was a disgrace to the nation as it was to its founders and the Mears' Foundry. Charles and George Mears threatended legal action if Denison did not withdraw his comments. Denison refused and he was subsequently sued by Mears for damages. The Office of Works would not let him have a piece of the bell so he had no defence and so lost. He paid £200 damages plus costs. However, Denison wrote again to *The Times*, on 8 July 1860, once more saying that Big Ben was a disgrace to its founders. This time Mears let it pass without further action. Perhaps Denison was right after all.

Although Denison wrote to the Office informing them that the bell could not now be rung, it has actually, after a slight turning in its position, been rung for the past 136 years! It will always be a symbol of our Parliament and heard every hour, via radio and television, by millions of people all over the world.

Regardless of the cracking of both bells, the completing of the finest clock in the world had been very successful and had made good use of his talents. He carried out many other public works and reference to the 'bell affair' was not often mentioned. Early in 1860 Dent was taken ill and decided to put his affairs in order. He was a wealthy man with a fortune of £60,000 and a business turnover of £8,000 a year. He consulted Denison about his will and left the bulk of his estate to him. However, he died intestate, his will apparently destroyed. Sir Charles Barry also died in 1860.

Lord Grimthorpe

In February 1886 Sir Edmund Beckett was raised to the peerage adopting the title Lord Grimthorpe and continued to be an active member of the House of Lords. He died in 1905. His estate was valued at two million pounds. Earlier, in 1886, he took part in a debate in the House concerning the proposed removal of the Holgate School in Hemsworth to Barnsley, supporting the former and could not resist a sneer at 'Black Barnsley'. Yet his ancestors, as we have seen, had very close connections with the town. Indeed, on family grounds, it would be appropriate to say that Barnsley had connections with the Westminster Clock and Big Ben.

Notes & References

The following sources have been used in the preparation of this study:

G J Alliott, *The Vanishing Relics of Barnsley* (1996)
Joseph Wilkinson, *Worthies of Barnsley and the District* (1881)
Brian Elliott, *The Making of Barnsley* (1988)
Peter Ferriday, *Lord Grimthorpe* (1957)
Peter Ferriday, *Victorian Architecture* (1963)
John H Burland, *Later Annals 1871-76*, Barnsley Local Studies and Archives (BLSA)
Dictionary of National Biography (1992), Oxford University Press
Barnsley Chronicle, 23 January 1869
Barnsley Independent, 6 May 1905
W G England *Pedigree of Local Families*, BLSA
Lodge's Almanack, 1906 BLSA

Acknowledgements

I would like to express my thanks to Mrs England for access to the books and notes of her late husband, W G England and also to Percy Fellows for the use of his photograph of Big Ben. Thanks are also due to the staff at the Barnsley Local Studies and Archives section of the Central Library; and to Diane Thornton for word processing the Beckett Pedigree.

5. JOSEPH BEAUMONT, 1792-1847: MINING STEWARD

by Geoffrey Hall

JOSEPH BEAUMONT WAS BORN IN 1792 but in what township or circumstances I have been unable to discover. According to his friends and obituarist Paul Rodgers he was 'left like an orphan', and 'set to work at a very early period at the coal pits near Scholes', a small village adjacent to the Chapeltown - Rotherham Road, between Thorpe Hesley and Kimberworth. Whilst growing up in humble circumstances Beaumont quickly learnt to maintain himself and assist in the support of his family. The turning point in his life came whilst working in one of the pits belonging to Earl Fitzwilliam. When the pit was put on a four day week he decided to make full use of this leisure time to improve his prospects in life. Although now a young man he was determined to educate himself and so became a scholar at one of the Greasbrough schools. He immediately took a liking to school and quickly realised that he was capable of becoming more than an ordinary collier. He purchased books to study and improve his education. Furthermore, to acquire knowledge and broaden his experience in mining matters, he worked at several collieries around Wentworth before moving to Worsbrough Dale in about 1818.

Joseph Beaumont married Mary Ann Swift at St. Mary's Church, Worsbrough on 23 November 1818. A sixty-three line poem *Epistle to Joseph Beaumont*, was written by Rodgers, a well-known local poet and lecturer, especially for the occasion. It included the lines:

> *In short, 'mong friends, I knew none other,*
> *So well deserved the name of <u>brother</u>.*
> *Joseph and I sworn friends for ever,*
> *Distance alone has power to sever!*
> *And now, that twice five miles divide us,*
> *Friendship had just as well ne'er tied us!*

The Beaumonts enjoyed twenty-eight years of married life but were not immune from sickness and suffering. They were blessed with six children but had the misfortune to loose four of them:

John, born 1820, died 13 January 1823, aged 3
Mary Ann, born 1824, died 30 July 1837, aged 13
Joseph, born 1829, died 29 August 1847, aged 18 (killed by falling
from his horse)
Elizabeth, born 1832, died 14 July 1841, aged 9

The surviving children were Sarah (b.1826) and James (b.1827).

Throughout his working life Joseph had earned the respect of
employers and workmates alike for his courage, discretion,
intelligence, honesty and practical knowledge of mining.
Furthermore he had gained first hand experience of dealing with
several small explosions of firedamp and other serious mining
accidents.

The largest mining company in the Worsbrough district was the
long established firm of Messrs. Field, Cooper, Faulds & Co of
Worsbrough Bridge who owned several coal and ironstone mines at
Worsbrough, Stainborough, Rockley and Pilley. A further company
asset was Worsbrough Furnace. One of the managing partners in the
business, Andrew Faulds, also carried out the duties of steward for
the firm, responsible for mining operations underground and on the
surface. Unfortunately he died on 19 March 1837, aged fifty-one. It
was now that the qualities and experience previously mentioned
reached fruition when Joseph Beaumont was appointed steward to
Messrs Field, Cooper & Co.

Beaumont had worked many years for the company prior to his
appointment and during this period had been involved in the
aftermath of at least five small explosions and several other accidents.
Indeed during the years 1832-42, eight small explosions and two
serious shaft accidents occurred at the company's pits: Stainborough
(2 explosions) and Worsbrough Park (6 explosions and 2 shaft
accidents) with the loss of 23 lives and 25 injured. He gave assistance
at other incidents which took place at pits in the neighbourhood and
frequently assisted Thomas Badger, the coroner, by providing advice
on mining matters.

In 1847 Beaumont was involved in the recovery work carried out
in the fire at Darley Main Colliery Worsbrough Dale and was also
called to the explosion at the Oaks Colliery, Hoyle Mill.

1. The fire at Darley Main Colliery, Worsbrough Dale (owned by Messrs Jarrett & Co): Friday 29 January, 1847

The fire occurred whilst men were driving a heading in the Barnsley
Thick Coal which is eight feet thick and of a fiery nature. About two

in the afternoon two colliers, Jenkinson and Barraclough, fired a charge of gunpowder to bring down the coal. After lighting the fuse the men took shelter and whilst waiting for the shot to detonate Jenkinson observed that the burning fuse had lit a feeder of gas. When the shot exploded it brought down about three tons of coal, releasing more gas which immediately caught fire over an area of five yards. The men tried to extinguish the flames using their jackets but were unsuccessful and so they went for help. A group of men coming to their assistance attempted to reach a place where a large water barrel was stored but failed due to the foul air and smoke.

After recovering in the fresh air, another attempt was made to smother the flames using buckets of water but they could not now approach within fifty yards of the fire. The men having failed to extinguish the fire came out of the pit and informed George Gomerson, the underground steward what had occurred. Immediately Gomerson went to the pit and gathered together a party of men to go down with him to extinguish the fire. The fire fighting team failed to reach the fire due to the foul air and smoke. Some of the men thought it was not safe to stay and returned to the surface leaving Gomerson underground with George Brown, Thomas Broadhead, John Gilberthorpe, Thomas Elstone, John Jenkinson and William Ellison. Gomerson, having failed to reach the fire, now decided to rescue the horses in the pit which were in danger of suffocation. After collecting the horses together they were taken to one of the shafts and left in the care of William Ellison. The remainder of the party collected their tools and then walked to the 'fourth bord-gate' and attempted to breach the stopping there which would have made it possible to walk the horses to the bottom of the downcast shaft and safety. Whilst working at the stopping they were all suffocated by the 'choke-damp'.

John Elstone, a relation of one of the men left in the pit with Gomerson, fearing for their lives, sent a message to Joseph Beaumont requesting his help. On his arrival at the Darley pit yard he immediately took charge. After gleaning as much information as possible regarding the situation underground he quickly organised a rescue party. Beaumont, with the rescue team, descended No.2 Shaft and quickly found Ellison and the six horses in a safe place. He was sent out of the pit after having informed Beaumont that the other men had gone to the 'fourth bord-gate' to breach a stopping. It was with great difficulty that the rescuers eventually found the remaining men all dead, lying about twenty-yards apart, as they had been fleeing from the choke-damp. Whilst recovering the bodies the rescuers suffered badly from breathing-in foul air and had repeatedly to take breaks in the fresh air before continuing with the work. It was midnight before all the bodies were recovered. No attempt was made to remove the horses as they were fastened up in a place which was ventilated by fresh air. The horses were brought to the surface on Sunday afternoon, but having not been fed since Friday they had eaten the coal baskets and any pieces of wood lying about. The men who lost their lives were:

> George Gomerson, understeward, aged 47 - wife
> and 5 children
> John Jenkinson, colliery, aged 45 - wife and 3 children
> Thomas Elstone, aged 34, wife and 4 children
> John Brown - aged 31 - wife and one child
> Thomas Broadhead, aged 46 - wife and 3 children
> John Gilberthorpe - aged 23 was unmarried

The funeral took place on Monday 2 February. The bodies were borne from their respective homes onto the main roadway leading to the church at the bottom of Worsbrough Bridge. It was at this point that the funeral procession was led by the six horses for which the victims had sacrificed their lives. The horses were mounted by the boys who regularly drove them at work in the colliery and in this unusual manner of showing respect they proceeded to St. Mary's Church. A large gathering of people joined the grieving families.

The Inquest

At the inquest Beaumont, acting as steward for Field, Cooper & Co, described how he had been 'sent for by John Elstone in consequence of what had happened at the Darley Main Colliery, to advise with them as the best means of getting the fire out'. He continued:

I went down Number 1 Pit and on the old level to the place where the fire started and found it was out. The accident arose from the lightly charged blast releasing an extra quantity of gas and the men not being able to put it out before it ignited the coal. Had I been there I would have made a stopping in the level and prevented the air from getting to the fire and it would have gone out of itself. The blasting of coal has been customary for twenty years in ours and many other pits and it is not considered so dangerous as to be stopped. If the men had remained with the horses they would have been safe, but they left to break-through the bord-gate to get the horses out and were overpowered in doing so by the

Figure 1. Gravestone in St Mary's churchyard, commemorating the death of the 'six workmen who lost their lives by suffocation in attempting to rescue six horses in the Darley Main Colliery when the coal was on fire', 20 January 1847. *Brian Elliott*
The verse below the list of names reads

> *Death by its overwhelming tide,*
> *Hath quickly laid us side by side*
> *Beware O man prepare in time*
> *We were cut down in all our prime.*

smoke. They had all turned back and one of them had nearly reached the pit bottom but the others had fallen at short distances from each other. The pit was exceedingly well ventilated.

Barnsley surgeon George Smith, told the inquest that he and his assistant were called to the colliery on Friday night to examine the bodies of the victims. After his examination he was of the opinion that all the men had died from the effects of inhaling carbonic acid gas, or 'choke-damp' **which is always the residue after an explosion of firedamp.** Smith attended Beaumont, Taylor and Thomas Harrison all of whom had been brought out of the pit in a state of stupor.

The Verdict

The coroner after summing up the evidence, said that all the witnesses agreed that the deaths of the six men had been caused by their remaining in the pit endeavouring to make a passage through which to take the horses, to a place they considered more secure than the one where they had left them.

A verdict of **accidentally suffocated** was returned by the Jury.

Finally, the last chapter of this story is to be found on a gravestone (Figure 1) at St. Mary's, beneath the east boundary wall of the church yard facing the back of the church.

(2) The Explosion at the Oaks Colliery, Friday 5 March, 1847

The dust had no sooner settled following the fire at Darley Main Colliery when, five weeks to the day afterwards, the local

Figure 2. An artist's impression of the Ardsley Main (Oaks) Colliery, taken from the *Illustrated London News*, 13 March 1847

communities surrounding Barnsley were stunned by the news of another calamity.

The Oaks Colliery, situated at Hoyle Mill, Stairfoot exploded on Friday 5 March, 1847, with the loss of seventy-three lives (Figures 2 and 3). Once again Joseph Beaumont was called upon to help, on this occasion by Mr G Wilson (Manager of the colliery) who asked him to come and bring some men with him to assist in repairing the pit.

On Monday 8 March, Messrs Firth, Barber & Co, the owners of the colliery, sent the following letter to Sir George Grey at Whitehall, London:

Messrs, Firth, Barber & Co,
Ardsley Oaks Colliery
Nr Barnsley
to Sir George Grey
8 March, 1847

It is our painful duty to inform you that a most serious accident, involving a loss of life to the amount of 73 persons, took place at our colliery, situate at the Oaks, about one mile from Barnsley, on Friday afternoon last the 5th instant. The coroner's inquest is being held to-day on the bodies of the unfortunate men and boys.

In the event of Government directing a commission to inquire into this most lamentable occurrence, we shall be ready to render to the Commissioners every information and assistance in our power to bring before them the cause of the accident, and we feel prepared to promote rather than to shun the investigation.

We have, etc
FIRTH, BARBER and Co

The following account of the explosion and subsequent events has been adapted from a report written on 22 March 1847, by Sir Henry de la Beche and Warrington W Smyth, who were commissioned by the *Home Office* to investigate the explosion at the above colliery.

The Explosion

The explosion occurred shortly after 3 o'clock on Friday afternoon and was so violent that it damaged both shafts besides the underground workings.

George Wilson, the colliery manager, quickly organised a rescue

Figure 3. The explosion at the Oaks Colliery as reconstructed in the *Illustrated London News*, 13 March 1847

party but they were delayed about an hour before the dust and smoke had cleared sufficiently for them to go down the pit. Before the rescue party descended a signal requesting the trunk to be lowered was received at the top of the downcast shaft. The trunk was a rectangular or square box in which men rode up and down the shaft. It was lowered and the first two men (bricklayers) were brought out of the mine, one alive and the other dead. The men had been working on a platform in the shaft at the time of the explosion, repairing the shaft walling. On reaching the pit bottom the rescue team found twenty-three injured miners gathered around the shaft who were quickly transported to the surface for medical treatment. Unfortunately three of them subsequently died. Despite the ventilation short circuiting due to the damage to the shafts and ventilating door in the pit bottom connecting road, there was sufficient ventilation for them to find and send up forty-five bodies. By this time it was about midnight and Wilson returned to the surface. Before going down the mine he had written a note to Field, Cooper & Co, requesting them to send Joseph Beaumont to the Oaks Colliery, with eight or nine men, to assist repairing the underground workings in order to restore the ventilation circuit and, if possible, recover the remaining bodies.

The Inquest

At the initial hearing of the inquest it was again thought that the source of the explosion was a heavy fall of roof in the unventilated goaf driving out the firedamp, 'which was ignited by the naked lights [candles] of the miners'. Systematic repair and recovery work commenced on the day of the explosion but it was not until the body of William Walton was found on Monday 15 March that the actual cause of the explosion was revealed at the adjourned inquest.

The Evidence of Joseph Beaumont and Benjamin Biram

(responses to questions are shown in italics)
Joseph Beaumont was examined on March 10:-
   Are you steward of the Worsbrough Park Colliery? -
   Yes, I am
   Did you not kindly assist in getting out the men after the accident at the Ardsley Main or Oaks Colliery on Friday the 5 March?
   I did: for Mr. Wilson wrote to our company to request me to come over and bring eight or nine men to lend assistance, which I instantly did as soon as I got the notice.

You have heard the evidence of George Armitage with respect to the finding of certain bodies, do you concur in the statements he has made?
Yes, I do.
After your experience in the mine since the explosion, and having studied the map now on the table would you state your opinion as to the locality whence you consider the explosion to have proceeded?
From B or C, as marked on the plan (both being at the edge of the waste).
Would you state your reasons for so considering?
The blast that took place has always thrown the stoppings in one direction, north, which shows the fire came from the points supposed.
After having given the subject the consideration which you have, should you think it probable that a heavy fall of the waste had forced the fire-damp upon the candles of the men working in the immediate vicinity?
It is quite clear that a break has taken place in the waste, and displaced the gas, and sent it down on the men's candles.
Is that your decided opinion?
Yes, it is.

Beaumont was re-examined on March 22:
Are you aware of the evidence adduced before the coroner as to finding the body of William Walton?
Yes.
Being aware of that evidence, what is now your opinion as to the cause of the explosion?
Since we found William Walton in the old break about 13 or 14 yards down, it is my opinion that it was he that lighted the gas in the old break.

Benjamin Biram, was examined on March 11:
Are you the superintendent of the collieries of Earl Fitzwilliam in this neighbourhood?
I am.
Did you not this morning descend the Ardsley Oaks or Main Colliery after having inspected the plan of the workings upon the table?
Yes.
Have you, after your examination of the colliery and the plans, formed any opinion as to the cause of the late explosion at that colliery?

I have: I consider that the explosion originated from the falling of the roof at the south waste as marked on the plan, such a falling having caused the carburetted hydrogen to be drawn out into the air-courses, where the mixture was fired by the candles of workmen.

Biram was re-examined on March 22:

Have you not attended the coroner's inquest held on the bodies of the sufferers who perished by the late explosion at the Ardsley Main Colliery?

I have.

Having so attended, and having heard the evidence adduced respecting the finding of the body of William Walton, what is now your opinion as to the cause of that explosion?

I think now that it scarcely admits of a doubt as to the gas having been fired by William Walton, from his body having been found so far out of the course of circulation of air, where I think a naked candle could not have been taken without producing an explosion; and from its having been given in evidence that he was not working with his lamp a short time before. If this be correct, I think the fall of the roof in the break was the effect of the explosion, and not the cause of it.

Verdict of the Coroner's Inquest:

The Jury are of the opinion, that efficient regulations are not enforced in this district to prevent the use of naked lights in those parts of coal-mines where inflammable gas is known to exist; and they are further of the opinion, that the recurrence of accidents involving so large a loss of human life demands the immediate attention of Her Majesty's Government, and would justify Parliament in framing such a code of regulations as would give greater security to persons employed in mining operations.

With these sentiments the Deputy Coroner, Mr G D Barker, expressed his entire concurrence.

Following the Oaks disaster Beaumont returned to living a normal life both work-wise and with his family. Unfortunately within a few months a personal tragedy struck his family on Saturday evening 21 August 1847. His eighteen year old son, Joseph was employed as a junior clerk in the offices of Messrs Field, Cooper & Co. After riding on his horse to Bank Top on company business he was returning home to Worsbrough Bridge when he met with a fatal accident. On approaching *Marrow House* at Ward Green, whether his horse took fright or stumbled is not known, but young Joseph was thrown to the ground and fatally injured. In the accident he received a fractured skull and it was evident from his other injuries that the horse had rolled on him when falling. Despite the best medical attention possible from Mr Smith, the surgeon, he died twenty four hours later. An inquest returned a verdict of 'Accidental Death'. Joseph Jnr was laid to rest in the family grave at Worsbrough St. Mary's churchyard.

The following extract is taken from the *Sheffield and Rotherham Independent* report on the accident:

> *We believe there has seldom been manifested more sympathy in the neighbourhood than on the occurrence of this accident. Besides that the youth himself was a general favourite, his father is the benevolent individual who on many occasions and particularly on the occurrence of the late Ardsley Oaks calamity, risked his own life to render aid to the sufferers. In fact had not a contingency intervened, a dinner and a splendid silver cup were to have been given to him by a number of neighbouring gentlemen, last Thursday for his benevolent conduct.*

Mrs Beaumont, distraught by the loss of her son, had not overcome her grief when she received another and more devastating shock barely three weeks later.

The Explosion at Pilley Lane Ironstone Mine
(Thursday 16 September 1847)

An unusual system of ventilation and set of circumstances were the cause of the explosion at Messrs Field, Cooper and Co's Ironstone mine, Pilley Lane.

The following method of ventilation was practised in the upcast shaft of this mine. The shaft was not fully brick-lined and in the sides of the circular shaft were several places where blowers (or feeders) of firedamp issued through breaks in the strata. It was the practice to keep one or two of these blowers always burning as they consumed the firedamp in quantities too small to cause any harm and at the same time induced a flow of air up the shaft.

At the time of the explosion a stage had been erected in the shaft at the Tankersley Park ironstone level which was about eight yards above the shaft bottom where there was roadway into the Flockton Thick coal seam. Furthermore the day was damp and windy and also two feeders of firedamp were lit just above the Tankersley Park ironstone level.

The Inquest (Held on Saturday 18 September at the *Gate Inn*,

Pilley)

On the morning of the explosion Joseph Beaumont and his nephew John Swift (underground steward and surveyor to Lord Wharncliffe and F W T Vernon Wentworth, Esq) descended the mine to measure the section of ironstone which was about to be worked. During the course of their visit they sat down and conversed with the men who were working in the pit before leaving them to return to the surface. Shortly afterwards an explosion occurred which blew the men's lights out. John Fisher, an ironstone getter, made his way to the shaft side to find out what was amiss and get a new light. On reaching the shaft side he found the stage was missing. He heard a moan and called out but received no answer. Fisher then called to the men on the pit bank to send the rope down with a corve attached and a new light. When the corve arrived at the landing he got in and was lowered down to the bottom. Here he found Swift lying unconscious on the broken stage and after lifting him into the corve they were conveyed to the surface. Fisher descended the shaft again but could not find Beaumont, so he called for assistance and was joined by two men, Musgrave and Thornton. After removing some timbers they found Beaumont buried about eighteen inches deep under the stage timber and debris. A large piece of timber lay across him which could not be dislodged until all the debris had been removed. He had been killed by the stage falling upon him. His head, body and legs were badly injured and the right thigh broken.

On the day of the explosion the weather was damp and windy. When Beaumont and Swift reached the stage in the shaft they found that the flames from the feeders of firedamp had been extinguished by the wind. Beaumont immediately attempted to light one of the feeders and it was at this point when the explosion occurred.

The explosion was caused by the following circumstances: approximately eight yards below the staging and access to the ironstone mine, was another roadway in the shaft side to the Flockton Thick coal seam. This roadway had collapsed, practically cutting off the ventilation and allowing the firedamp to accumulate below the stage. Due to the inclement weather the barometer had fallen, drawing out the firedamp from below the staging and old Flockton workings into the shaft. It was stated that the pit was well ventilated and when the feeders were burning they considered that there was no danger. The Jury returned a verdict of 'Accidental Death'.

At the closing of the inquest the coroner, Thomas Badger, was reported as saying that he had had during a succession of years many cases of violent deaths to enquire into, and had witnessed the fruits of death in all forms, but had scarcely known one instance which had given him so much pain. He stated that he had known Mr Beaumont many years, had communications with him in various ways, often had his most valuable advice and assistance in different cases, had conferred with him in the inquest room, and conversed with him in private, and on all occasions found him to be 'a man of sound sense, of great good nature, and of indisputable courage'.

The newspaper reporter recorded that

> *Mr Badger, both at the commencement and close of the inquiry, made a deep impression on all who heard him, by the feeling manner in which he spoke of the unfortunate occurrence, and of the estimable qualities of the departed.*

A further compliment was paid by Beaumont's obituarist: 'he was wise in counsel, brave in action, his life was spent mainly in useful and profitable deeds'.

As we have seen, a silver cup, purchased by public subscription, was to have been presented to Beaumont at a dinner held in his honour. On the first occasion it was due to three members of the subscribing committee being away on business and on the second due to the unfortunate death of Beaumont's son. Shortly after the inquest the subscribers committee held a meeting at the *Red Lion*, Worsbrough Bridge and agreed that two of their members should privately present the cup. The appointed members went to his home and presented the cup to Mrs Beaumont and her surviving children.

The following inscription was engraved on the memento:

> *Presented to Mr Joseph Beaumont, Colliery Agent to Messrs Field, Cooper and Co, of Worsbrough Bridge, as an enduring testimonial of the benevolent and disinterested exertions which he has at all times displayed in the perilous emergencies of colliery accidents, and particularly in approbation of his undaunted courage, skill and judgement in the terrific explosion in the Ardsley Oaks Colliery on the 5th March 1847, when 73 human beings were lost.*

Beaumont's funeral took place on Saturday afternoon, at St Mary's Church in Worsbrough village. About three hundred people went to pay their last respects. The chief mourners were members of the family, the colliery owners Messrs Field, Cooper & Co, the Ardsley Oaks and Darley Main Collieries and Benjamin Biram of Earl

Figure 4. The Beaumont family gravestone in St Mary's Churchyard *Author*

Fitzwilliam's Collieries with his underground viewers. Also in attendance were many gentlemen from Barnsley along with workmen and other people of the neighbourhood.

Today in St. Mary's churchyard the gravestone (Figure 4) stands proudly there for all to see.

In conclusion, the following words of Ebenezer Elliott serve as a most appropriate tribute:

Father, our brother's course is run,
And we bring home thy weary son,
No more he toils, no more he weeps,
And shall we mourn because he sleeps.

Sources

This article is based on accounts in contemporary newspapers and from official reports.

Acknowledgements

I thank the following for their help: Arthur Clayton, Mrs Winifred Taylor, Brian Elliott, Russell Whitaker, John Goodchild, Cyril Rayner, and the Archive and Local Studies Staff at Barnsley and Sheffield Libraries.

6. CHILD LABOUR IN MINES IN THE BARNSLEY AREA IN THE EARLY VICTORIAN PERIOD: EVIDENCE FROM THE CHILDREN'S EMPLOYMENT COMMISSION

by Melvyn and Joan Jones

THE VICTORIAN PERIOD IS RICH in detailed investigations of the social and economic conditions of the 'working classes'. Among the best known are Henry Mayhew's study of *London's Labour and the London Poor*, Charles Booth's *Life and Labour of the People of London*, Edwin Chadwick's report on the *Sanitary Condition of the Labouring Population of Great Britain* and Friedrich Engels's *The Condition of the Working Class in England*. One series of investigations that deserves to be better known locally is that connected with the Children's Employment Commission of the early 1840s enquiring into the employment of children in mines, factories and workshops. The sub-commissioner responsible for collecting evidence and writing up the report on the employment of children in mines and factories in the South Yorkshire area was Jelinger C Symons Esq. His report on children in mines in West and South Yorkshire, which is dated July 1841, covers 42 pages with 17 pages of appendices followed by 73 pages of depositions from 299 separate witnesses gathered in early 1841.[1] Symons interviewed mine owners, managers, miners, the children who worked in the pits and a variety of other witnesses including doctors and clergymen. He investigated practices and conditions in collieries and ironstone pits, large and small, including adit mines (day-holes) and bell pits (Figure 1).

The reformers who pressed for these Commissions to take place were concerned about the physical and spiritual welfare of the children. Others saw the child labour force as a necessary evil and it was condoned not only by capitalists large and small but also by parents, the latter seeing children from a very young age not as dependants but as important components of the family economic unit. The underground steward at a coal pit near Thorpe Hesley told

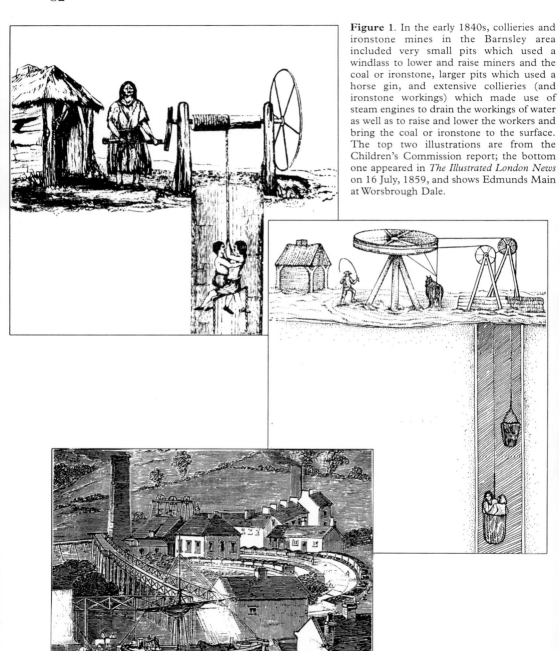

Figure 1. In the early 1840s, collieries and ironstone mines in the Barnsley area included very small pits which used a windlass to lower and raise miners and the coal or ironstone, larger pits which used a horse gin, and extensive collieries (and ironstone workings) which made use of steam engines to drain the workings of water as well as to raise and lower the workers and bring the coal or ironstone to the surface. The top two illustrations are from the Children's Commission report; the bottom one appeared in *The Illustrated London News* on 16 July, 1859, and shows Edmunds Main at Worsbrough Dale.

Symons that 'it would do great harm to a man who has a large family to prevent a lad from opening a [trap] door or being in a pit till he is 11 years old.' One divisive issue even among those who condoned child labour was the employment of girls underground, and as we shall see, Symons witnessed girl miners on many occasions in the Barnsley area although two of the biggest employers - Earl Fitzwilliam and Newton Chambers at Thorncliffe - did not allow this form of labour. In what follows we hear views from both sides of the argument and also those of the sub-commissioner himself. Some of the children interviewed were painfully honest; others may have been 'briefed'. The same must be true of the adult witnesses who would not have wanted to be dismissed for showing their employer in a poor light. However, even with these reservations in mind what comes across is a graphic portrayal of heavy, debilitating work, often in atrocious conditions, usually in semi-darkness and with the strong possibility of physical injury. Symons describes graphically what it must have been like for young children being introduced to a pit for the first time:

> *The springs which ooze through the best cased shafts, trickle down its sides, and keep up a perpetual drizzle below. The chamber or area at the bottom of the shaft is almost always sloppy and muddy, and the escape from it consists of a labyrinth of black passages, often not above four feet square...*

Many must have been afraid and faced the next day's work with fear and loathing. During their childhood they might have first-hand experience of accidents caused by explosions of fire-damp, suffocation from black-damp, roof falls, breaking of ropes and chains in the shaft, inundations and blows from runaway corves.

The rest of the article follows the order in which Symons organised his 1841 report with the insertion of eye-witness accounts as appropriate.

Age of Commencing Work

According to Symons 'there were well attested instances of children being taken into coal-pits as early as five years of age...'. Edward Ellis Esq., a Silkstone surgeon, said that he had 25 years' professional experience among colliers and he was of the opinion that children went into pits at the age of five very frequently. The Rev Richard Morton, curate of Dodworth, said that parents got their children into the pits 'as soon as they think they can do anything', adding 'I have been told that some have gone by the time they have been five years old'. Symons thought such cases were rare but that many did begin work at seven. He reckoned eight was the normal age for beginning work underground. It is clear from the evidence that many coal owners did not know how young many of their workers were or conveniently ignored what was going on. They consistently gave the age of commencing work underground as being higher than it actually was.

Symons reported that in thin seam pits there was a temptation to bring in young children simply because they were small and could cope better with the low roofs. One Sheffield coal manager actually said in his evidence that 'Christians are handier than horses...'.

Hours of Work

On average miners, including the children, worked between 10 and 11 hours a day six days a week. Each day each team of miners - and the children were key members of these teams - 'got' a certain quota of coal or ironstone. Towards the end of a week or fortnight, depending on when they got paid, longer hours were frequently worked, to make up for any lost time.

Work usually commenced between five and six in the morning and work began as soon as the coal face was reached; this was almost immediately in a small pit, but could take up to an hour in an extensive deep colliery where the miners had to wait to take the cage to the pit bottom and then walk to their work place. A collier at Messrs Day and Twibell's pit in Barnsley told Symons that young children were 'taken out of their beds at four o'clock, and between that and five, throughout the year.' The miners usually left the pits between three and five in the afternoon. Night work was unusual.

Meals

Symons' initial summary in his main report suggests that meal-taking was a well-ordered, substantial affair:

It is the general practice among colliers to breakfast before they go to the pit, and to take their substantial meal after they return home. The meal taken in the pit (in at least five cases out of six) is a luncheon consisting of bread, and sometimes bread and meat, or bread and cheese. They have oatmeal porridge and milk for breakfast, and sometimes onion porridge. They have generally meat and potatoes for dinner when they come out of the pit - a small portion of meat and a good deal of Yorkshire pudding with it. The parents often have tea or a little beer for their drinking, but children usually have nothing after their dinner.

He went on to say that the engine (for drawing coal to the surface) stopped generally for an hour for dinner 'and always 40 minutes', during which time the engineer and the banksman (who received the coal wagons (corves) at the surface) had their dinners. Down the pit, he records, there was no fixed duration of time to take a meal break. The getter (the miner who actually hewed the coal), he said, resumed working after a short rest, often helped - willingly or otherwise - by the older children. He went on to say that in some of the pits near Chapeltown work scarcely stopped 'above a quarter of an hour'.

It is clear from the evidence that Symons collected in the Barnsley area that the children often began their work without having any breakfast, often took meagre rations to work, and were often too tired to eat when they got home. When he interviewed Elizabeth Day, a 17 year old hurrier at Hopwood's pit in Barnsley, she said she had bread and a bit of fat [dripping] for her dinner in the pit; some of the hurriers also had 'a sup of beer'; she said she drank the water that ran through the pit. One collier told Symons that hurrying was 'very slavish work', yet he had known boys work twelve hours without more than 'a bit of dry bread to eat.' A Mr Crooks, a Barnsley surgeon, in a letter written to Symons, said that on his rounds that day he had ridden by a group of miners' cottages and a neighbouring farmer had told him that many of the children there worked underground and that many 'who had thoughtless parents' were badly fed. He said some of them were sent to work without breakfast, took little to eat with them and had 'but coarse fare when they returned'. In contrast, when interviewed by Symons he said that he had heard that 'there is enough bread lying about in a pit to feed a pig, and when they come out they have hot dinners generally.'

Washing

Symons claimed that washing after work was 'very partial' and 'confined in nineteen cases out of twenty, to the upper parts of the body, except on Saturdays and Sunday mornings.' Neither, he said, was there any change of clothing: the men and boys put on their shirts, waistcoats and coats, and the women and girls their gowns.

The nature of employment

Children were employed underground in four different ways: as trappers, horse-drivers, jenny boys and hurriers.

In a deep pit ventilation air was drawn down a 'downcast' shaft, then circulated through the workings and ascended an 'upcast' shaft (in this period often the same one that coal was wound up, and up and down which the miners were carried from and to their work). In order that the fresh air made no short cuts, trapdoors were placed along the main underground roadway (main gate). The responsibility for making sure that the trap doors were always closed between the passage of full or empty corves was with the *trappers,* and this role was entrusted to the youngest children in a pit - they were not yet big or strong enough to do other jobs (Figure 2). Symons described it thus:

> *Their duty consists in sitting in a little hole, scooped out for them in the side of the gates behind each door, where they sit with a string in their hands attached to the door, and pull it open the moment they hear the corves at hand, and the moment it has passed they let the door fall too* [sic]*, which it does of its own weight. If anything impedes the shutting of the door they remove it, or, if unable to do so, run to the nearest man to get him to do it for them. They have nothing else to do; but, as their office must be performed from the repassing of the first to the passing of the last corve during the day, they are in the pit the whole time it is worked, frequently above twelve hours a day. They sit, moreover in the dark, often with a damp floor to stand on, and exposed necessarily to drafts* [sic] *though I have seldom found the temperature lower at their posts than 58°, and often higher.*

Figure 2. A young trapper at work

He went on to say that 'Trappers are on the whole, more cheerful than might be expected; and it is not unusual to hear them singing as they sit in their holes.' Samuel Hirst, a nine year old trapper at Earl Fitzwilliam's pit at Jump was questioned by Symons. He recounted that he liked it 'middling'. He said he sat by himself and didn't have a light. He said he sat still all day and never did anything except open and shut the door. He said he'd rather be at school than down the pit. He said 'it's only sometimes that they pay [beat] me'. When Symons interviewed another trapper, George Lindley at Gawber pit, who was nine and had been trapping for three years, the boy told him that when his light went out 'I smoke my pipe. I smoke a quartern of tobacco every week.' At the same pit he encountered Sarah Gooder, an eight year old trapper. She told Symons that she trapped without a light and was scared. She said she went to the pit at four or even half-past three in the morning. She said she sometimes sang, but only if she had a light. She said she dare not sing in the dark.

The best occupation for children, according to Symons, was that of *horse driver*. Horses were used to take corves to the pit bottom in large collieries where the main gate was long and the coal seams sufficiently thick to allow the use of animals. Horse drivers were involved in little heavy work, only being called upon to exert their strength if a corve accidentally came off the rails on which it was travelling. The horses were well trained, and the drivers sat in the front corf (they were usually in trains of six to eight) when taking empties back to the coal face. At Earl Fitzwilliam's pits at Elsecar and Jump each horse driver had an assistant. There were 21 horse drivers and their assistants employed there.

Older children, usually boys of 11 or 12 to 15, were also employed as *jenny boys*. Jenny boys were required where, because of faulting, there was a rapid descent down a gate. In these places a pulley system was set up and corves brought by horses had to be detached, hooked on to the pulley system and allowed to descend to the next level. The speed of the descent was controlled by a brake operated by the jenny boy. The weight of a full corf caused an empty one to be drawn up from the lower to the higher level. Symons found a 'great muster of these lads' at the Elsecar collieries.

By far the most common form of employment of children underground was that of *hurrier* or *trammer*. Hurriers were employed to convey coal in corves from the coal face to the pit bottom, or where horses were used, from the coal face to the main gate (Figure 3). Symons described the corves as:

Figure 3. A hurrier. *Children's Employment Commission report, 1842*

> *...oblong waggons, on small wheels of 9 to 12 inches diameter, running on railways, which are laid down in nearly all the gates of every colliery. These corves vary greatly in size, carrying from 2 to 10 cwt of coal and weigh about 2 or 2½ cwt themselves, making a weight of about 8 cwt in all. The operation of propelling these corves is called hurrying, and, in some places, tramming; it is done by placing both hands on the top rail of the back of the corve, and pushing it forward, running as fast as the degree of inclination of the road or the strength of the hurrier will permit.*

Unlike the trappers, horse-drivers and jenny boys, the hurriers were employed directly by the miners (getters). During a day's work the hurriers pushed their corves considerable distances. At Mr Clarke's collieries at Silkstone, Symons calculated that, on average, the hurriers had to push a loaded corf (weighing 8 cwt) 150 yards from the coal faces to the horse gate and back again 20 times during a shift - a distance of three and a half miles. At Traviss and Horsfall's pit at Worsbrough the distances worked were considerably longer: hurriers had to convey their corves 400 yards full and 400 yards empty 20 times during a day's work - an overall distance of more than nine miles.

At Messrs Thorpe's pits at Gawber, Symons likened the work of two sisters he saw hurrying there to slavery: 'I have no hesitation in adding that were they galley slaves their work could not be more oppressive, and I believe would not in all probability be so much so.' And yet Mr J C Sutcliffe, the general agent for the pit, while admitting that the corves in the pit were heavier than in other local pits (12½ cwt when full), was of the opinion that 'a girl of sixteen can hurry one of these corves very well and do her day's work with ease.' This evidence contrasts markedly with that given by Ann Eggley at the same pit:

> *The work is far too hard for me; the sweat runs off me all over*

Figure 4. A hurrier at work in a thin seam pit. *Children's Employment Commission Report, 1842*

sometimes. I'm very tired at night. Sometimes when we get home at night we have not power to wash us, and then we go to bed. Sometimes we fall asleep in the chair. Father said last night it was both a shame and a disgrace to work as we do, but there was nought else for us to do.

Where the gates were steep great strength was needed either to hold the full corf back or to push the empty corf uphill back to the face. Symons said it was not uncommon to see bald hurriers 'owing to pushing corves up steep board-gates with their heads'. In thin seam pits there were often no rails and the roofs were so low that the corves had to be pulled like sledges on chains fastened round the hurriers' waists by belts (Figure 4).

It must be remembered that it was the miners (the getters) who hired the hurriers. There were certain advantages for miners in employing members of their own family as hurriers. The main advantage was that earnings were kept within the family. If they were young they could be more easily controlled and directed than other employees. They could also be worked harder at no extra, or even less, expense. Evidence in Symons's report suggests considerable abuse in situations where miners employed their own children, with an insistence on very long hours and unrealistic output targets. The mineral agent at Thorncliffe (Newton Chambers) told Symons that

Those who have got their own children at work with them use them worse than others. I am quite sure of this. Where the lads are hired ... they will stick up for themselves and will not work more than the time agreed on, but where the undertakers employ their own children, they can make them do as they like.

Rates of Pay

In South Yorkshire, Symons said, trappers earned generally 6d per day. The hurriers, in the thick coal pits, earned about 5 shillings a week at 11; those of 14 earned 8 shillings and those of 17 were paid 8 shillings. Miners' earnings varied according to their strength and industry. Young able-bodied getters in thick coal pits earned 20 or 25 shillings a week. In the thin coal pits wages were 10 or 20 per cent less. In some pits weekly wages were as high as 30 shillings but, according to Symons, in those circumstances the miners lived more luxuriously, drank more, and missed more days through illness brought on by heavy drinking.

Moral Condition

Symons was of the view that the vices of the children of colliers were much less than those of 'the manufacturing class'. He put this down to the fact that they were 'much more closely confined and tired when their work is done' and because they did not work together for long periods. Having said that, he believed that their ignorance was just as great as the children who worked in factories, if not more so. He also reported that there was a 'fearful amount' of swearing and indecent language in the pits.

There was general concern about the lack of education among the mining population. They were at work during the day, and too tired to wish to take advantage of sunshine and fresh air at the weekends. The opinion of William Newbould, a coal master, seems quite out of touch: 'They could learn in the evenings if they chose; they are not too tired with their work to do so.' Timothy Marshall's view (he was a miner at Darton) seems more realistic: 'they are both tired and disinclined to learn when they have done work.'

Symons had much to say and report about the employment of girls underground. Girls, he said, performed all the various mining jobs, trapping, hurrying, filling, riddling, tipping, and occasionally getting. He went on to say that one of the most disgusting sights he had ever seen, at the day pits at Hunshelf Bank, near Penistone, was that of 'young females, dressed like boys in trousers, crawling on all fours, with belts round their waists and chains passing between their legs. He said the gate in the pit was not more than a yard high, and in some places not much more than two feet. The corves had to be pushed and dragged in the closely confined space. At the same pit he witnessed a girl of fourteen getting coal with 'the regular pick used by men.' She was half sitting and half lying at her work in a place not two feet high and 'of course, she didn't like it.'

At Messrs Charlesworth's pit at Silkstone Symons interviewed Ann Fern, a hurrier, who had been working there for five years. She seemed resigned to her fate. She said she was up at half-past four, went down the pit at five and got out at four or five in the afternoon. She said she liked the pit but would rather be in service 'but had never tried.' She said it was hard work but 'should be worked hard anywhere I daresay.' She had had a broken leg while working as a trapper when she was younger.

The sub-commissioner was concerned about the degree of nakedness among the girls and the effect this had on the girls themselves and miners with whom they worked:

In great numbers of the coal-pits in this district the men work in a state of perfect nakedness, and are in this state assisted in their labour by females of all ages, from girls of six years old to women of twenty-one, these females being themselves quite naked down to the waist.

When he went down Hopwood's pit at Barnsley he found:

assembled round a fire a group of men, boys and girls, some of whom were of the age of puberty, the girls as well as the boys stark naked down to the waist, their hair bound up with a tight cap, and trousers supported by their hips. Their sex was recognisable only by their breasts, and some little difficulty occasionally arose in pointing out to me which were girls and which were boys, and which caused a good deal of laughing and joking.

He also had something to say about what he called 'bastardy' in the pits, going on to say that the character of the miners in general was such that it was the general practice to marry the girls they had seduced.

The evidence he obtained from leading local citizens about the employment of girls underground was unanimous in its condemnation of the practice. Michael Thomas Sadler Esq, a Barnsley surgeon who had lived in the town for eighteen years, said that he strongly disapproved of females being in pits, adding that 'the female character is totally destroyed by it; their habits and feelings are altogether different; they can neither discharge the duties of wives nor mothers.'

George Carr, a 50 year old ironstone miner from Tankersley where girls were not employed, gave his opinion of the practice:

I make no more money than the colliers at Silkstone, nor so much,

but I would be hard put to it before I would bring a lass of mine to
the pits - no, not if I was ever so ill put to it. I would live upon one
meal a day sooner. I don't consider it right, no way; it is never done
here … I have wrought above 40 years in ironstone pits. I have got
several children, three only are working here, all boys, and I have two
boys and two lasses at home. I am sure colliers could do without
putting their lasses in pits...It's a shameful practice.

Symons concluded that the mining children were growing up   in
what he variously called 'a state of Heathen ignorance' or 'a state of
absolute and appalling ignorance'. Because they started work at an
early age, were out of sight during the day and took advantage of the
fresh air and light on Sundays, the mining population lived, he said,
'out of sight of the rest of the community, and almost wholly out of
its ken: they are reached by none of our institutions.'

Conclusion

Mr George Traviss, a Barnsley coal owner, told Symons that he did
not think children were overworked so as to hurt them. 'They always
appear to me', said Traviss, 'to be very cheerful, and run about and
play when they come out of the pit in the evening'. The same
sentiments were also expressed by other coal owners and managers.
Symons's riposte in his report was typically direct and neatly sums up
the situation of the many children working underground in pits in
the Barnsley area at the beginning of the Victorian period:

The evidence given by some witnesses, that the children are cheerful
when they get out of the pit, is somewhat akin to evidence that people
are cheerful when they get out of prison.

To a late twentieth century reader, Symons's report contains
compelling evidence about the wrongness of committing children to
work underground from a very early age: it was likely to have a severe
impact on their physical health, their morals and their education let
alone the psychological damage that was done. The practice seems to
us callous and depraved. And yet it was not thought to be wicked by
coal owners and many of the parents of the children involved. The
coal owners had a vested interest in getting out of the pits the largest
amount of coal for the least cost and the parents saw their children,
when they had reached a certain age, as contributors to the family's
income rather than as dependants. It needs to be remembered that
there was no compulsory education system, no old age pensions, and
trade unions were in their infancy.

The outcome of the enquiry was that when the report was laid before Parliament in 1842, a bill was brought forward by Lord Ashley (later the Earl of Shaftesbury) and an Act of Parliament was passed on 4 August of that year forbidding the employment of girls and women underground and making unlawful the employment of boys in pits under the age of ten. The Act became law from 1 March 1843. The penalty for non-compliance was relatively small - a fine for each case of not less than £5 and not more than £10. An inspector to enforce the Act - he was called the Commissioner for Mines - was appointed in December 1843. With just one person to cover the whole country evasion of the provisions of the Act was not difficult at first.

A contemporary - but not unbiased - commentator, Friedrich Engels, writing two years later was of the opinion that:

> *The Bill ... has remained a dead letter in many coalmining regions because no mining inspectors were appointed to enforce its provisions. If a coalmine is situated in a rural area evasion of the law is in any case a relatively simple matter. So it need cause no surprise to discover that last year (1843) an official memorial laid before the Home Secretary by the Miners' Association stated that over sixty women were employed on the Duke of Hamilton's collieries in Scotland. Nor need it cause surprise to learn that the Manchester Guardian reported that a girl had been killed in a colliery accident - if I remember rightly - at Wigan.*[2]

Notes and References

1. *Royal Commission on Children's Employment (Mines)*, 1st Report (1842) Parts I and II, Parliamentary Papers (380) XV and (381) XVI, Irish University Press.

2. Engels F, *The Condition of the Working Class in England* (1844), translated by Henderson W O and Chaloner W H, 1971 Basil Blackwell, pp. 284-85.

Further Reading

Lake, Fiona and Preece, Rosemary *Voices from the Dark: Women and Children in Yorkshire Coal Mines,* 1992, Yorkshire Mining Museums Publications, Overton.

Machin, Frank *The Yorkshire Miners: A History,* 1958, Volume 1, National Union of Mineworkers (Yorkshire Area), Barnsley.

7. UNCLE BEN IN AMERICA: A LOOK AT THE ILLINGWORTH LETTERS

by Philip Hansen and Geoffrey Tweedale

PERSONAL LETTERS CAN BE an invaluable historical source, yet usually - unless their authors were rich and famous - they do not survive, or remain inaccessible to the historian. It is even rarer for such letters to relate to the lives of English emigrants, especially those who left to begin new lives in America in the nineteenth century. Only a handful of such letters are known to have survived for the South Yorkshire region.

In this article, we describe a series of letters relating to the Illingworths, a little-known - yet in their day influential - family, who lived at Snowdenhill, near Stocksbridge. In particular, we look at the career of Benjamin Illingworth, Figure 1, whose letters to his relatives in Stocksbridge provide a unique source on a forgotten transatlantic link.

Who was Benjamin Illingworth? The family name seems to have originated around Halifax and probably Benjamin's forebears arrived in the Barnsley and Sheffield district, by way of Silkstone and Cawthorne, sometime during the late eighteenth or early nineteenth century. The Illingworths eventually made their home near Stocksbridge at a place named Hunshelf, a hilly township which included the hamlet of Snowdenhill, Figure (2a). It was a predominantly rural area, with oats, wheat, and barley as the main crops. Even as late as the 1890s, wheat in this area was cut mainly with scythes. In the early nineteenth century, stone-quarrying was the only industry to operate on a large scale.

Benjamin's parents were Robert Illingworth (1798-1870), a farm labourer, and Mary Broadhead (1799-1866), who married at Penistone Church on 21 May, 1823. The early

Figure 1. Benjamin Illingworth (1823-1914) *Peter Long*

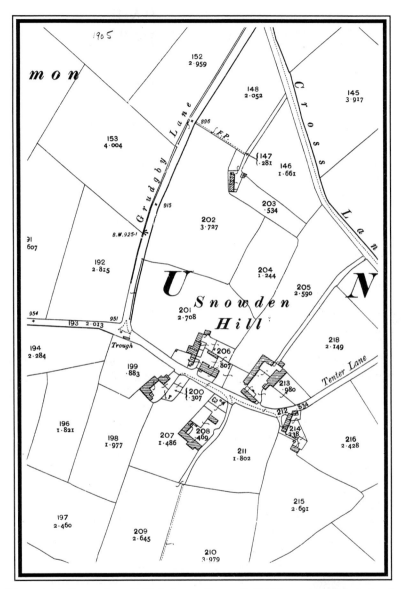

Figure 2(a). Extract from 1905 Ordnance Survey (1:25000) map showing the hamlet of Snowdenhill. The Illingworth cottage is linked by footpath to Grudgby Lane - located between fields numbered 202 and 147

history of this 'frugal couple', who lived in a small Snowdenhill stone cottage, Figure 2(b), has been told by Stocksbridge's local historian Joseph Kenworthy, who was related to the Illingworths. Benjamin was the first child born to the couple on 11 July, 1823, and in the following twenty years they had eight more children (Samuel, Joshua, Charles, George, John, Rachel, William and Martin). Robert Illingworth supported his large family by his work as a farm hand and shepherd, and also grew his own crops on the four acres of land surrounding his cottage. According to Kenworthy:

> *The quiet, patient old man, who in later years collected the rates for Hunshelf township, and who, as a farm hand and shepherd, never received more than eight shillings per week, and ten shillings with 'drinkings' thrown in at lambing times, had to take his little lads from their lessons in the school taught at Hawksworth's fold, and send them down to the Old Wire Mill to 'scour' wire. I have heard those lads, as men in after years, with repressed emotion, tell of their father meeting them on dark nights at the stepping stones, and how, in time of flood, he carried or guided them over the stones.*

Figure 2(b). The cottage of Robert and Mary Illingworth at Snowdenhill where Benjamin was born

As the Illingworth children grew up through the 'hungry forties', life in these rural areas was harsh.   Charles Illingworth later told Kenworthy: 'I must have eaten some tons of porridge and oat-cake in my time'.   It was the staple diet for labouring men, as bread and meat were such a rarity.

However, Snowdenhill was already feeling the impact of the rapid industrialisation that was happening in the valley at Stocksbridge; and even greater developments were taking place several miles away in Sheffield.   Hunshelf may have been mostly rural, but Stocksbridge and its environs had a more mixed economy with several important industries.   At Wortley, Thurgoland, Oughtibridge, and Wadsley the metalworking industry had been long established.   In 1842, Samuel Fox had launched his famous wiremaking business in Stocksbridge, which was later to become a leading alloy steel manufacturer.   The region was also a major centre for the refractories and mining industry.   Consequently, some of the Illingworth's offspring began moving out of agriculture into industrial occupations.   For example, the fourth son, Charles Illingworth (1830-1912), as a boy of nine and with the help of a brother, scoured wire at the Wire Mill in Thurgoland.

Benjamin Illingworth was another son who did not follow his father into farming.   In 1837, he was apprenticed in the steel trade. The 1841 Census enumerates him living at Wharncliffe Side, with the Dickinson family.   One member of that household, George Dickinson, owned the Holmes Works, a tilt on the River Don upstream from Oughtibridge at a place known as Brightholmlee.   It was there that Benjamin was apprenticed as a tilter.   How he came to be introduced to the Dickinsons we do not know, though clearly Benjamin proved good at the job.   According to one American biography: 'his mechanical aptitude and rapid progress as a skilled workman soon engaged the attention of his employers, and at the age of twenty-one he became foreman of the works'.

In 1848, however, Benjamin made a crucial decision.   He was persuaded by Joseph Dickinson, George's brother, to accompany him to America to help in the establishment of a steel works run by American entrepreneurs.   Benjamin later related to Joseph Kenworthy the details of his first trip on the good ship *Cornelia*:

The ship was more than six weeks on the sea.   There were no steamships in those days.   Our ship was a four-master and a very big one.   She carried [good?] *many passengers, mostly Irish.   Sometimes we were becalmed for a few days at a time, and sometimes in a gale we would be blown a few hundred miles out of our course and in some gales we would be blown a few hundred miles towards Liverpool. All passengers had to provide their provisions. The shipping company advised us to bring bread, flour, oat-meal, potatoes, crackers, tea and coffee, and each family had to cook for themselves. In the galley there was a range about twenty feet long, with a good fire burning all day long. I have set many a tea-kettle on that galley-fire, and many a pot of potatoes, and many a pan of bacon. But provisions ran out in about four weeks, and the ship furnished us with Irish potatoes, hard tack and cold water.*

It was an inauspicious start, but Benjamin's spell as a forger proved successful and he decided to stay. If he emigrated to America to better his standard of living and improve his job prospects - as seems likely - then Benjamin's expectations were certainly fulfilled. Either when he arrived or soon afterwards, he became manager of the hammer department at the Jersey City Steel Works, one of the pioneering American crucible steel works located in New Jersey. Benjamin even found a job as hammerman at the same works for his younger brother, John Illingworth (1836-1920), who arrived in the USA in 1855 (Figure 3). Three more of his brothers - Samuel (b.1827), Joshua (b. 1829), and William (1841-1919) - followed Benjamin and all found steelmaking jobs in the same area.

Figure 3. Benjamin's younger brother, John Illingworth (1836-1920), who 'simply lived to make money' in America

Benjamin and John became leading figures in the East coast steel trade. Benjamin apparently worked as manager at the Jersey City Steel Works (which in 1853 was leased for ten years to J R Thompson & Co) until about 1860. He was also involved in the building of other new steel works in New Jersey: first at Rockaway, near Lake Hopatcong, and then at Pompton Lakes. By the American Civil War, Benjamin had made his fortune and his reputation as an authority on steel manufacture. In 1861, when the lease on the Jersey City Steel Works expired, Benjamin Illingworth and a group of friends incorporated it as the Jersey City Steel Works of J R Thompson & Co. The company became the largest crucible steel works in New Jersey, and was bigger than many of the leading Pittsburgh producers. For twenty-five years, Benjamin was one of the principal partners in this venture, until his retirement in 1888. John Illingworth, meanwhile, went on to even greater things: after 1864 he was a partner in Newark's first cast steel business, which as Atha & Illingworth, became another leading special steel firm in America.

The Illingworths were clearly one of the most successful immigrant families in adapting to American life. Much of their story, however, remains shadowy and can only be pieced together from newspaper obituaries, American state and county histories, and other printed sources. However, we are fortunate that Benjamin kept in close touch with his family who stayed in Stocksbridge. In particular, he wrote regularly - on average at least twice a year - to his brother Charles, who was one of the few Illingworth brothers who do not seem to have been attracted by the New World. In his later letters to Charles, he also added a few lines - signed 'Uncle Ben' - to Hannah née Nichols (1886-1958), who was Charles's grand-daughter. Apparently, Benjamin began corresponding soon after he landed in America, but these letters have not survived. Even in his old age, though, Benjamin was still writing home and after the turn of the century many of his letters - some thirty in number - are extant.

By July 1900 - the date of the first extant letter - Benjamin was living in comfortable retirement. He was no longer involved with the steel trade, though he continued to keep his family informed of the progress of the American Illingworths in the steel business. Besides information on American industry, Benjamin's letters provide insights into contemporary social life. He discusses his American way of life and the perspective from across the water enables him to offer some fascinating contrasts with life in Snowdenhill. Benjamin's personality also surfaces in the letters.

Both Benjamin and John accumulated considerable wealth in the New World. According to an obituary in *The Newark Evening News*, 23 February, 1914, Benjamin had made 'a small fortune', even before the American Civil War; and the profits of his New Jersey company added to his estate. John seems to have been particularly money minded - 'he simply lived to make money', was one relative's comment - and he died a dollar millionaire in 1920 in the days when that really meant something. Benjamin's first surviving letter immediately takes us into a world that was far different from distant

Hunshelf.

In his retirement, Benjamin spent his summers holidaying on the New Jersey coast. One resort the Illingworths frequented was Belmar. In July 1900, Benjamin wrote :

> *This place is 150 miles from Jersey City. R H [Illingworth] & family joins us in renting a furnished house for which we pay $500 for the season, thear [sic] is four large rooms and kitchen on the first floor and 8 bedrooms above and a piazza on 2 sides and front, thear [sic] is 4 servants in the house and so everything goes nicely and we live on the best the land produces, we drive a good deal, especially the ladies and children. R.H.I and Mr Dawson goes to the town every day, except Saturday. John's place is just above here, and so on the 11th of this month I went up there. When I got home from John's that day at 6 o'clock p.m. dinner was ready and so as many as could get a round [sic] me did so, to escort me into the dining room, and the first thing I so [sic] on the table was a big chocolate cake with 77 lighted candles stuck into it and by my plate a new white felt hat, a knapkin [sic] ring, a box cigars, a well filled portfolio with all kinds of writing material and several letters wishing me long life and prosperity, and then I realised that it was my birthday ...*

A better idea of the social circumstances of the Illingworths in New Jersey, can be gleaned from Benjamin's description of a euchre party:

> *Most of our relations and a few intimate friends in America join together & meet once per weekend to have a good social and pleasant time ... We set 6 small tables in the parlour & 4 players at each table & so them is 24 players & the rest looks on. 5 points is game & the first two that gets 5 points goes forwards to the next table & soon until [sic] all the games are played & the lady of the house gives 6 prizes to be played for & she also gives all refreshments & they are ample & the best the country affords. We don't indulge in roast beef & plumb [sic] pudding but we have squab quail chicken turkey, new strawberrys and ice cream. We had 10 courses & a different kind of wine for every course & the last course we commenced on champagne & we kept it up untill 1 o'clock in the morning, & then we went home with the girls in the morning. We engage black men waiter[s], they wear evening dress suits & white gloves ... I wish you could join us at those social gatherings. I know you would enjoy them, but the only danger would be you might split your sides with laughter.*

An even more remarkable measure of the Illingworths' status in the New World is their travel arrangements for visiting England. For his trip in 1912, Benjamin boarded the RMS *Germanic* and to say he travelled in style would be an understatement: he had a state room, the number one suite on such ocean liners. What a contrast to the hard tack and potatoes of his first American trip and what a remarkable comment on the upward mobility of the son of a poor Snowdenhill shepherd! The business career of one of Benjamin's nephews, Robert Henry Illingworth (1861-1922) the son of Samuel, underlines the family's new-found status. Under John Illingworth's wing, Robert progressed rapidly in the family's New Jersey steel company and after 1900, when the business became part of the Crucible Steel Company of America, his rise continued. The dynamism of Robert and his growing executive responsibility - eventually he became vice-president of Crucible, the largest special steel firm in America - were a constant topic in Benjamin's letters. When Robert visited Europe, he could afford to give his family a farewell dinner in the Waldorf Astoria Hotel in New York - in Benjamin's words, 'the largest and the grandest Hotel in the world and the most expensive ... [where] dinner[s] thear [sic] cost fifty dollars a plate, wine not encluded [sic]'. Robert could also afford first-class transatlantic travel: in 1908 he returned to New York on the RMS *Lusitania*, booking a state room on what he described as 'the finest boat in the world ... and largest I ever crossed in'.

As hard-working, talented young men, with steelmaking skills that were much in demand in the world's fastest growing economy, the Illingworth brothers epitomised the 'go-getting' ethos of the New World. They were clearly one of the most successful immigrant families in the American steel trade. 'The Illingworths is getting high up in the steel business', reported Benjamin in 1902: 'I am proud of all my nephews, they are all high up'. The opportunities in the USA were frequently mentioned by Benjamin and his earlier letters home - though they have not survived - must have been an important factor in the emigration of his younger brothers. Even in his later years, he was still extolling the opportunities in America, though he did not underestimate the possible sacrifices involved (regarding emigration, he once stated that 'the young stand it well, but it takes the starch out of the older people'). One wonders what the family in Stocksbridge would have made of the letter sent to Charles after Thanksgiving in 1902:

> *The President of the US issues a general proclamation to all this*
> *subject, requesting all who is religously* [sic] *inclined to go to their*
> *respective places of worship & to give thanks to Almighty God for all*
> *the Blessings you have received during the year. One minister*

preached on the prosperity of the country telling about the breadth &
length of the country & its great crops & great manufactures & the
great rail road & he said that the people of the US had more cause
to give thanks than any other people, because of their abundance of
everything. They have enough to spare to feed several other countries.
I so a piece in the papers a few days before Thanksgiving day in 48
hours time thear come into New York 300 tons of turkeys. We have
one every Sunday all through winter. We had one on Thanksgiving
day 17lbs & it was the tenderest one I ever carved & we had 15 of
our friends to help us give Thanks over it, & we had a plumb [sic]
pudding made after Aunt Sarah's receipt & it was a grand one.

In November 1902, he mentioned to his brother Charles, the
experience of William Mather, the eldest son of his wife's sister:
'When he was 14 years old he ran away from Canada & came to see
his Uncle Ben. He started in the night, without a penny in his pocket,
400 miles away. Nothing succeeds like success, a boy with a spirit like
that, is sure to succeed. He is now a rich man'. Meanwhile, Joseph
Dickinson, who had been instrumental in Benjamin emigrating, had
become the manager of a big steel works in Pittsburgh and his
brother John was the foreman in the rolling mill at John Illingworth's
works at Harrison, New Jersey. Meanwhile, Jack Dickinson had
charge of the hammers at the works, and they were all, in Benjamin's
words, 'making lots of money'. Even in the early twentieth century,
the Illingworths were personally still recruiting skilled labour in
Stocksbridge for their New Jersey Works. In 1912, for example,
Robert Illingworth persuaded Fox's first chief analyst, Mr A Jobson,
to join his company in America.

Other insights can be gleaned from Benjamin's letters. As
historians have highlighted, immigrants had a range of motives for
writing to friends and relatives in their homeland. They might write
to arrange the migration of other members of the family; they might
wish to obtain financial help from home; or they might send letters
simply to keep in touch with their roots and their loved ones, partly
as a means of coping with the lonely and disorienting experience of
living in a foreign country. Any letters that Benjamin sent (if any)
that either encouraged his brothers to emigrate or asked for money
have not survived. However, the letters that are extant do show a
strong wish to keep in touch with his family in Stocksbridge. He
often asked about his brother's farming activities and still showed a
keen interest in agricultural matters (though he himself lived in
Jersey City and did not farm Figure 4). In a letter to Charles in

1900, he wrote: 'Robert says you had not commenced to cut grass on account of cold and wet weather. But hope it will be favourable for you to gather in your hay and corn. We could easily spare you 6 or 7 weeks of hot weather that would ripen your corn and enable you to cut your grass and get it in the same day'.

Even though he clearly never regretted leaving Yorkshire for the land of milk and honey, Benjamin in his old age could still become euphoric and sentimental at the thought of his boyhood surroundings. In 1901, after hearing that his brothers George and Charles were to meet, he wrote:

> *I hope you will have a good time together. Oh wouldn't it be grand if I could join you in climbing them mountain sides and then take a walk to Penistone, Snowden Hill and Bolsterstone and Sheffield and then take a trip to Bridlington and Blackpool and Scarbro, and into Derbyshire [sic] ... The hills of Stocksbridge on the peaks of the lofty mountains which seem to reach the sky. The glistening snow is deep I know as the fleeting years go by. If ever I should tire of wandering I'd bend myself that way and if this should be I'll once more see the sunlit Hill some day.*

'Old England with all her faults I love her still', was a recurrent lament in Benjamin's letters. In his old age, he still visited his birthplace, and wrote in 1902 to Charles that he and his family intended to set 'our feet on the old sod once more' (Figure 5). Benjamin was now nearly eighty years old. In that summer, he toured the Stocksbridge area, taking time to see his brothers and revisit old haunts. He noted approvingly the farming activity of his friends, the Wood family at Penistone:

> *They were carting hay in a hay shed ... The farm is 120 acers [sic] and [h]as*

Figure 4. Benjamin's first house in New Jersey, built in 1860

Figure 5. This portrait postcard shows Benjamin (left) and (probably) his brother, John Illingworth. Addressed to brother Charles, it reads:

> *Come and see us, nothing can compare with Belmar. It is lovely sweet and embracing, it tempts you out of doors, it sends the blood tingling through the veins, it makes you brisk, alert, good humered [sic], it makes you glad to be alive, it makes you understand that life is worth living, it will make you feel so good that you will never want to die. Here is happiness worth the journey. Here is pleasure unrefined, the prize so worth the cost.*
>
> *I am always yours Benj. Illingworth*

50 acers of moing [sic] *grass, he* [h]*as 3 stables for horses and 3* [?]
*cows and a pig sty with 16 compartments, a poultry building, a duck
building, a goose building and the house and all the out buildings are
lighted by gas and electricity even in the pig sty. The house is large
and beautiful and flower and vegetable gardains* [sic] *are extensive.
His two sons were at home superintending the hay making.*

After a good meal and a cigar at the Woods', Benjamin with Joseph
Wood visited his birthplace at Snowdenhill: 'I went to the house and
I enterduced [sic] myself and told [the occupier] that I was born in
that house 79 years ago and she looked frightened thinking it must
be my gost [sic] coming back again'. A visit to a local steel works and
a day out at Bridlington (where he was 'disgusted with the weather.
It rained and was verry [sic] cold. The thermomiter [sic] was down
to 48 degrees') were the other highlights of the trip. By the end of
August, Benjamin was on his way home, pleased to see Snowdenhill
again (it was his last visit), but also glad to be leaving an 'inclemant
[sic] climate, for the land of sunshine by day & moonshine by night'.

Something of Benjamin's personality shines through his letters
(Figure 6). By the turn of the century, he was a widower. He had
married Sarah, the daughter of Joseph Dickinson, in about 1850:
but after nearly fifty years of married life, she died in 1899 (Figure
7). Benjamin was left with a daughter, Ada (who later married a
manager at the Prudential Insurance Co, New York). Benjamin,
however, evidently retained his zest for life. A gregarious family
man, he delighted in the company of his American family and his
English relatives. Charles' grand-daughter, Hannah, in particular
seems to have been the apple of his eye. He had a hearty appetite
and food was one of his favourite subjects. He liked a good cigar and
fine wine and spirits, with the fondness of a man who could still
remember the days of porridge and oatmeal in Snowdenhill. He told
Charles: 'Well every night I take a smile looking at you & as the old
song says, be it understood every morning I take an eye opener & at
noon I take a bracer because the thirst in one is such I never can
drink a drop to[o] much'.

Benjamin's hard upbringing had not made him into a socialist. He
was a Republican - as befits a robust self-made man in America -
though neither Benjamin (nor his brother, John) seem to have taken
any interest in politics. For all his great wealth, Benjamin was
apparently without a trace of self-importance. His letters still
retained traces of Stocksbridge dialect - such as in 'thear' (for there),
'boath' and 'smoaking' — even after fifty years in America. He had
a warm sense of humour and enjoyed a joke - either polite or ribald

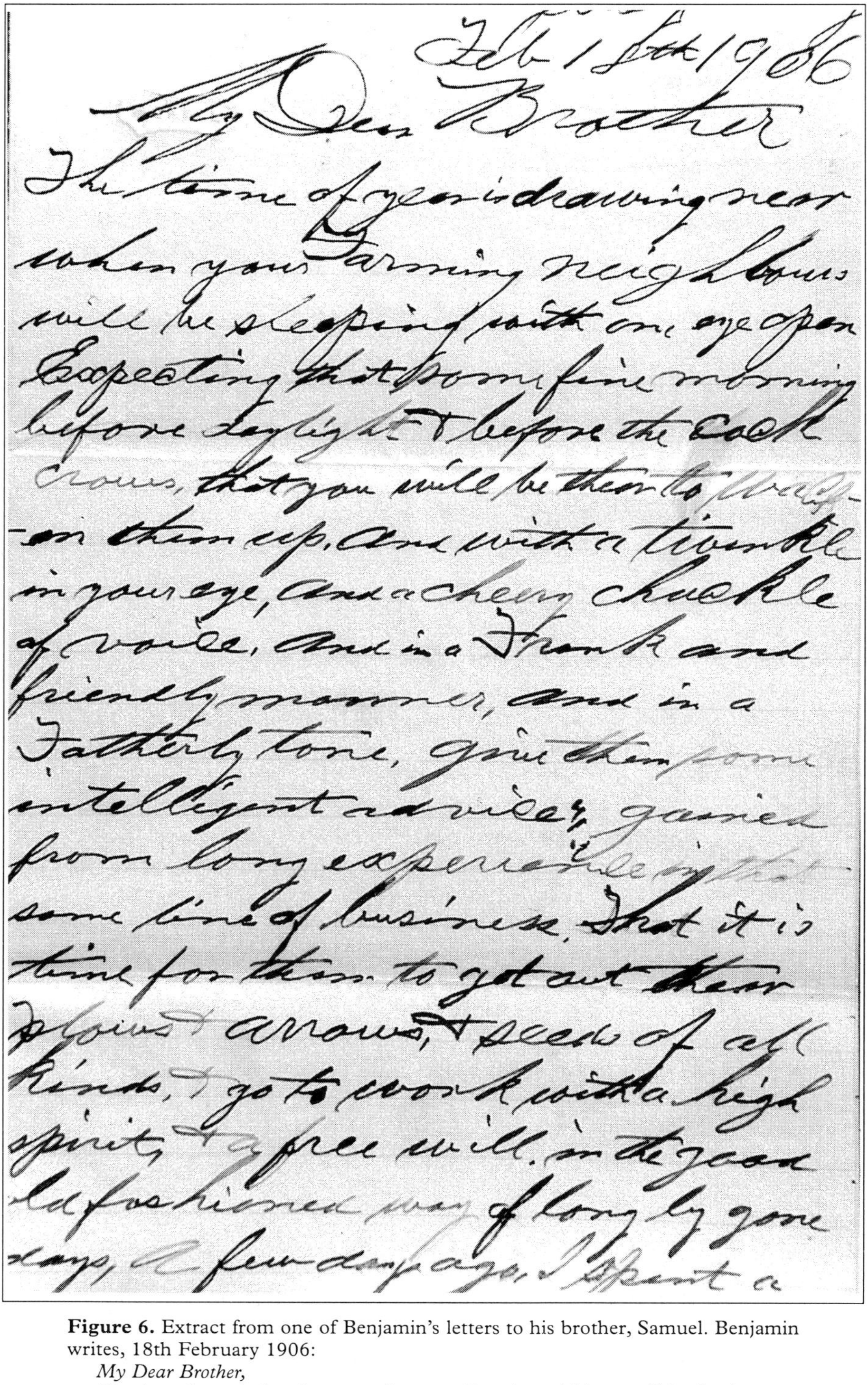

Feb 18th 1906

My Dear Brother

The time of year is drawing near when your Farming neighbours will be sleeping with one eye open Expecting that some fine morning before daylight & before the cock crows, that you will be thear to wacken them up. And with a twinkle in your eye, And a cheery chuckle of voice, And in a Frank and friendly manner, And in a Fatherly tone, give them some intelligent advice; gained from long experience in that same line of business. That it is time for them to get out their plows & arrows, & seeds of all kinds, & go to work with a high spirit, & a free will. in the good old fashioned way of long by gone days, A few days ago. I spent a

Figure 6. Extract from one of Benjamin's letters to his brother, Samuel. Benjamin writes, 18th February 1906:

My Dear Brother,

The time of year is drawing near when your Farming neighbours will be sleeping with one eye open Expecting that some fine morning before daylight and before the cock crows, that you will be thear [sic] *to wacken* [sic] *them up. And with a twinkle in your eye, and a cheery chuckle of voice, and in a frank and friendly manner, and in a fatherly tone, give them some intelligent advice; gained from long experience in the same line of business. That is the time for them to get out their plows* [sic] *and* [h] *arrows and seeds of all kinds and go to work with a high spirit and a free will in the good old fashioned way of long gone* [sic] *days.*

- even if it was at his own expense. After his return trip to New York in 1902, he told Charles how:

Figure 7. Benjamin's wife, Sarah née Dickinson, who died in 1899 *Peter Long*

> *after leaving Queenstown we ran into a storm that made us all sea sick except Maggie & Ida & a few others & so after a good breakfast I was full up to the top & so becoming sea sick all at once I ran to the rail of the ship and threw up & behold my false teeth & altogether went overboard to the bottom of the sea & so [saw?] the gold plate glisten as it went down. I hope that some old wale [sic] & shark will make use of them. But thear I was with only a few last teeth in my head & so after I got well I asked my waiter to grind my meat. But he said that he would not be allowed to do so in the dining room & he said if it was done in the kitchen I would be the last attended to. And so I resolved to do the best I could, & so I got along nicely with porrage [sic] and chicken & fish & fruits ...*

He liked poetry and in his letters to Hannah he often added a verse or two, in which the sentiments (If you have a smile to show/ Show it now/ Make hearts happy, roses grow/ Let friends around you know/ The love you have before they go/ Show it now) combine a touching love of his family with his own kind nature.

Benjamin was a religious man, who worshipped at Grace Church in Jersey City, where he was a vestryman and later warden for many years. His interest in church affairs and his own personality are shown in this account of his meeting with a New Jersey bishop, at about the time he moved into a new house at 477 Jersey Avenue in 1870:

> *one Sunday after service* [at Grace Church] *Dr Rise our minister said to me. The Bishop will be here next Sunday & I want you to entertain him while he is in the City. Well them words nearly paralysed me. I felt as if all the stuffing had blown out of me. But I managed to say. Well Dr I am the worst stick in the whole world to entertain a Bishop. Oh he said you will find him the pleasantest man you ever met. He said you will have nothing to do, but to give him plenty to eat & you will find him the most genial and social person*

*that ever graced your table. Well I could say no more. But I thought
of that poar* [sic] *Irish man that had been ill so long & he surprised
his wife & Family by saying my greatest desire after my death is to
be buried in a Jewish cemetery. But he would not give his reasons for
that untill* [sic] *near the end, & then he said it was because he
thought it would be the last place in the whole world where the devil
would be looking for a Irish man. Well in a day or two I got a letter
from the Bishop saying that he had been informed by Dr Rise that he
was to be my guest while he remained in the City, & that is train
would be due at the station at 4.30 p.m. Saturday. Well I answered
his letter & said that Mrs I & myself would be glad to have the
Bishop as our guest as long as he remained in the City. Well I drove
to the station to meet him. I knew him among all the passengers, I
had seen his photo in the papers, & he was over 6 feet tall. I went up
to him & said Bishop I have a carriage outside for you. O he said
are you Mr I. I said yes, he said I am glad to meet you & to make
your accuaintance* [sic]. *Then he said let me introduce you to Mrs
Starkey his wife. I told her I was delighted to see her, but it wasn't
exaccly* [sic] *true. Well we drove home and I enterduced* [sic] *them
to Mrs I. She received them pleasantly. The Bishop said Mr I do you
smook* [sic]. *I said yes. Well then he said I know you will have some
good cigars. He made himself at home & made me laugh more than
I ever had done in the same time before. Well* [illegible] *we went into
dinner. Mrs I had prepared a good one. But the Bishop eat sparingly.
He said he was obliged to be careful what he eat, & so Dr Rise* [?]
*words came true, I never met his equal for pleasantness & sociability
… [Afterwards] I got a letter from him thanking us for our
hospitality & kindness shown to them, & they was our guest once per
year up to the death of Mrs I …*

Benjamin continued to enjoy life into his eighties (Figure 8). In
December 1903, on a 'Monday blowing & snowing', he related to
Charles how 'the thermomiter [sic] was down to 18 degrees this
morning', but he still set forth outside 'bundel [sic] up in a big Ulster
over coat, & a seal skin cap & artic [sic] boots lined with red flannel
& fur lined buckskin gloves & a cigar in my mouth, & then I am ready
to face the artic [sic] reagons [sic]'. He advised Charles: 'I know it
will be cold on your mountainside, & so you will bundle your self up
in the same way'. After his summer holiday in 1904, he told Charles:

*I gained 5lbs, am stronger, can walk further, can see to read good clear
print without glasses for a short time only*[.] *people tell me that I look
better & younger than I did 6 or 7 years ago. I thank them for the*

Figure 8. Benjamin Illingworth standing on the steps of his mansion at 477 Jersey Avenue in Jersey City, New Jersey

compliment & I tell them that I feel well & I live well & sleep well & work moderately & as [sic] an easy conscience & for all these benefits I am truly thankful and desire to say that because I am in good health & spirits & active & energetic.

However, Benjamin wrote less after his eightieth birthday and there were to be no more trips to England. In the summer of 1913, he wrote the following poignant lines to Hannah:

I think my life is nearing its end ... On the 11th day of July last, I was 90 years old. I do not think I shall live much longer. My life is nearly spent. A friend to whom I said this could not controle [sic] his surprise ...[but] ... there is no sorrow in my voice. Just Resignation[.] And when the call comes I think it will be a sudden one[.] We should all be ready for the Call Because we don't know how suddenly it may come. My friend asked me if I was in good health. Yes I answered. I still feel young and capable of performing several more years of labor. But I think I shall soon pass away. Perhaps I may live another year or more longer. We are never sure. You know; it is our souls that makes us young or old. If our souls be young though our bodys [sic] be as old a[s] Mathtuselah [sic] we are young indeed.

Benjamin's words proved prophetic and in the following February, after a short illness, he died. Robert Illingworth gave Hannah the details in a letter dated 23rd February 1914:

It is with regret that I notify you of Uncle Ben's death Sunday, February 22th [sic] at about 8:30. He has been ailing for the last four weeks ... [and because] ... of the terrible weather we have experienced during the month of February, he was unable to get out and take his customery [sic] walk ... A week ago last Tuesday, February 10th, he took to his bed and he remained there until his death ... Yesterday morning at eight o'clock Ada asked him if she would bring him some breakfast, consisting of coffee, a cereal and an egg. He said Yes, that would be very good. She went down stairs [sic] to get it and was not away over a half hour. Alice, the oldest daughter, brought up the breakfast and found that he had rolled off the pillows which propped him up in bed and that he was dead. They immediately called the Doctor and he said that his heart had merely stopped acting. His mind was absolutely clear until the last second of his life and we are all very happy and thankful for the perfect and peaceful ending of a long and perfect life. He was talking about all his friends on the other side next to the last time I saw him, which was about a week ago. He never ceased lamenting the fact that he had made his last trip across the ocean.

He was buried in New York Bay Cemetery on a bitingly cold day: yet this did not deter a full church of mourners from attending. As Robert pointed out, this was 'something not often seen when a man practically buries all his old time friends and relations'. That in itself was a fitting memorial to one of Snowdenhill's most famous sons.

Acknowledgements and References

Derek Stapley kindly brought the Illingworth letters to our attention and introduced us to their owners - Douglas and Ethel Walton - who allowed us to transcribe them. As a direct descendant, Ethel Walton was able to make available to us her knowledge of the family's history. Peter Long has also been kind enough to supply two Illingworth family photographs. In the USA, another decendant of the family, Helen Illingworth, provided further valuable information and correspondence. We would like to acknowledge the help of Sheffield City Library and Stocksbridge Library; and the following scholars and institutions: Charlotte Erickson, David Franz (New Jersey Historical Society); Robert B. Gordon; Bierce Riley and Bob Holton (Society for Industrial Archaeology); and John Ingham.

A copy of both the letters and our transcription has been deposited at Sheffield Archives. The bulk of our quotations are from these sources. Others can be found in the following:

William Brown (ed.), *Biographical, Genealogical and Descriptive History of the State of New Jersey* (1900). Contains short biographies of Benjamin and John Illingworth.

P Crossland, '*Historic Hunshelf*', in Brian Elliott (ed.), *Aspects of Barnsley: Discovering Local History* (1993).

P Crossland, 'Thurgoland Wiremills', in B. Elliott (ed.), *Aspects of Barnsley: Discovering Local History II* (1994).

C J Erickson, *Invisible Immigrants: The Adaptation of English and Scottish Immigrants in Nineteenth-Century America* (1972; reprinted, 1990).

P Hansen and G Tweedale, '*The Lads of Snowdenhill and the New Jersey Steel Trade*', *Historical Metallurgy* (forthcoming). Examines Benjamin's steel career in detail.

J Kenworthy, 'History of Snowdenhill ... [and] ... The Story of the Lads of Snodnal Town who went Forth to Help in Laying the Foundations of the American Steel Trade', published in *The* [Stocksbridge] *Express* (April- September 1921).

The Newark Evening News (23 February, 1914). Obituary of Benjamin Illingworth.

G Tweedale, *Sheffield Steel and America: A Century of Commercial and Technological Interdependence, 1830-1930* (1987).

8. BARNSLEY COMES OF AGE: THE TOWN IN THE 1860S

by Harold Taylor

-No sooner do people step onto the station platform than they are prompted to say 'Save us from Barnsley' and promise themselves that their visits to the town shall be like those of the angels, short and far between!

'TOWNSMAN', WHO MADE THESE heartfelt complaints in a letter to the *Barnsley Chronicle* in January 1869, was but one of many who had grumbled over the years about a station which was 'a disgrace and injustice to the town'. Civic pride was hurt, for Barnsley had made much progress over the last ten years.

The station certainly did not measure up to expectations. The waiting room was so tiny that it was reserved for women travellers only, the menfolk being obliged to:

suffer the smoke, dust and draughts of a narrow platform, having crossed a yard as like as not ankle-deep in mud. [1]

In 1860 it had been brought to the notice of the Local Board of Health that the station was:

a truly disgusting and abominable place - a stinking nuisance . [2]

Yet the railway companies had indeed contributed to the progress which Barnsley had been making during the 1860s, although it was still necessary to board an 'omnibus' outside the *Royal Hotel* in order to meet a train at the other 'Barnsley Station' at Cudworth, on the Midland Railway's main line.

In December 1859 the Manchester, Sheffield and Lincolnshire Railway Company had at last completed its link to the town from the Trans-Pennine line at Penistone, running into the existing station of the Lancashire and Yorkshire Railway. This link had been brought as far as the MS&L goods station, just off Regent Street, in 1857. Even though the final connection would wait two more years, the achievement of 1857 was treated as a major event, depicted in *The Illustrated London News* (reproduced as Figure 1) with enormous

Figure 1. The opening of the Penistone-Barnsley line at the MS&L Railway Goods Depot, 12 February 1857. Regent Street Congregational Church (completed 1856) in the background. Great liberties were taken by the artist in depicting the alignment of streets! *Illustrated London News, 7.3.1857.*

artistic licence. A procession is shown entering the station, the Congregational Church in the background. Headed by the Barnsley Brass Band:

> *accommodated on a wagon drawn by seven very powerful horses,*

this procession had set off from Summer Lane Station, the platform there having been:

> *covered with canvas and relieved by numerous arches, tastefully decorated with evergreens.*

The Directors of the MS&L, along with shareholders, had arrived at five past noon and had been joined on the train by, 'the principal

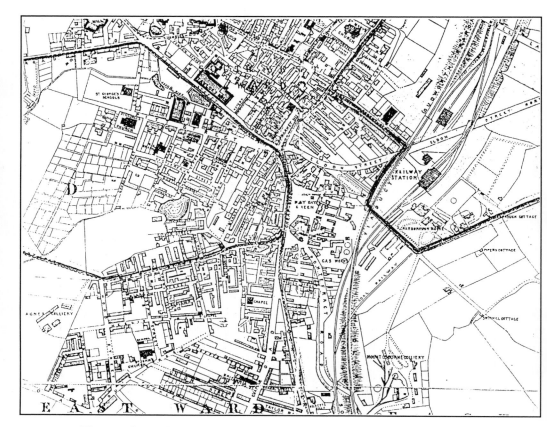

Figure 2. Part of Barnsley on the map produced in 1869 to define the Wards. Working class streets in the south west and south centre. Agnes and Mount Osborne Collieries. The 'Station' was the 'beastly hole' of the L & Y Railway. The Cudworth Branch track had been laid but was not yet in service. Linen mills in the Townend area are heavily outlined. Note the millponds *BLSA.*

inhabitants of the town and neighbourhood'. The train, drawn by the locomotive *Idis*, had moved slowly to the terminus, arriving to loud cheers.

'It now rested with the manufacturers and coal companies to give their support,' stressed the Company Chairman at the opening ceremony. During the afternoon a large and enthusiastic crowd of workmen called out Joseph Locke - local man and accomplished railway engineer - from the party at the *King's Head Hotel*. Locke's address to the men brought loud cheers.

Barnsley was growing at a great pace, both in population and in extent. Numbers had increased by almost twenty per cent between

1851 and 1861, and the increase over the next ten years was to be much greater, amounting to over 5,000 in a total of 23,000. Nearly a thousand new dwellings were built during the 1860s.

In-migration had been a major contributor to this growth, the linen industry in particular acting as a magnet for men or for whole families seeking work. The 1861 Census reveals that only around two heads of household in every five had been born in the town. Many of the rest were natives of surrounding villages or other parts of Yorkshire, but there were significant numbers from Ireland (over 230 families) and from across the Pennines, notably from the Wigan area. Others hailed from Nottinghamshire and Lincolnshire and there were small numbers from as far afield as Kent and Northumberland. Some had arrived in Barnsley after earlier migrations. Such was the story of John Riches, a brazier, living in Nelson Street in 1861. Born in Devon, he and his Irish-born wife, Mary, had been living in Chester, a few years previously.

The greater part of the working class population lived in the crowded rows and courts in the south and south-western parts of the town (Figure 2), their numbers swollen by a host of lodgers, most of these living-in with families, but others in Registered Lodging Houses. One of these, in Baker Street, housed sixteen, born in places as far apart as Liverpool, Plymouth, Belfast and Dundee. Many of the cottages in this part of the town, built to house handloom weavers, featured cellar loomshops and external flights of steps. Figures 3 and 4 illustrate a style and layout commonly found in that area, though there were considerable variations, some of the most

Figure 3. Part of Court No. 5, Joseph Street (seen below). Weavers' cottages with cellar loomshops and characteristic external flights of steps *BLSA*.

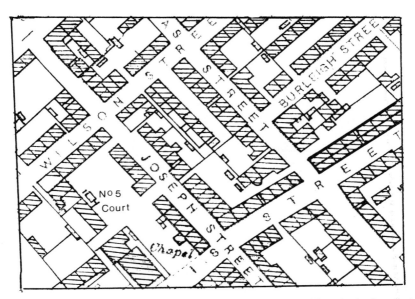

Figure 4. Part of the crowded streets of south-west Barnsley. Note the back-to-back dwellings *BLSA*.

crowded accommodation being in 'back-to-back' cottage rows.

In Joseph Street most families were headed by Barnsley-born people, but eight of the others were Irish and there were natives of Bristol, Darlington and Sussex, as well as people from Manchester, Leeds and Huddersfield. The majority in this street worked as

Figure 5. The northern area of Barnsley in 1869. Note the developing middle class residential area between Sackville Street and the loop of the railway. Only a few plots had been taken up in Victoria Road at that time *BLSA*.

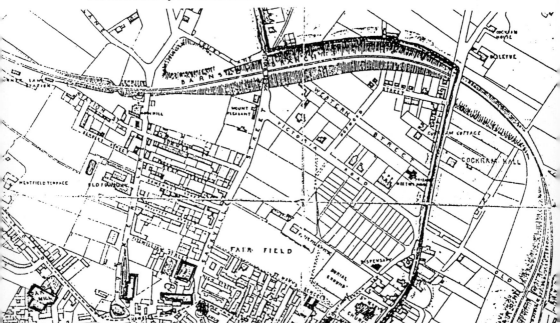

Figure 6. Middle class dwellings in Sackville Street. *Providence Villa*, part of Temperance Terrace, built in 1851 for James McLintock, owner of the Utilitas Works in Summer Lane and prominent member of Blucher Street Chapel *Tasker Photographic Trust.*

handloom weavers, but there were miners, a wiredrawer, a shoe maker and a foundry operative among the others.

Middle class families were largely to be found, distanced from the main working class areas, on the northern side of the town. Figure 5 shows a spacious layout of streets there with plots waiting to be taken up by the more prosperous members of the community. By 1871 Victoria Road would be lined with imposing stone villas. In 1861 Regent Street was already the home of successful men with their families and their servants - manufacturers, merchants, a master builder, a solicitor, an accountant, and an engineer. Figure 6 shows some of the substantial homes which had been built in Sackville Street in mid-century. Part of Dodworth Road too had been developing as a middle class suburb.

The Breath of Heaven

Although Barnsley was indeed growing, and would achieve Municipal Borough status by the end of the decade, there was an acute awareness that major improvements were necessary if the town was to be worthy of the hoped-for higher ranking. The 1866 Report of Dr Sadler, the Medical Officer of Health, underlines the deplorable standards of housing and of sanitation in large areas of the south and south western parts of the town.

> *Many of the privvies are in an indecent state, and it is in many instances next to impossible, at least very difficult, to keep them decent, where there is only one place of convenience for several houses, especially where there are many children; the consequence is that there are many disputes as to whose duty it is to keep them clean.*

Sadler pointed to the relatively high death rate among tenants of the crowded courts and the 'highly objectionable back-to-back houses'. In Copper Street alone thirty six of the forty four houses were of this type:

> *the bedrooms having no chimney to act as ventilator, being as a result most unhealthy places. Such places give a fearful power to the spread of diseases, especially when they are crowded.*

'Let the breath of heaven have fair play,' he urged.

Figure 7. The reservoir at Smithies, constructed for the Barnsley Water Company in 1848. Water extracted from the Dearne was pumped to storage reservoirs on higher ground in Huddersfield Road and to Jordan Hill *Author.*

As a step towards improved health Sadler strongly advocated the building of public baths by the Local Board of Health, the town's elected administrative body since 1853. There had been an unsuccessful call for this amenity a few years earlier, urging that it would be:

> *beneficial not only to the physical but also the moral condition of all classes*

John Vallance, weaver and noted radical, put the view of the meeting in simpler terms:

> *The working classes had few opportunities of enjoying the luxury of a good wash!*

Work had commenced on new sewerage installations in 1862, but major works to improve the outfall to filtration beds at Hoyle Mill had to wait until the 1870s.

T'Ingbirchworth Wattar'

By 1861 the town's water supply had become a problem. The scheme, developed by the (private) Barnsley Water Company in the 1840s, but purchased by the Board of Health in 1854, drew water from the River Dearne at Smithies. The reservoir, shown in Figure 7, is still to be seen. Now the river was not only polluted but inadequate in volume. In 1861 the problem had been intensified by the loss of a supplementary supply normally pumped from the 'New Gawber Hall Colliery', but where there had been a serious explosion. By late August the reservoirs held no more than three weeks' supply. It would appear that the Sough Dyke too was no longer able to fill the ponds which supplied the linen mills with water for steam raising and processing work, for 'manufacturers in the town' were using the same water over and over again to such an extent that the millponds - such as those around Townend - were alleged to be:

> *centres of disease, whose foul gases would greatly increase the malady if the town was visited by an epidemic.*

Determined steps were now taken to obtain water from Ingbirchworth, 'though the scheme would not be fully completed until 1871'. This important development inspired one of the local 'poets' to compose appropriate verses for *T' Bairnsla Foaks' Annual an Pogmoor Olmanack*:

> *Yo Bairnsla foaks can swagger nah,*

Yo hardly knaw what's matter
Wi that big pond o' drinkin stuff-
We mean t'Ingbirchworth wattar.
T'poor collier lads can nah look smart,
'Cos t'wattar's nah much softer;
An all can say we've time to wesh,
An don wersens up ofter.

An Ornament Worthy Of The Town

There were other urgent needs. Barnsley needed a General
Cemetery, for by 1860 an Order in Council had closed the
churchyards in the town.[3] There seem to have been other problems
too. A clergyman had complained to the Burial Board in 1859 that
the scene which often confronted him when he went to inter a corpse
on a Sunday:

> *presented the appearance of a tea garden, owing to the number of*
> *young men smoking cigars and short pipes.*

The opening of the new cemetery in May 1860 was deemed a major
event. Thirty seven designs had been submitted for the chapels and
ornamental gates. The winning design, with its suitably sombre
Gothic style, seen in Figure 8, was by a Leeds firm, Perkin and
Backhouse. The foundation stones of the chapels were laid:

> *in the presence of an enormous concourse, a vast procession formed of*
> *clergy, gentry, clubs and Sunday School scholars, having walked to*
> *the site.*[4]

Heading the procession were Parochial Constables with staves,

Figure 8. The chapels and gatehouses of the new Barnsley Cemetery
Illustrated London News.

followed by no fewer than four brass bands, spaced at suitable intervals along the column - the Ecclesfield, the Wharncliffe-Silkstone, the Thorncliffe and the Dodworth Band. Four bands and the voices of the crowd of around thirteen hundred people would make the singing of *The Old Hundredth* at the conclusion of the ceremony a moving experience.

An editorial in the *Barnsley Herald* pronounced the new cemetery to be:

> *an ornament worthy of the town, presenting to future generations a monument of the liberality of those who preceded them.*

It was a suitable recognition too of the fact that death was an all too familiar visitor to many homes in that period.

Public works were not the only significant developments in the 1860s, for the fledgeling Barnsley British Co-operative Society took off in February 1862, later to become such an outstanding feature of the Barnsley scene. One of the Quarterly Meetings, held in the Market Street School, heard that 'the balance sheet showed the Society to be prosperous'.[5] The original shop, shown in Figure 9, was now inadequate, and by January 1863 removal to new premises had 'stimulated an increase in membership to 201'.[6] A dividend of one shilling in the pound was declared.

'A Noble Gift.'

Private generosity also made major contributions to the development of the town's amenities in this period. In 1864 John Staniforth Beckett endowed a hospital and dispensary at a cost of £8,000.

Three years earlier the widow of Joseph Locke, had made possible the purchase of a large area of land at High Stile Field as a site for a public park dedicated to the memory of her husband, who had died in September 1860. The opening of Locke Park was:

> *one of the most imposing events that ever occurred in Barnsley. The streets were crowded with people. Flags waved from almost every house, and all the shops were closed. The day was beautifully fine and was observed as a general holiday.*[7]

At 2 pm a procession formed in Church Field amidst the ringing of bells and the firing of cannon. The Barnsley Rifle Corps Band and a troop of Yeomen Cavalry headed the procession, followed by 'Secret Orders' and Friendly Societies, Clergy and Ministers, Magistrates, officers and Members of the Board of Health and about 4,600

Figure 9. The first shop of the Barnsley British Co-operative Society, 16 Market Street, *The Coronation History of BBCS Limited, 1862-1902.*

scholars, many of them wearing medals struck for the event.

At the park a crowd of about 20,000 assembled:

> *on an eminence before a large platform, which had been erected for the notables. The spectacle was remarkably striking, the exultation of the people, the music, the booming of cannon and the appearance of innumerable flags, all conveyed the impression that the subject had entered deep into the hearts of the public.*

Some idea of the gathering can be gained from the photograph (Figure 10) which was taken on the day. John Burland perhaps caught the mood in his verses, which end:

> *High Stile Field no more! This is now Locke Park,*

Figure 10. From a photograph taken at the opening ceremony at Locke Park, 10 June 1862. The stage to accommodate the 'notables' can be discerned top centre. Note the gentlemen in top hats near the camera and the vast crowd beyond *Barnsley Civic Review, 9.1951.*

Where Barnsley's denizens may hear the lark,
The luxury enjoy of shrub and tree,
And perfume breathing flower! Ever free
Alike to rich and poor! A noble gift,
Won for us by hard mental toil and thrift!
A boon with pleasure, health and beauty fraught!
So let us all esteem it as we ought!

A more down to earth description appeared in *T'Bairnsla Foaks' Olmanack*, part of which is reproduced as Figure 11.

In the evening of this momentous day the 'notables' sat down to dinner at the *King's Head Hotel*. Henry Richardson, who was later to become Barnsley's first Mayor, rose to propose the health of Mrs Locke, but went on to enthuse about the town's prospects:

Barnsley possessed the power of becoming a noble and grand town. It could command resources which were unexceptionable as a means to prosperity. It was the centre of the great Yorkshire Coalfield, and it maintained the excellence of its linen manufactures; it would soon possess an abundant water supply and it now had a park.

T'Happanin a Lock's Pairk.

NIVVER ta be forgottan TENT A JUNE, wal Bairnsla's Bairnsla, or theaze a hahce stanin, or a livin creater in it! Noa, nivver ta be forgottan; for hah can it, when it wor t'day at which LOCK'S PAIRK wor handad ovver ta t'publick az ther awn for ivver? An nivver cud a day been more suitad, noa not if it hed a been a t'foaks' awn mackin. T'sun shane i dubble breetness, nay, more then it hed homast ivver dun before; an t'claads hung rhaand i snaw-white festoons, at a respecktfull distance, it clear blue skye, an t'wind waftad nice an gently, just soa az ta mack ivvry boddy feel moderatly cooil an cumfatubble. Soa far wor t'day, weatherologically speikin.

Then cum t'next, t'livin pairt at scene; an a scene it wor, truly. T'bairns, like as menny pidgeons waitin for dayleet, wor laupin in an aht a bed, an runnin up an dahn t'staircase, az thay wackand before t'sun hed weel begun ta peep, an az ther faithers an muthers turnd aht too, not bein able ta get a wink a sleep for ther noisy tongues, an rattle a ther feet, aht a t'windaz popt fleg after fleg, till ivvry street, az heigh az chaimber an garrit stories whent, wor hacktly blockt up; beside theaze, hahce rigs, chimley tops, an t'owd Cherch taar hed flegs, Union Jacks, an streamers floppin an crackin on em, wal thear worrant a sparra ta be seen, awther up at slates, spahts, or onny where else abaht, all bein off az fast az ivver thay cud fly, wunderin wot ivver thear wor ta do it tahn; an dogs, too, wor runnin yelpin a three legs, a ivvry side, tryin ta find a quiet spot or corner. In fackt, thear wor nowt nor noabdy still; even t'dust it street wor up, ta join t'throng, an t'smook aht a t'chimley tops seemd ta curl itsen inta sum fantastical form. Az for foaks' ees, thay nivver

28

Figure 11. The opening of Locke Park as reviewed in *T'Bairnsla Foaks' Olmanack*, 1862-63.

'May Every Miner Soon Be Free!'

Barnsley's key role as the centre of an expanding coalfield was now clear. Although there were still over a thousand handloom weavers in the town, over six hundred power loom workers, and many others employed in the bleaching and dyeing trades, it was to be coal, not linen, which would form the basis for future growth. Already there were over a thousand colliery workers in the town alone, and the visual evidence of mining pressed hard on the very edge of the built up area - the Mount Osborne pits to the east, Agnes Colliery to the west, Willow Bank and Gawber not far away to the north. The mining industry would make its presence known in a more dramatic way in the appalling disaster at the nearby Oaks Colliery in December 1866.

The coal trade was recovering after a downturn in prices during the late 1850s. The canals still carried much coal, but it was the continued growth of the railway system that opened up new and bigger markets. The new MS&L line had stimulated the shipment of coal through Liverpool, and raised great optimism about exports to the USA. The Great Northern railway now carried coal southwards, supplying much of London's needs and raising hopes of shipments to France. Locally ironworks and gasworks were important customers. Bigger wagons were being introduced and some colliery companies felt sufficiently encouraged to build their own wagons.

Labour relations were, however, less happy. Wages had been cut in the late 1850s, stimulating a greater interest in trade unionism among the miners. There were strikes and lockouts in the early months of 1860 and serious disputes too in 1864, culminating in lockouts lasting for many months, some owners bringing in Staffordshire miners as strike breakers. Leaflets carrying anonymous verses expressing the colliers' point of view pleaded for public support:

We are poor Barnsley miners,
Standing by our rights.
We hope you all will help us
By giving us your mite.
May every miner soon be free
From bondage and from misery
Forsake our sins without delay
Press on and we shall win the day.

Yet there were happy occasions. By 1866 the South Yorkshire

Miners' Association, now over 5,000 members strong, held its 'Demonstration' at Barnsley in the September of that year, marking the Association's growing confidence. This was a 'fraternal meeting', joining with miners from Derbyshire and Nottinghamshire, and twenty eight public houses in town had been booked as billets for use by visitors during the day.[8] From an early hour the streets were lively, and by mid-morning May Day Green, Queen Street and Sheffield Road were 'crowded to suffocation'. A large number of miners and their families began to arrive in spring carts or waggons, and fully loaded trains steamed in from Sheffield.

As the miners' Lodges assembled on Church Field behind their banners the *Chronicle* reporter was moved to write that:

> *No one could fail to own that the union in South Yorkshire is a reality - a power-*

but added that:

> *A characteristic of the gathering was the clean, respectable and orderly appearance of the individuals of which the assembly was composed. Contentment sat on every brow, while a cheerful smile animated nearly every countenance.*

The procession moved off, cheered by bright sunshine and the lively music of four bands, to the cricket ground at Beechfield to hear the Association's Secretary, John Normansell, and other speakers make clear the aims of the union.

The linen industry was still important, however. There were over twenty linen manufacturing companies and over ten more handling

Figure 12. Hope Works of the linen manufacturing firm of H and H J Spencer in Sackville Street, 1980s, subsequently demolished. This enterprising firm carried out a wide range of processes - spinning cotton, weaving 'union cloth', bleaching, printing and dyeing *Author*.

bleaching and dyeing.[9] A cluster of mills had grown up around Townend, as shown on Figure 2, and the town had a widely recognised reputation for quality fabrics. In 1862 Carter Brothers, whose Oak Mill was just off Racecommon Road, confidently entered items for an International Exhibition:

> *High quality damasks of chaste patterns, pretty drills, bleached sheets, bath towels and tea cloths.*

There were some good trading years in this decade. In the summer of 1861 some of the largest firms were preparing patterns for the French market.[10] At their Hope Works Spencers (seen in Figure 12) had successfully pioneered new processes of colour printing.

Yet even in the good years the earnings of the handloom weavers were still small, mainly producing, as they did in this period, the lower grades of fabric. The poverty of the cottage weaver was a sad feature of the town. John Burland's bitter lines of 1850 would still reflect the despair of many weavers:

> *Pick the shuttle! Swing the fly!*
> *On a pauper's death bed lie;*
> *Hush, old whitethroat says tis God's ordaining;*
> *Clickit, clickit, sweat and die!*

In 1861 there were forty weavers in the Workhouse, only half of them elderly people, aged over sixty.

By the 1860s the linen mills were chiefly recruiting female workers, since the menfolk could earn more at the pit. Now the town's linen industry was perhaps at its peak; thereafter there would be a long period of decline.

For many families the spectre of poverty was never far away in the 1860s, and it made its face conspicuous through the appearance of soup kitchens from time to time, especially to meet crises caused by lockouts in mine or mill or downturns in the very vulnerable handloom side of the linen industry.

In 1860 and 1862 demand was such that soup kitchens almost ran out of funds(11). 1862 was a particularly difficult year, with severe distress in February and over eleven hundred people on 'relief', but as funds dwindled away, 'two gentlemen canvassed the town and raised nearly £150'.

Self Help

Material improvements were not the only form of progress in the

Barnsley of the 1860s. A good number of both middle and working class men were caught up in the quest - so widespread at the time - for 'self-improvement'. Samuel Smiles' best seller, *Self Help*, had appeared in 1859 and its opening chapter began with the words: 'Heaven helps those who help themselves'. Organisations already existed to promote adult education, the Franklin Club having been founded by Burland and others in the 1840s. Although it had lost some of its original working class character by the [8] 60s, it offered to all its members a reading room, lending library and a lecture programme covering literature, drama and philosophy. One of the lectures in 1862 introduced Geology, one of the enthusiasms of the period, and a science so accessible to the amateur.

The Mechanics' Institute too offered similar facilities, and meetings covering literature, politics, history and philosophy. Burland, hearing readings from *Macbeth* in December 1860, was quite carried away by the experience, remarking afterwards on 'the wonderful power and pathos of the play'. Political issues received attention, one of their debates condemning war as 'unscriptural and opposed to reason and sound policy'. There were other difficult topics. The 1862 programme included a lecture on 'The Beautiful and the Sublime in Nature and in Morals'. Another society met in Tinker's Coffee House for lectures and debates.[12]

The mid-Victorian ideal of self-improvement extended to music too. Thirty pupils were attending the 'Tonic Solfa' classes of the Albert Institute in 1862, benefiting from this simplified form of musical notation.[13] They may well have been drawn from the enthusiastic choirs of the town's numerous Nonconformist chapels, and had very likely been among the singers of the Barnsley Choral Society in February 1860, when a performance of *Messiah* was given to a packed house.

Oratorio was very much in vogue in this period, both nationally and locally. The lecture and concert at the Mechanics' Hall in April 1860 had therefore been a sure draw! An 'absolutely crowded hall' listened intently to a lecture on oratorio music given by C J Bincombe of York:

> *Oratorio music had produced an elevating and ennobling influence upon the people of this country*

he claimed, and by way of illustration the evening continued with selections from three contemporary favourites - *Messiah, Creation* and *Elijah*, performed by 'a large party of vocalists'.

There were other events to delight the music lover too in the same year. During March the English Opera Company gave a series of performances - *Il Trovatore, La Somnambula, Maritana, The Bohemian Girl* and *The Daughter of the Regiment*, before moving on to Bolton, their next venue.[14] The large audience included John Burland, indefatigable reporter of the Barnsley scene over many years, who commented on the 'highly respectable audience'!

Opera may well have drawn its audiences mainly from the middle classes, but the brass band movement, which had taken off in the 1840s, opened up a fine musical experience for working class people too, as did the chapel choirs. Several thousand spectators enjoyed the Contest on the Beechfield Cricket Ground in 1860. The Dodworth band was there, but most contestants had travelled some distance, from Doncaster, Hemsworth, Heckmondwike and as far away as Stockton. Popular operatic selections appear to have formed the bulk of the fare.

The town's theatres offered further variety. In 1860 Duval's Theatre put on *Othello*, which drew large audiences, but 'more popular plays' were presented at other times.'[15] The *Chronicle* correspondent reported in February of that year that:

> *This place of amusement continues nightly to attract numerous and delighted audiences at the series of plays given during the week.*

Even more popular was the Pantomime, put on in January 1865 at the Royal Queen's Theatre, which had opened in Eldon Street three years previously.[16]

On a higher plane that year was the Art Exhibition, showing at the Central Chambers in Church Street. The paintings on view conformed well to the high moral tone rated so highly in this period. (Figure 13 illustrates the lead given in this direction by the widely distributed journal: *Sunday at Home*.)

The *Chronicle* advertisement gave notice of:

> *Positively the last week to see The Day of Judgement, The Great Day of Wrath, and The Plains of Heaven. These grand and solemn works of art, painted by the late John Martin, are valued at £15,000. The pictures will be brilliantly illuminated.*

Occasionally a circus came to town, giving a lift to the townsfolk from the drudgery or the routine of everyday work. The visit of *Ginnet and His Company of Equestrians* in March 1860 produced the most exciting event of the year. As the circus paraded through the town the 'Educated Bull, Don Juan', was presented standing on a carriage drawn by horses, 'his hoofs on a footstool', riding at such a

"MY SON, IF SINNERS ENTICE THEE, CONSENT THOU NOT."

Figure 13. 'The high moral tone' of the period! Instructive Sabbath reading in the periodical *Sunday at Home*, May 1857.

height that he could peer into second storey windows. As he was untethered, 'he might have leaped down upon the crowd, had he been disposed for a frolic'. Fortunately Don Juan was 'remarkably docile and obedient'.[17] Visitors to the 'big top' were able to enjoy;

> *the artistic and graceful riding of Lady Ella and the art and drollery of Dan Rice and other clowns.*

Two years later *Tom Taylor's Mammoth Circus* arrived in Churchfield. The principal attraction this time was the sparring exhibition between Tom Taylor's champion and Young Brook from Birmingham. Not surprisingly this spectacle pulled in large numbers of men from the surrounding villages as well as from the town.

In May the Barnsley Fair offered a welcome change from the daily round. For those who could afford it the railway companies offered trips to Worksop, Retford, Grimsby (for Cleethorpes), Sheffield, Manchester and even London. The railway, with its excursion fares, had opened up quite new possibilities of travel for working men and their families. The Sunday Schools had been taking full advantage. Trainloads of scholars and teachers had been to Cleethorpes in June 1860. On Whit Monday 1861, 1,500 scholars were taken to Liverpool, 400 to Belle Vue Gardens and a large number to Matlock, blessed by 'a sun shining in splendour through an almost cloudless day'. Sadly a complaint by the railway company after a trip two years earlier makes familiar reading! Some of the carriages had been defaced by children writing on them in chalk and 'damaged by nails driven into the side for the purpose of hanging up labels'.

Barnsley Feast Sunday, however, appears to have been a day for enjoying the town itself. In August 1860 trains brought in such a large number of visitors from the district that the 'principal thoroughfares were full of people, on a day remarkably fine'.

For the sporting buff there were remarkable cricket matches in the 1860s. On Barnsley Feast Monday, 1860, a Grand Cricket Match between eleven of England and twenty two of Barnsley and District began at the Clarence Ground in Shaw Lane. A 'highly respectable company of ladies and gentlemen' were present on each day, making a total of nearly 8,000 spectators.[18] Barnsley's twenty two, put in to bat, could only collect a meagre forty six runs from the bowling of Jackson and Tinsley in their first innings. Nevertheless the spectators were in for:

> *a rare treat when the celebrated opponents, Daft and Clark, displayed their skill with the bat.*

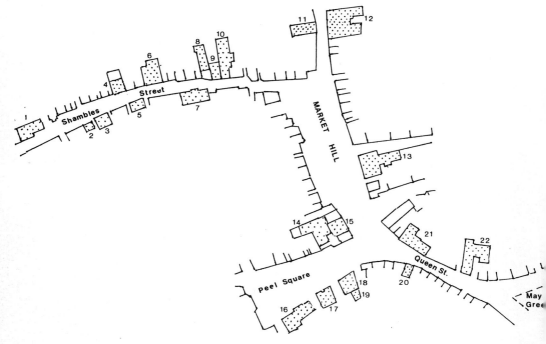

Figure 14. Some of the inns and public houses in central Barnsley in 1851 (excluding 'Beer Houses')

The Monk Bretton band supplied additional entertainment. A similar contest took place in 1861, but in the following year the odds were somewhat altered when All England met a mere fourteen Yorkshiremen. Perhaps this was the 'Grand Cricket Match' planned by the Barnsley Cricket Club when it was formed at a meeting on June 12 at the Royal Hotel.

Although opportunities for 'self improvement' were very much in evidence, many preferred to spend their leisure time in alternative ways in Barnsley's numerous inns, pubs and beer houses. Eighty three of them are listed in a Directory of 1862, and ten years later there were more than a hundred. A stroller along Shambles Street, along Cheapside and on to the beginning of Sheffield Road might be tempted to partake of a pint of ale at any of twenty seven establishments which lined the route. Figure 14 shows most of these and Figure 15 illustrates the pattern in Shambles Street where inns stood cheek by jowl.

In the country as a whole beer consumption was rising and would

Figure 15. The Old White Bear in Shambles Street, cheek by jowl with the Sovereign Inn *Tasker Photographic Trust.*

peak in the 1870s.[19] Alcohol was widely blamed for many of the social ills of the time, yet it is not to be assumed that all Barnsley pubs were places of rough behaviour. At the Brewster Sessions in September 1860 only nine cases of complaint were presented for the whole Division, and 'most of these were of a trivial nature'. A year later the Session reported a decrease in drunkenness, the 135 cases for the pubs in the district being 'considerably below average for previous years'. Yet in the second half of 1863, the record of Barnsley Petty Sessions lists fifty six cases of drunkenness and 224 cases of assault.[20]

Certainly the members of the Temperance movement in Barnsley were convinced that the drink problem was a major issue, requiring strong measures to defeat it. They faced a difficult task in view of a popular belief among working men that 'beer was manly and strengthening'. The struggle forms the subject of verses in *T'Bairnsla Foaks' Olmanack* of 1862 where 'Ale Pot' and 'Teapot' argue the matter and Ale Pot sings:

> *Its the grandest stuff me brave lads*
> *Withaht onny boastin an braggin;*
> *For a man i this wurld here a ahrs*
> *When wurkin, an toilin an faggin.*

By 1850 the Barnsley Temperance Society was celebrating its twenty fifth anniversary, with activities ranging over several days. On the first one:

> *A goodly muster sat down to tea in the Salem*
> *schoolroom, Castlereagh Street, a group of ladies*
> *furnishing the tea gratuitously and presiding*
> *at the trays.* [21]

Later everyone crowded into the Mechanics' Hall to hear addresses and listen to temperance songs. Already the Society had its own Juvenile Drum and Fife Band. Five years later they added a 'Temperance Choir'. Through music and copious verse the Society presented its uncompromising message: 'Intemperance had poisoned millions and blasted the prospects of millions more'.

The Petition

Over the years the progress of the town confirmed leading men of the town in their opinion that Barnsley was worthy of Municipal Borough status. It was the Ratepayers' Association, formed in 1866 that first suggested an all-out effort to achieve Incorporation. Although there was opposition, chiefly on the grounds that there would be additional and unsustainable charges on the rates, beyond the means of weavers and miners, the eventual outcome of a series of meetings was a vote in favour of the plan. [22] A Petition was to be prepared addressed to the Queen's Most Excellent Majesty in Council with a plea for the granting of a Charter of Incorporation.

The petition put forward a strong case for acceptance. Immense capital had been invested in extracting valuable seams of coal; there were excellent rail and canal connections; there were ironworks, linen and other manufactories and the town had a thriving and increasing market; the Board of Health had over the last thirteen years expended upwards of £100,000 in Work of Public Character; the population was increasing rapidly; there was a good range of public buildings, ten chapels and two churches, a Dispensary and a Cemetery, several banks and a public park.

The Petition Document, bearing over 1,800 signatures, each stating the man's occupation, offers a fine vista of the range of manufacturing and commercial activities in the town, and more than a hint of social status. Entries range from the thirty three 'Gentlemen' to a large body of labourers.[23] The importance of boot and shoe manufacture is clear; the range of skills in the foundries, the paper and the glass industries are all apparent, as well as the dominance of mining and textile manufacture. It is clear too that there was much work in the building trades, reflecting the continued expansion of the town. There was a host of retail shopkeepers, among them 56 grocers, 34 drapers and 53 tailors. There were dealers in a wide range of commodities, a small army of

BARNSLEY COAT OF ARMS.

Figure 16. Barnsley's Coat of Arms, 1869.

warehousemen, and around a hundred men providing the transport necessary for the whole urban machine to work. Accountants, solicitors and doctors featured among a well-represented professional class.

The Charter of Incorporation, effective from 5 July 1869, was laid before members of the town's governing body, the Board of Health, on Saturday, 17 July:

> *The precious document, with its ponderous seal of yellow wax, was examined minutely, and read out to the assembled body by the Clerk. No sooner had he finished reading than the bells of St. Mary's Church began to send forth merry peals, which were repeated at intervals throughout the day.*[24]

Appropriately, the Coat of Arms (Figure 16) suitably reflected the important part played by outstanding men - the families of Beckett and Locke - in the town's progress to its goal, as well as the industrial heart-beat of the town.

Barnsley had come of age!

Notes and References

1. *Barnsley Herald*, January 1860, Barnsley Local Studies & Archives (BLSA).
2. Burland J H *Annals of Barnsley* (BLSA).
3. *Barnsley Herald*, (BLSA).
4. Burland (BLSA).
5. *ibid*
6. *ibid*
7. *ibid*
8. *Barnsley Chronicle*, 8 Sept 1866 (BLSA); Machin F *The Yorkshire Miners* (1958), v.1 (BLSA).
9. Kaijage F J *Labouring Barnsley* 1816-56, 1975 (BLSA).
10. Burland (BLSA).
11. *ibid*
12. *ibid*
13. *ibid*
14. *ibid*
15. *ibid*
16. *Barnsley Chronicle* (BLSA).
17. Burland (BLSA).
18. ibid
19. Best G *Mid-Victorian Britain*, 1971, p240
20. Barnsley Petty Sessions Records, BLSA.
21. Burland (BLSA).
22. England G W *The Growth of Local Government in Barnsley*, 1913 (BLSA).
23. The Petition Document (BLSA).
24. *Barnsley Chronicle*, 17 July 1869 (BLSA).

ACKNOWLEDGEMENTS

I am grateful to the staff of Barnsley Local Studies Library and Barnsley Archives for their invaluable help in locating sources of information. Also to the Tasker Photographic Trust for permission to use Figures 6 and 15, and to Norman Wroe for help in locating Figure 10.

9. BARNSLEY CHARACTER (AND CHARACTER EXPERT): THE SUPERLATIVE PROFESSOR BEST

by Dr James Walker

T H Best, Phrenologist and Magnetic Healer, wishes to inform his Numerous Friends and the Public Generally that he can be Consulted Daily from 10 a.m. to 10 p.m.

THOMAS HERBERT BEST arrived in Barnsley Town in 1900 having pursued his studies and refined his arts 'in other towns for many years' and established his practice in a small, unassuming terrace on Cemetery Road. For those seeking his healing talents, the building was to be a symbolic stopping-off point on the hill descending from the busy Sheffield Road (which bustled with life) to the capacious graveyard that was Barnsley Cemetery.

Figure 1. Queen Victoria herself subscribed to Phrenology and had the heads of her children 'read'

It was exactly a century earlier that German anatomist Franz Joseph Gall founded the doctrine of Phrenology on the premise that the human character, along with the intellectual and moral qualities, could be revealed by the pattern of bumps and protuberances on the head. Queen Victoria, as can be seen in Figure 1, became interested in the subject. Twenty years before Best's debut, Barnsley had lost its first practitioner of the art, Old Mill poet Thomas Lister, despite the therapeutic attentions of Smedley's noted Hydropathic Establishment. Magnetic healing (Figure 2) had achieved notoriety through the theatrics of Austrian physician Franz Anton Mesmer, a near contemporary of Gall, who claimed to manipulate the 'Universal Fluid' which conveyed the influences of the planets to the human system via 'magnetism'; later recognised as

Figure 2. Magnetic Healing

the hypnotic state. John Elliotson, a London physician and heart specialist, was an early forerunner of T H Best in merging the two disciplines together in the 1830s to form 'Phreno-Mesmerism', although he was obliged to renounce his professional status in consequence.

Capturing the popular imagination, phrenology, palmistry and fortune-telling intermingled readily in the sideshows of Victorian fairgrounds, promising enlightenment to local townsfolk for the price of a hard-earned penny or two.[1] In similar vein, and stage-managed with a backdrop of electrical gadgetry, Mesmerism carried on the show business tradition of its founder (with his flowing lilac robes and iron wand) and in the mid-nineteenth century provided 'a series of entertainments' in the Corn Exchange, Market Hill, to the accolade of crowds which 'increased nightly' (the preceding engagement at that venue, a travelling American preaching the virtues of Temperance, was not reported to create such excitement).[2]

The various self-appointed experts in the healing and clairvoyant arts who were visitors to the town over the years no doubt prompted Best to generate custom of his own via a publicity photograph (Figure 3) and entries in the local newspaper of the day. From April 1900 his press announcements addressed not only the general public but also 'Numerous Friends', whether promoting himself as Professor, Popular Character Reader and Palmist or by use of his slogan, 'I make Health a Special Study'.[3] The photograph depicts him standing amidst the diverse paraphernalia of his trade, with two phrenology heads, a pile of learned tomes, a printed document (perhaps a diploma) to endorse his credentials, the bones of a human foot, and a crystal skull to add a suitable air of mystery.

Despite making a name for himself in this way, his business off to a sound start and his precious artefacts secure behind the solid stone frontage of his Cemetery Road consulting rooms, Best could still not afford complacency. In the Public Notices section of the *Barnsley Chronicle* of 7 January 1901, a Madame Cinderella proclaimed her

Figure 3. Professor T H Best, Barnsley's 'Character Expert & Magnetic Healer'
Elliott Collection

proficiency in Phrenology and Palmistry, attending premises at 6 Wesley Street (which formerly joined Sheffield road with Pontefract Road, only a short distance from Best's practice) during her sojourn in Barnsley. Originating from the mysterious East (from among the seaside attractions of Bridlington, to be exact) she had reputedly caused 'Immense Sensation in the Principal Towns of the United Kingdom' and now invited patronage at fees of 'one shilling and upward'. Our erudite Professor, not to be outdone, was swift to respond with his own assertions in the same column a week later:

THE BEST Phrenologist, Physiologist and Palmist in Barnsley is undoubtedly your Friend and Neighbour T.H.Best. Consultations daily 10 a.m.-10 p.m. Testimonials from clergy, gentry, professional and business men. Terms reasonable. Bazaars and Entertainments attended.

Madame Cinderella's entry the following week was, by way of contrast, laconic and modest:

Madame is expert: No self-praise. Consult testimonials from the press and public.

The war of words and competing claims continued, but like her fairy-tale namesake at the ball, Cinderella's stay was limited. Subsequent notices informed the reader of the impending departure of the 'World-Famed Madame' as if exhorting potential clients to make haste. After just a few weeks, perhaps due to poor trade or perhaps fearing the imminent transformation of her horse-drawn transport into a pumpkin, Cinderella left town, allowing Best to corner the local market in heads, hands and healing.

His rival did make the occasional brief return in the months ahead, but by and large she faded from the limelight and by the following January the only Cinderella making the headlines was the lavish twelve-night production at the Public Hall, Eldon Street. 'Ee by Gum,' ran the billing, 'Griffin and Drake's Barnsley Pantomime CINDERELLA' featured 'Mr. Walter Griffin directing' with such on-stage wonders as an 'Electric Carriage' for the heroine, not to mention the 'Expensive Engagement of the Great Augustine Brothers in their Marvellous Barrel Act (the Sensation of the Age)'.

Meanwhile, at the end of his first year of reading characters and reading destinies, Thomas Herbert Best's magnetism had attracted enough fee-paying customers for him to embark on a 'Summer Tour' in May 1901, a luxury that he could afford to repeat over the next few years, with notice of his return from distant travels published in the *Chronicle* every autumn.

We are left to speculate how much insight Best had in predicting his own fortunes, as well as those of his Barnsley clients, but the Edwardian era was just beginning and foretelling the changes and upheavals of the twentieth century that lay ahead would have been no easy task...

Notes and References

1. Publicity claims had to be worded carefully; e.g. promising to read the future risked prosecution under the *Vagrancy Act* of 1824 for 'professing to tell fortunes'.
2. Burland J H *The Annals of Barnsley and its Environs* for 1852 and 1853.
3. *Barnsley Chronicle*, Public Notices sections, 1900-03.

Acknowledgements

Thanks to Brian Elliott for loan of the 'Professor Best' photograph, and to Mavis Sadler for her assistance.

10. BARNSLEY'S PHOTOGRAPHIC PIONEERS, 1842-1870

by Brian Elliott

The 1840s: 'Likenesses, as if removed from the surface of a mirror'.

IN DECEMBER 1842 IT WAS REPORTED in the *Doncaster, Nottingham & Lincoln Gazette* that 'a considerable number of most respectable parties' had visited the Nobeman's Stand at Doncaster Race Course for the creation of 'Likenesses, as if removed from the surface of a mirror'. Edward Holland of Sheffield, the pioneering photographer responsible, also advertised his intention to visit several other Yorkshire towns **including Barnsley**.[1] This was a remarkably early example of entrepreneurship since the invention of photography had been proclaimed only three years earlier.

William Fox Talbot of Laycock Abbey, Wiltshire, referred to his pictures as 'photogenic drawings' in a paper read to the Royal Society on the last day of January, 1839. His presentation, based on four years of experimentation, was prompted because of the announcement in Paris, three weeks earlier, that Louise Daguerre had developed a new photographic process. The French showman had in fact refined and capitalised on his late partner's (Joseph Nicephore Niepce) earlier work. The *daguerreotype* process resulted in a small, delicate but pin-sharp image being chemically fixed on a copper plate, the fragile whole protected in a glass-fronted case, similar to a miniature painting (Figure 1). Although the process was expensive and the plates not reproducible, 'Daguerreotypomania' dominated commercial photography in the 1840s and early 1850s.[2] Talbot's negative-positive process or *Calotype* enabled multiple prints from a single paper negative, had 'softness' of tone and therefore appealed to artistic amateurs but the public were enthralled by the daguerreotype image which could even be colour tinted.

Early photography was restricted because of the patents of the respective processes. Licences were an expensive extra cost for anyone wanting to set up a new studio. Antoine Claudet, an immigrant glass wholesaler from High Holborn, received personal

Figure 1. A daguerreotype of a young American woman in a 'Union' brand thermoplastic case, c.1860 (image size:182mm.x 70mm). The braid on her cape, wide skirt and simple hairstyle suggests a date of about 1860. Daguerreotypes remained popular for longer in the U.S.A. than in Britain

tuition from Daguerre in Paris in the autumn of 1839, and bought a licence to practise in England.[3] Claudet was a great enthusiast rather than an opportunist unlike the London speculator, Richard Beard who obtained the exclusive English rights to the Daguerrotype. Beard opened his business in the roof of the Royal Polytechnic Institution on 23 March 1841, the first professional portrait studio in England.[4] Chadburns of Sheffield, manufacturers of scientific instruments and optics, purchased a licence from Beard in the summer of 1842 and by January 1843 were taking portrait photographs in purpose-built rooms at Brightside.[5] With Sheffield in the hands of the Chadburn Brothers, Edward Holland's licence was restricted to certain other Yorkshire towns. Holland left Doncaster in the middle of February 1843 and is known to have visited Bradford and Halifax but then appears to have surrended his licence because of non-payment of dues.[6] Although Holland and the Chadburns are unlikely to have visited Barnsley, they provide us with four salient features of the early trade:

(1) The market was almost exclusively limited to the wealthier classes.

(2) Only fashionable centres or larger towns and cities could support a purpose-built studio.

(3) Many early photographers were itinerants, travelling between select venues.

(4) The cost of setting up in business and the 'mystery' surrounding the operation of such a novel process gave considerable artistic and social status to the early photographer.

The 1850s: 'True to life that one would almost deemed they breath'

The 1840s were the very early years of photography when it was little more than a minority curiosity. In 1851, the year that marked the death of Daguerre, an innovation occurred which, because it was unpatented by its inventor, allowed the free expansion of photography. This was the Wet Plate Collodion process, devised by Frederick Scott Archer. It involved making negatives on sensitised **glass** plates and, like Daguerreotypes, the image quality was excellent. The main drawback was the need for exposure and development to take place in one operation - no problem in the comfort of a studio - but for outdoor work the intrepid Victorian photographer had to carry an entire dark room with him (Figure 2). The outstanding results achieved in hostile environments by

Figure 2. A mobile hand-cart dark room for the wet plate process

Figure 3. Roger Fenton needed this adpated wine merchant's van to house his 'press kit' at the Crimean battlefront, c.1855

pioneers such as Francis Frith (in the Middle East) and Roger Fenton (in the Crimea) involved a test of both determination and ingenuity (Figure 3). In England, Robert Howlett's photograph of Isambard Kingdom Brunel, set against the anchor chains of the *Leviathan*, remains as one of the most evocative of all Victorian photographs.[7] Locally, as we can see in Harold Taylor's article in this volume, an unknown photographer was able to capture some of the pomp and ceremony of the opening of Locke Park on 10 June 1862.[8] This view would have probably been taken by a large wooden sliding box camera using a 'whole-plate' (6 x 8 inches/16.5 x 21.5cm) and requiring an exposure time of at least five seconds, hence the blurred figures.

Prints were usually made on albumen, paper manufacturers having to obtain huge amounts of egg whites to meet demand.[9] However, influenced by the popularity of Daguerre miniatures, similar but cheaper examples, known as 'Ambrotypes', were also produced (Figure 4). The cheapest innovation, however, was the introduction of the 'Tintype', where a positive image was exposed and treated on a thin iron sheet. Cut to size, these near-instant images were popular with the growing band of itinerants, and survived at seaside and fairground locations until about 1950.

The patent-free wet collodion process lead to the phenomenal rise of the professional photographer. The census of 1851 and 1861 saw an increase from only 51 listed to over 2,500.[10] In Sheffield the number of photographers in business in the ten years after 1854 increased from 4 to 30.[11] By 1861 there were 25 professional photographers in Leeds and 9 in Bradford.[12] Even smaller industrial towns such as Barnsley could support three or four studios, at least one photographic shop and a lively trade in second-hand equipment. Photography had arrived.

Figure 4. Ambrotype (glass positive) in a pinchbeck type frame of a young woman c.1856. Image size(visible): 50mm x 60 mm *Author's Collection*

Understandably, there was an overlapping period when the portrait painter and the photographer competed for trade. But the realistic and cheap representations achieved by the new art form reduced the importance of the painter; and, as if to seal the latter's fate, photographers hailed themselves as 'photographic artists', advertisements and the backs of *cartes de visites* proclaiming their aesthetic skills. Yet photography as an art form was not without its critics in mid-Victorian Barnsley. A feature in the April 1857 edition of the *Barnsley Record*, whilst praising the 'magic' of the art, also condemned 'fancy portraits', the writer preferring plain 'untouched', 'true to life' and 'genuine' versions:

> *...a good photograph needs no artistic effort introduced, but why this modern fancy of face-making - because the public expect, ask, and pay for it, wishful for a picture as well as a portrait, and when fancy pictures are thus made it is often good bye to the portrait, the photographer ought only to 'flesh' the face and hands, and with this stop, or he is in danger of maring the truthful and delicate delineations of the sun-drawn portrait.*

This photographic critique was almost certainly the work of Thomas Dale, the *Record's* enterprising proprietor, a disillusioned purist who gave up photography four months later. Dale was astute in recognising the key relationship between science and art in photography, as shown in the opening paragraph of his far-sighted article:

Photography is one of the purest and most instructive sources of amusement we know, as an Art it has acquired a marked celebrity and universal acceptation, it is in fame and favour with and bearing upon other fine arts and business departments; its discovery is but of **yesterday** *- its* **today** *commands our surprize and meditation - its* **tomorrow** *or future will be the* **ne plus ultra** *of artistic attainment and scientific adaptation.*

He concluded by identifying the four basic requirements for the 'Beginner of the Art': 'a good lens, good chemicals, cleanliness and patience', each indispensable to the other; and recommended getting 'a good 1s. Primer or Handbook', followed by practical help from a friend 'on the mystical manipulation of the art' - and, with down to earth Barnsley realism - 'if you then don't succeed it is your own fault.'

Early Photography in Barnsley [13]

Who were Barnsley's photographic pioneers? It is difficult to identify with certainty who was 'first in the field' but the following examples, not therefore in chronological order, were all active during the 1850-70 period:

(i) M Holt

Holt, from premises at 1 Albert Street (between Market Street and Cheapside), described himself as *Photographic Artist* in a notice placed in the *Barnsley Times* of 7 March, 1857. One wonders if he was able to establish a proper commercial studio from this address. Yet his advertisement offered 'Portraits or family groups taken all weathers, from 9 a.m. till dark.' It is possible that Holt functioned either on a small scale or had a portable studio. He does not appear in the 1851 or 1861 census, so may have been an itinerant, living in lodgings on a temporary basis.

(ii) Thomas Dale

Dale was probably a serious amateur rather than a professional studio photographer but had a very impressive range of the latest equipment advertised for sale from his own Pitt Street auction mart (*The Athenaeum/* Temperance Hall) in the summer of 1857. His business interests which included proprietorship of the *Barnsley Record* newspaper combined, as we have seen, with a general disillusionment of the artistic aspect of photography in promoting his

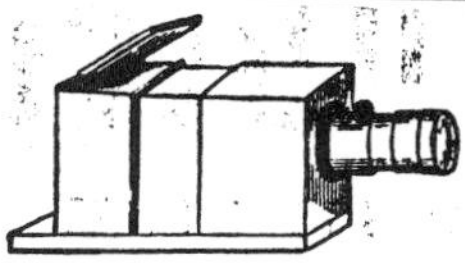

PHOTOGRAPHY.

CAMERAS, LENSES, MATERIALS.

TO BE SOLD CHEAP, the following Photographic Apparatus, all thoroughly good, in working condition; they are the property of, and have been used by, T. Dale, whose other engagements now prevent his further practising the Art, he, therefore, wishes to clear all off. To the Amateur a fine chance presents itself for securing Lenses, Cameras, and other Articles at a Cheap rate and of known Correctness.

The whole will be exhibited at No. 29, Pitt-street, where the Lenses may be tried,

LENSES

1 A whole plate 8½in. by 6½in., double combination, French Lense, by Jamin; gives a beautifully clear and well-defined Portrait, quick in action, mounted in brass with rackwork.

2 A quarter-plate English Lense for Portraits 4¼ by 3¼, sharp and clear, mounted in brass with rackwork.

3 A quarter plate French Lense, *new*, for Portraits 4¼ by 3¼, by Jamin, mounted &c.

4 A very superior single Lense, for Views, to cover a Plate 9 by 7, with Stops, mounted in brass with rackwork.

5 A prime single Lense, for Views, to cover a plate 6½ by 4¾, with rackwork mounted.

6 A very good single Lense, for Views, to cover a plate 5 by 4, sliding tube.

7 A Meniscus Lense, mounted in brass to slide, with a Camera thereto, by Abrahams, of Liverpool.

8 One of Abraham's of Liverpool, best Stereoscopic Cameras, mahogany, with a double combination Lense of rare quickness and brilliance.

9 An unequalled 1-9th Lense for Locket Portraits, not surpassed by a Voigtlander.

CAMERAS

10 A whole plate size Walnut Camera complete, with the addition of two slides with sky adjustments, adapted for either a double Lense for Portraits, or a single Lense for Views. No. 1 and 4 Lense have been used with it.

11 An extending Camera, for enlarging Portraits or making copies the size of original; will work from 6in. to 20in., focus Lense, so made that the dark Slides and Lense Slides to No. 10 fit it.

12 A ¼ plate Camera in Walnut, used with No. 2 Lense.

13 A ¼ plate Camera in Walnut, *new*.

14 A Tourist's Folding extending Camera for Views, 5 by 4, made in deal wood, very light and portable, three legs as tripod fitted. No. 5 Lense being used with it.

15 A Stereoscopic Camera, in deal, adapted for 2 Lenses.

16 A mahogany Stereoscopic Camera, for 2 Lenses.

17 A Photographic TENT, for working in the country, readily put together, and as easily taken apart, rendered impervious to light by black cloth, stretching cords, stakes, &c.

18 A Photographic Gallery, 13ft. long by 7½ft. wide, with glazed top and side lights, interior dark room, made to travel, having folding floor, sides, and roof.

19 A Tin-box comparted for Chemical Bottles and Lense, suitable for a tourist or landscape operations.

20 A Wood-box, ditto.

21 A quantity of Stereoscopic subjects, on paper, glass, & silver-plate, in lots.

22 A Box to hold Stereoscope & subjects, with lock & key.

23 A large Printing-frame, with hinged back, strong plate glass, mahogany frame.

24 Ditto ditto.

25 Ditto ditto.

26 Ditto ditto.

27 Albumenized Paper

28 Photographic Paper unalbumenized or salted.

29 Porcelain and Gutta Percha Dishes; Horizontal and Vertical Silver Baths, cased and covered.

30 Photographic Colours, in mahogany box, with brushes &c. complete.

31 Books on the Art—The Collodion Process, by Le Gray; Compendium of Photography, by F. Cox; Photographic Manipulation, by T. H. Hannah; A. B. C. of Photography, a Guide to Painting Photographic Portraits, with Draperies, &c., by A. N. Rentoul; Plain Instructions in Draphanie.

32 Plate-boxes, in all sizes, to hold 50, 24, & 12 in each, in White wood and Walnut:

33 Leather Cases for single and double Portraits, Pass Partouts, Frames, Mats, Preservers, Glasses.

34 Stereoscope hand-glasses.

35 A Background representing the interior of a room with window to open or close, and distant Landscape.

36 Lot of stoppered Bottles, Glass Jars, Travelling Boxes, &c., &c.

Figure 5. Sale advert for Thomas Dale's extensive collection of photographic equipment, *Barnsley Record*, August 1857. Notice the graphic of a sliding box camera

decision not to 'further practise the Art'. His equipment, as can be seen by reference to Figure 5, included a 'Photographic TENT, for working in the country' and a 'Photographic Gallery, 13ft. long by 7.5 ft. wide with glazed top and side lights, interior dark room, made to travel, having folding floor, sides and roof'. Dale offered for sale a similar gallery two years later (Figure 6).

Figure 6. Dale's further sale notice of his unwanted 'Photographic Gallery', *Barnsley Record,* 25 June 1859

PHOTOGRAPHIC GALLERY FOR SALE.

TO BE SOLD CHEAP, a Wood-built Photographic Gallery, (made in parts, easily removed,) good Side and Top Lights and Dark room, size 12 feet by 7 feet. The Gallery is in the Country and may be seen.

For Price and reference apply to T. Dale, Pitt-street, Barnsley.

(ii) George Campbell

A little more information is available about Campbell who appears to have functioned from several town centre premises, according to a notice in the 1 May 1858 edition of the *Barnsley Times* :

G.Campbell begs to inform his Friends and the public

generally that he has removed from Mr Guest's Yard to premises opposite the Devonshire Arms, near the railway station. G. Campbell is prepared to take portraits of every description from 1s. upwards.

Campbell's move may have been strategic in the sense of locating his trade at a site that would attract the interest of both residents and visitors arriving by rail.   In the 1861 census he was resident at 3 Nelson Street, aged 44, described as *Photographic Artist*, his family (wife and daughter, aged four) sharing with a mother who had two young children and a female weaver, aged seventeen.[14] According to Tasker, Campbell was at 25 Eldon Street (later site of *Magnet Hotel*) in 1862-66.[15] This was of course a prime business street and much favoured by later photographic establishments.   It appears that Campbell's business affairs were far from easy in the 'early days' as we find him petitioning against creditors in 1855.[16]   It is also interesting that two years later we find Campbell giving notice, in the *Barnsley Times* (and from yet another address), that his availability was limited, though this may have been an advertising ploy, to attract more custom:

GEORGE CAMPBELL'S stay in Barnsley is now very short, and very respectfully urges upon Ladies and Gentlemen the importance of an immediate visit to his gallery, in Crescent Street, if they wish to secure a FAITHFUL LIKENESS of THEMSELVES, FAMILIES or FRIENDS, taken so TRUE TO LIFE that one would almost deem they breathed.

Campbell emerges as something of a showman - just the kind of approach that was needed in order to attract a wide clientele. No identified examples of his work have been obtained but he must have been of some status since a vignette, shown as Figure 7, based on one of his photographs, was used by Rowland Jackson in his *History of the Town and Township of Barnsley*, published in 1858. A year later he was, via the *Barnsley Chronicle* (12 March), offering 'A NEW AND IMPROVED STYLE OF PHOTOGRAPHY, giving portraits the appearance of, MINIATURES ON IVORY', also described as 'ALBASTRINE PHOTOGRAPHY.' He also offered a printing service from 'AMATEURS' OWN NEGATIVE PHOTOGRAPHS' from his 'GALLERY NEAR THE RAILWAY STATION', probably the first photographic processing establishment in the town.

Figure 7. This small engraving of Market Hill, used as a frontispiece for Rowland Jackson's 'History of Barnsley' was based on one of George Campbell's photographs, c. 1857

(iii) Job Walker (established c1854)

A former miner established one of the the earliest and most enduring studios in Victorian Barnsley. Job Walker (1832-1899) worked underground, at West Melton, the same pit that employed his father, but at the age of 22 pledged never to enter a pit again following a near fatal accident.[17] Fond of music, Walker had mechanical skills and had been able to repair instruments in his spare time. From this background he took up photography 'when the art was only in its infancy, and in a short time became an accomplished manipulator, displaying considerable artistic taste and skill in the portraits which he turned out.'[18]

Job Walker opened a studio - said to be 'the first in Barnsley' - in Peel Square, at what became known as *Chronicle Buildings* (now the *Tommy Wallocks* pub). Advertisements were appropriately placed in

Dale's *Barnsley Record*, such as this example, from the 25 June,1859, edition:

WALKER, artist in Photography, Peel Square, Barnsley,
N.B. Families attended at their own Residences on the most Reasonable Terms. Miniature Portraits taken for Lockets, Brooches, Rings etc.

It is interesting that he offered an 'at home' mobile service, probably for the more wealthy clients. A more detailed advertisement, lodged in the edition of 29 October, 1859, - and shown here as Figure 8 - suggests that his business was proceeding well and that he was successful in 'securing likenesses of children, coaxing them for a few minutes into that which is very difficult, viz., a sweet yet lively stillness' which, as we shall see, was quite a feat given the practicalities of early studio photography!

Walker appears to have established a good reputation, attracting custom from Barnsley and the surrounding districts. He was probably the first professional to take portraits of 'ordinary' people, particularly in the later years of his business and was official photographer to the West Riding Constabulary (Barnsley Division). Directories show that by c1871 he had removed to Eldon Street, confirmed as at number 48 (Figure 9, later site of the *Odeon* cinema) where he remained until his retirement, in 1889.[19]

The census of 1871 shows his private residence as being 20 Pontefract Road, where he lived with his wife, Elizabeth, children Arthur (aged 7), William Henry (3) and Elizabeth (3 mths); and Annis Paver, his 'photographic assistant', aged fourteen.[20] Walker also established a music shop at 21 Sheffield

---

FIRST-RATE LIKENESSES
AT SECOND-RATE CHARGES!

J. WALKER, Photographer, (Gallery near the Drinking Fountain) Peel-Square, Barnsley, wishes to express his thanks to the many who have visited his Gallery for the purpose of having their Portraits taken by him ; and begs to impress on the public and those who have not visited him, that his likenesses are distinct, clear, and true to life ; that he studies the position of the sitter, in order to give a pleasing picture ; that his portraits are finished with all dispatch and artistically coloured in complexion and dress.

J. W. is very successful in securing likenesses of children, coaxing them for a few minutes into that which is very difficult, viz., " a sweet yet lively stillness."

Specimens may be seen ; a visit to and sitting for a portrait will not be regretted.

Likenesses taken for Lockets, Brooches, Pins, Rings, Bracelets, &c.

Likenesses as low as 6d., 9d., 1s., 1s.6d. and 2s.6d. and prices up to 15s.

Figure 8. 'First-rate Likenesses at Second-rate Charges' was the slogan used by Walker in an advertisement in the *Barnsley Record*, 29 October 1859

Figure 9. Job Walker's two-storey Eldon Street shop and studio, probably purpose-built so as to allow plenty of light into the upper, studio, area. It stood next to the Empire Palace. Here we can see the premises photographed in 1905, having just been vacated by another well-known Barnsley professional photographer, Will Randall who had been in occupation about two years, moving to Peel Street. Another photographer, J G Alexander, had succeeded Walker at this address in 1892, staying in business until Randall arrived on the scene. The premises were demolished in c 1954 (when it was R W Atkin's sweet & tobacco shop) to make way for the new Gaumont cinema. *Tasker Photographic Trust*

Road which was to be managed by his eldest son. The photography business was described as 'Job Walker and Son' about the time of his retirement and appears to have been run by the son for a few more years, the music (and also cycle) shop functioning until about 1917.

A Congregationalist and a Liberal, Job Walker was, according to his obituarist, 'widely known' and 'highly respected', though he 'never took part in town matters.'[21] His will, dated 2 February 1899, just twenty days before his death, shows that he was then living at 3 Bond Road (off Huddersfield Road), one of the most fashionable residential areas of Victorian Barnsley, describing himself as 'Gentleman'.[22] His wife was given household furniture and effects as well as income from his personal estate during her lifetime; and, after deduction of the running costs of the Sheffield Road shop, the tenancy and proceeds went to a younger son, Ernest. The remainder of his estate was shared between his children, Arthur Walker and Kate Walker.

(iv) Wilson and Bullock

During the mid-1860s Thomas Wilson and a Mr Bullock established a small photographic business in Barnsley. Trade directories indicate that they operated from 68 Sackville Street which appears to have also been the residence of Thomas who is listed under that address, described as 'photographer', aged 60, in the 1871 census. A fine miniature 'vignette' portrait of a young woman (Figure 10) suggests that their work was of a good standard. We can see that on the reverse the trade address is given as *Gordon Terrace, Barnsley*.

Figure 10. Head and shoulders profile of a young woman in vignette form, c.1865 by Wilson & Bullock

(v) James Denton, est.1869

Right at the end of our period, James Denton, aged 39, a joiner and hardware dealer established a business that included professional photography on Sheffield Road. This was the beginning of a very well known family firm serving several generations of Barnsley people.

(vi) T E Brooke

Like some of the later local photographers Brooke came from a background of picture framing and also printed funeral cards. He operated from a private address, Popular Terrace, Barugh Green (Darton township) in the 1880s and probably for a decade or so earlier. The easel on the 'coat of arms' - like trade card logo (Figure 11) suggests that he was one of the growing breed of artistic photographers. His presence shows that there was sufficient demand for studio commercial photography that it could function in village locations.

Figure 11. Reverse of one of T E Brooke's earliest *cartes de visite*

(v) Suppliers for the 'Black Art'

We have seen that in the 1850s and 1860s photography or 'The Black

Art' as it was becoming known (due to tell-tale chemical stains on the hands of practitioners) was attracting more custom. It remained, however, a very exclusive amateur or professional activity. The cost of obtaining equipment and supplies, and the necessary artistic and scientific knowledge was a barrier to wider participation, and remained so for several decades. Yet there was sufficient demand for materials that a specialist shop was established in Barnsley in 1859.

M. Wright of 31 Pitt Street, according to his advertisement in the *Barnsley Record* of 12 March, 1859, (Figure 12), offered amateur and professionals the latest collodion process, a selection of cases, frames etc and other items 'used in the Photographic Art'. We can also see that he had a 'Cheap' second-hand walnut camera – with a Lerebour (French) lens – for sale, the latter 'sharp in definition and remarkably quick in action'. One month later Wright placed a notice in the same newspaper informing the public that he had moved to 55 Sheffield Road and his advertisement (Figure 13) shows that he continued to stock the latest equipment and materials. It is also interesting to see that he sold the *Photographic Weekly News* and offered a mounting service for funeral cards. Although a shopkeeper,

---

. PHOTOGRAPHY.
PORTRAIT & LANDSCAPE COLLODION.

M. WRIGHT, 31, Pitt-Street, Barnsley, calls the attention of Photographers to a new make of Collodion he is now supplied with; it is chemically quick, gives good whites, blacks, and half-tones, has a tough firm film, and by a slight alteration in the ordinary developing solution, is adapted for negatives. Any Photographer prefering the modern feature in Photography of converting positives into negatives, should use this Collodion.

Union, Velvet, and Leather Cases, Passe Portouts, Frames, Chemicals, Varnishes. Colours, Brushes, Printing Paper, Stereoscopic Slides, Glasses, and other articles used in the Photographic Art.

Also, To be Sold Cheap, a Second-hand half-plate Walnut wood CAMERA and LENS, the Lens is by LEREBOUR, gives a clear sharp definition and remarkably quick in action ;—in good repair, and not sold because at all defective in any one point.

Figure 12. M Wright of 31 Peel Street, Barnsley offered for sale a 'new make of Collodion' in an advertisement placed in the *Barnsley Record*, 12 March 1859

WIGHT, HAMPSON, AND CO.,
9, PEEL-STREET, BARNSLEY,

ANNOUNCE to amateurs and professionals in Photography, that in consequence of Mr. W. Wright having declined business in the sale of Photographic Chemicals and Materials, they have opened a PHOTOGRAPHIC DEPOT for CHEMICALS, COLLODION, VARNISHES, FRAMES, PASSE PARTOUTS, CASES, &c. Their supply of Chemicals are from one of the first houses. Genuiness and purity may be relied on. The Materials are of varying qualities and prices.

W. H. and W. have received the appointment of the sale of RAMSDEN'S celebrated COLLODION. They have also an Ambrotype Collodion of inestimable excellence. Transparent Varnishes, to dry with or without heat, Black Varnish, which dries quickly, and does not crack. Likenesses mounted in Frames or Cases.

Wight, Hampson, and Wight wish also to inform the public that in the recent alterations they have made on their premises, in Peel-street, they have provided a GALLERY FOR TAKING LIKENESSES, which they mount in the pure Photograph or embellish with artistic backgrounds, in oil colours.

Specimens and prices known on the premises.

Figure 13. Wright announces his removal to 55 Sheffield Road where he continued to offer photographers a wide range of products and services, *Barnsley Record*, 9 April 1859

Wright must have been at the very least an enthusiastic amateur photographer, because of the new and highly specialised nature of the trade.

Wright's photographic trade did not appear to prosper. In the autumn of 1859 **Wight, Hampson and Company** announced the opening of a new 'Photographic Depot for chemicals, Collodion, varnishes, frames, passe partouts, cases etc' at 9 Peel Street. The notice (Figure 14) shows that the business began 'in consequence of Mr W. [sic] Wright having decline business in the sale of Photographic Chemicals and Materials. They appear to have taken over Wright's stock but also provided a new feature: a 'GALLERY FOR TAKING LIKENESSES'. In the same edition of the *Barnsley Record* a small advertisement informed the public that 'The Photographic Shop' on Sheffield Road, was now 'A Butter and Provision' establishment.

PHOTOGRAPHIC DEPOT.
No. 55, SHEFFIELD-ROAD, BARNSLEY.

M. WRIGHT, announces to Photograph-ers and the Public, that he has removed from 31, Pitt-Street, to No. 55 Sheffield-Road, Barnsley, and begs to direct attention to the following requisites for the fascinating process of the Photographic Art, either in Portrait or Landscape Studies, a new make of Collodion which he is now supplied with; it is chemically quick, gives good whites, blacks, and half-tones, has a tough firm film, and by a slight alteration in the ordinary developing solution, is adapted for negatives. Any Photographer preferring the modern feature in Photography of converting positives into negatives, should use this Collodion.

A re-developing solution for producing those superb pictures, The Alabastrine, equal to the most costly miniature, Specimens taken by the above Collodion and finished with the above named solution, may be seen.

Union, Velvet, and Leather Cases, Passe Portouts in variety; Frames, astonishingly cheap; Pure Chemicals, Varnishes, Colours, and Brushes; Glasses, and other articles used in the Photographic Art.

Albumenized and Salted Paper, Stereoscopic Slides, Stereoscopes with prism and round eye pieces

Cameras, Lenses, Tripods, Head Rests, Glass Porcelain and Gutta Percha Dishes, Baths, &c.

Agent for Ramsden's Collodion, and the Photographic Weekly News.

Funeral Cards mounted.

M. Wright, No. 55, Sheffield-road, Barnsley.

Figure 14. Wight, Hampson and Company's new 'Photographic Depot' was centrally located at 9 Peel Street (near Job Walker's studio), *Barnsley Record*, 22 October 1859.

Photography Mania

Two innovations enabled photographs to be easily available in most mid-Victorian homes. The first was the introduction of the stereo viewer whereby a pair of small (3 x 3 inch) prints were superimposed by the relationship between the eye and the device, resulting in a remarkably vivid three-dimensional image. Hand-held viewers, such as the example shown as Figure 15, were fairly cheap though luxury table-top versions were available for the middle-class drawing room. Albumen prints pasted on cards, usually measuring 7 x 3.25 inches (90 x 180mm), were bought in sets and were available in a huge range of subjects. By 1858 the London Stereoscopic Company had 100,000 titles. The craze for collecting coincided with

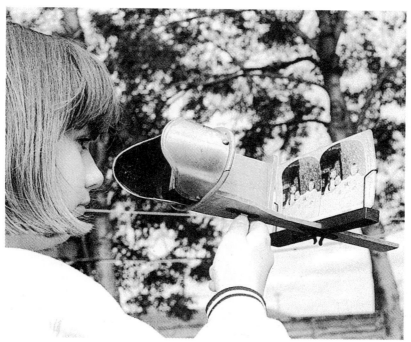

Figure 15. A typical hand-held stereo viewer   *The Author*

the boom in travel begun by Thomas Cook in the 1850s. With stereo viewers our recent ancestors travelled the world. In Barnsley, Thomas Dale had three stereoscopic cameras, including a mahogany example by Abrahams of Liverpool 'with a double combination lens of rare quickness and brilliance' and a variety of stereo subjects for sale in 1857. About the same time stereoscopic slides were stocked in M Wright's 'photographic depot' in Pitt Street. Such was the demand that enterprising printer and stationer **G Moxon** of 22 Market Hill ran a 'Stereoscopic Circulating Library', perhaps similar to the video-hire section of shops of today.

As the use of the stereo viewer faded in popularity (though there were later surges of interest), photographers began making glass slides for magic lantern shows but the second great innovation placed photographs - especially portraits - within reach of ordinary people and the age of the 'Family Album' began. The story began in 1854 when Disderi, photographer to the French court of Napoleon III patented a new type of camera that had four lenses, therefore allowing eight different photographs to be taken on one plate.

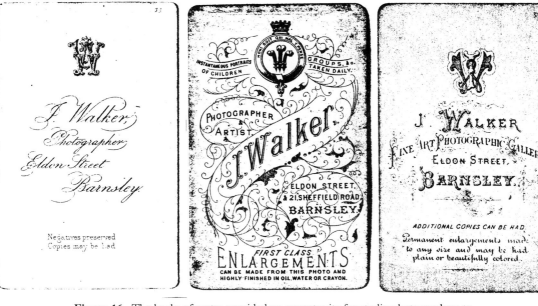

Figure 16. The backs of cartes provided an opportunity for studio photographers to proclaim their skills, the graphics becoming more complex with the passage of time, as can be seen in this series, taken from Job Walker's studio, c1860- 90.

Pictorial calling cards or *cartes de visites* were produced but never really caught on until photographs of well known people were made. Queen Victoria invited the American photographer J E Mayall to Buckingham Palace in 1860 for the purpose of producing a series of cartes of herself and her family. She was so pleased with the results that Mayall was given permission to publish a Royal Album for public sale. When Prince Albert died, a year later, some 70,000 memorial cartes were bought **in one week**, making him far more famous dead than alive. Cartomania had began in earnest and sitting for a portrait was now within the pocket of most homes. Before the introduction of cartes a portrait photograph would have cost £2 to £3, about twice the income of the average family. Cartes initially cost half a crown but soon tumbled to one shilling and eventually just sixpence. Working people put on their Sunday best and flocked to the new studios. By 1869 annual sales of cartes reached an astonishing 16-18 million. [23]

The photographic image was mounted on backing cards measuring 3.25 by 2.25 inches (90 x 57mm) which had the photographer's name and address on the reverse. After a few years' many photographers produced increasingly flamboyant logos, as can be seen by reference to an interesting series of graphics relating to Job Walker, Figure 16.

Purpose-made family albums were produced in many thousands, leather-bound with splendidly embossed covers held in place by gilt clasps, and pages having slots where the cartes could be conveniently positioned. Grandmother could be placed next to Queen Victoria, Prime Minister Disraeli or a local worthy. A typical album might house 48 cartes as was the case with a local example which contained photographs dating from c1860 to c1890 and included the work of Job Walker, Wilson & Bullock, T E Brooke, Thomas Edson and Warner Gothard. A selection of local cartes is shown at the end of this study (Figure 19, a-m).

A visit to Job Walker's Studio

In the 1850s and 1860s a visit to a studio was a social event and Job Walker, like many of his contemporaries saw himself as a professional artist as well as a commercial photographer. His own appearance and manner had to be appropriate and was probably not unlike the example shown as Figure 17. Understandably, the sitter or sitters also 'dressed-up' for the occasion and Walker would be able to advise beforehand on the most suitable attire - black silks and satins being

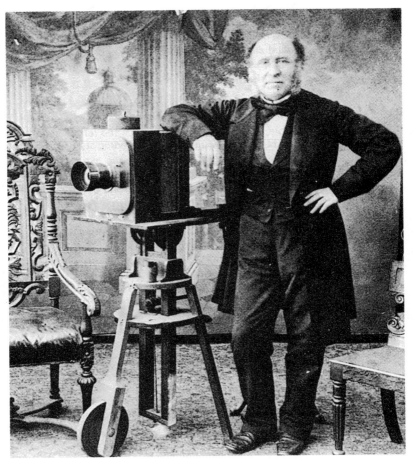

Figure 17. An unknown portrait photographer in his studio, albumen print, 1850s. The base of a head clamp is just visible behind his feet. The photographer's attire, his general manner and the quality of the studio fittings suggest that his business catered for a fairly exclusive clientele

preferred since some colours did not reproduce well in the 'black and white' cartes (yellows, reds and oranges came out black; purples, pinks, mauves and light blues as white). For most working class people their image was therefore untypical of their normal appearance. It is likely that the sitter was positioned where 'flattering' north light was dominant, probably from high side windows (artificial lighting was rare at this time). There would be a suitable backdrop - a rustic scene, a hint of classical architecture etc on a painted scenery roll.   Firms even specialised in the making of

Figure 18. A typical *Punch* cartoon of the period, mocking the new artist photographers. Here we can see a sitter, of small stature, being 'accommodated' by the use of small-scale furniture; in other words a critique on the lack of reality in many 'Likenesses' *Author's Collection*

prestigious chairs and tables for studios. The need for complete stillness over many seconds was absolutely vital, so Job's studio manner was crucial in putting people at ease, especially for children, the elderly and those of a nervous disposition. It must have been a daunting experience for many ordinary people to pose for a photograph. It was common to employ head clamps to steady the posture. Walker appears to have a good rapport with his sitters since, as we have already seen, he boldly proclaimed his speciality - portraits of children - on later advertising. The dull expressions of sitters was indeed entirely due to the need to keep still, smiling being an extremely rare occurrence, in fact convention deemed that it detracted from dignity, respectability and self-control. Not surprisingly, cartoons in *Punch*, Figure 18, frequently mocked a visit to the photographer's studio, even for the middle classes. Walker also offered to 'attend families in their own residences' though this was likely to have been taken up by the better off customers. Walker and his professional colleagues did not have the gift to create the poignant intimacy as portrayed by contemporaries such as David Octavious Hill and Robert Adamson - nor the talents of Julia Margaret Cameron and Lewis Carroll but their work does provide lasting images of Barnsley people for future generations.

By 1870 we have seen that early photography had made an impact in mid-Victorian Barnsley, as it also had in other provincial towns, and over the next twenty years professionals such as Job Walker were to be challenged by newer studios, most notably that of Warner Gothard who was to describe himself as 'Photographer to the Royal Family'. But it was Walker, the former miner, and a handful of other 'artistic professionals' who were the real photographic pioneers of Barnsley.

The gradual introduction of the dry collodion process, especially after the innovation of the use of gelatine by Richard Leach Maddox in 1871, heralded the beginning of photography as a popular past-time, facilitated by George Eastman and the Kodak camera, but as we shall see in a forthcoming article, there was a continuing demand for the studio photographer.

Figure 19. A series of *cartes de visites* covering the period c1860-1890:

(a) An early carte c1865 from Warner Gothard's studio at Great Grimsby, Lincs. The ladies in crinoline dresses, bodices, necks and shoulders braided. Gothard prospered when he moved to Wakefield and then to Barnsley in the late 1880s

(b) Typical formal pose (similar to a painting), full-length portait from the studio of Wilson & Bullock c1867. Head clamp just visible behind the subject's feet. Impressive side wiskers! Plain background, apart from draped curtains confirming early date

(c) Early Job Walker carte. Seated subject framed in oval with rustic scene in background, c1865. Informal attire of a working man?

(d) Another early Walker portrait but of a 'full-length' seated figure, rustic background

(e) Military cartes from Walker's studio. Here we can see two soldiers in full uniform. Nice touch is the informal seating of the right figure

(f) A close view of a military subject (same uniform)

(g) Interesting carte from the studio of T E Brooke of Barugh Green. It must have been quite an achievment to arrange this threesome, c1875

(h) A fine carte of a young woman by 'Art Photographer' George Rushworth of Dodworth Road. The fringe of the dress matches that on the chaise longue and dates the image to c1875

(i) Children were difficult subjects to capture naturally - and keep still! Here G E Wales of Sheffield Road has done well to pose this youngster by seating her on a well upholstered chair. The 'white' dress does not reproduce well

(j) A fine child portrait by Warner Gothard, late 1880s, the subject somewhat precariously perched on a chair

(l) A local worthy: Bruce Wentworth of Wentworth Castle, Stainborough, in fashionable check suit, photographed by Gothard in c1890 (probably a gift to one of his servants)

(n) Cabinet print by Job Walker (c1880) of John (1810-87) and Ann (1816-88) Crossland who lived in the Churchfields area. John was a bleacher and warehouse man, probably employed at Spences Calender Works. The collar that Mrs Crossland is wearing probably relates to the Good Templars *Julie Woodward*

(k) A fine three-quarter vignette style portait of a young woman - rare in the sense that she almost has a smile on her face. From the studio of Eddison of Sheffield Road, late 1880's

(m) A fine head and shoulders vignette of a young woman from Job Walker's Eldon Street studio, 1890s. As photography improved, the camera focussed more closely on the subject's face. Notice the jet broach and matching earrings and popular 'Princess Alexander' fringe

Notes and References

1.   Adamson K, 'Doncaster's Earliest Photographer', *Yesterday Today* , Local History Quarterly Review (Doncaster Library), 2, April 1991.

2.   Daniels P *Early Photography*, 1978, p 18.

3.   *ibid*; for a general view of Daguerreotypes see Harker M F *Victorian and Edwardian Photographs* ,1982 (revised edition) in the Letts Collectors' Guides series, pp 9-11; also Pols R, *Dating Old Photographs* (Federation of Family History Societies), 1992, pp 6-7.

4.   Daniels, *op cit*, p 21.

5.   Smith D M, 'The Birth of Photography in Sheffield,1840-1870', *Transactions of the Hunter Archaeological Society*, v.14, 1987, pp 64-66.

6.   Adamson, *op cit.*

7.   Daniels, *op cit*, pp 26-27.

8.   *Barnsley Civic Review*, Sept 1951.

9.   Pols, *op cit*, pp 10-11. In 1866 it was estimated that some six million egg whites were being used in the preparation of photographic paper; Dresden, Europe's largest producer, used six thousand eggs **per day** as late as 1894. Albumen paper was superseded by gelatine-chloride printing-out papers in the 1890s.

10.   Lambert M *Fashion in Photographs*, 1860-1880 (1991), p 10; Pols, *op cit* p 12.

11.   Smith, *op cit*, p 67.

12.   Dewhirst I *Gleanings from Victorian Yorkshire* (1972), p 119.

13.   Information from census returns, business directories, newspapers and original photographs have been used to build a reasonable picture of the early years of photography. Identifiable photographs are a wonderful source but are rare for this period. They can be occasionally found in the hands of antique dealers, though most are 'anonymous' and, for portraits, the sitter is seldom named. Sadly, thousands of family photographs have been destroyed or thrown away as rubbish. Thankfully, small *cartes de visites* (visiting card size photographs) and larger 'cabinet' size prints for the later years of the century are plentiful and even turn up at car boot sales. The writer's aim has been, over several years, to collect a representative selection of the work of local photographers but inevitably there are gaps for the earliest known practioners. For noted photographers - such as Gothard - a fair sample can be obtained over the entire period of operation.

14.   Tasker Census Index (TCI), Barnsley Local Studies & Archives (BLSA).

15.   Tasker E G *Barnsley Streets*, vol 6, p 39.

16.   TCI, BLSA.

17.   Obituary notice, *Barnsley Chronicle*, 25 February 1899.

18.   *ibid*

19.   White F *W R Directory* 1871-72; Tasker *Barnsley Streets*, 6; TCI/BLSA.

20.   TCI/BLSA.

21.   Obituary notice, *Barnsley Chronicle*, 25 February 1899.

22.   Proven 22 June, 1899, Somerset House, London.

23.   Smith *op cit* p 71

Further Reading

Roberts, Pam *Under Exposed: A Guide to Collecting, Identifying and Conserving Old Photographs* (BBC Publications), 1966.

Wade, John *A Short History of the Camera*, 1979.

Landsell, Avril *Wedding Fashions, 1860-1980* (History in Camera series, Shire Publications), 1983.

The Dalesman *Old Yorkshire in Pictures*, 1970.

Craven A B *Victorian and Edwardian Yorkshire from Old Photographs* (Batsford), 1971.

Jackson B *Cawthorne 1790-1990*, 1991.

The Frith Collection *Photographic Memories of Yorkshire*, 1995.

National Museum of Photography, Film and Television, *The Book*, n.d. (Guidebook).

The Photohistorian: quarterly journal of the Historical Group of the Royal Photographic Society.

Acknowledgements

Thanks to Mr and Mrs Lockwood and Mr and Mrs Mathers for the loan of a Victorian family album and cartes; to Kath Parkin of the Barnsley Chronicle for publishing my appeal for information relating to Job Walker; to Mr R Walker and the Tasker Photographic Trust for reproduction of a photograph of Job Walker's Eldon Street premises and to Mrs Julie Woodward for her great[2] grandparents' portrait photograph.

11. Barnsley's Wellington Street Theatre

by Kate Taylor

LIVE THEATRE IN BARNSLEY has had a chequered history. This account focuses principally on the theatre in Wellington Street although references will be made to its rivals of which only the Public Hall in Eldon Street remains active as a venue for live performances today.

Travelling players may well have visited Barnsley long before 1789 but the first available evidence of their presence lies in two entries in the register of the parish church of marriages in that year involving 'comedians' (a conventional term for actors at that time).[1] Until 1788 it was illegal to act for financial reward, although this does not seem to have been a serious deterrent, but an Act of Parliament of that year legitimised acting for hire provided that the company obtained a licence from the local magistrates and played for no more than sixty days in any one town. From 1792, when West Riding Magistrates' Quarter Sessions' Order Books first note the grant of a licence - to William Pero for performances in Halifax - it becomes easier to trace players' visits. [2]

In 1798 William James Colyer (or Collier) and William Huggins were granted a licence to perform for up to 21 nights in Barnsley (Figure 1).[3] The company was no doubt a modest one, of perhaps a dozen players including some women, and seems to have travelled principally in Nottinghamshire and Lincolnshire but the previous year they had played in Rotherham and were to return there after their Barnsley visit. They played in Rotherham again in 1799, in Barnsley in 1800 and in Rotherham in 1801 and 1802.[4] By the time of the next licensed visits to Barnsley, in 1807 and 1812, Huggins was in partnership with Clarke.[5] The visits, some at least of which were in July, are unlikely to have lasted much more than a fortnight and would have involved a change of bill each evening with two main items with some kind of interlude - a dance or a song - in between.

Before Barnsley gained a purpose-built theatre, the company performed in Strutt's laithe (or lathe), a barn near the top of the old White Bear Yard in Shambles Street (Figure 2).[6]

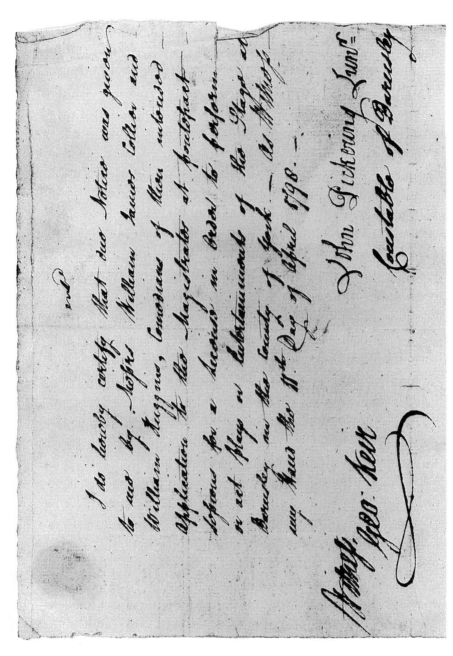

Figure 1. Certificate showing that William Collier and William Huggins have given due notice of their intention to apply for a licence to perform in Barnsley. This is the first recorded instance of their coming to town

John Goodchild Collection

It was Huggins and Clarke's company that played in Barnsley's first purpose-built theatre, in Wellington Street, when it opened on Wednesday 26 July 1815.[7] The evening's programme included *The Miller and his Men* and a farce, *Love, Law and Physic*. The theatre, 'an unpretentious looking and externally unadorned little structure'[8] had been built in 1814 at a cost of about £1,400 by William Depledge and John Wilkinson.[9] Depledge had inherited money from a relative who had managed the Irish estates of Lord Fitzwilliam.[10] It is said that the company was 'well patronised by the gentry of the town and neighbourhood' and that 'on bespeak nights', (ie when a patron gave his name to the evening's entertainment and bought many tickets for it) it was no unusual thing to see outside a string of carriages extending from the front of the building in Wellington Street down to the top of Peasehill's Nook' (Peel Square).[11] There was, however,

Figure 2. The Old White Bear Yard in Shambles Street (From a sketch by Kenneth Graham). Collins and Huggins brought their company to Strutt's Laithe, a barn here, before Barnsley's first theatre was built

considerable opposition from religious bodies, in particular from a Quaker missionary, Thomas Shillitoe.[12]

The new theatre may have been used very little but this was not uncommon at this time. Huggins and Clarke gained a licence to play there again in 1818[13] but William Huggins died in Gainsborough on 22 November, 1821,[14] and his eldest son, Francis, died only two years later. There was a Grand Concert at the theatre in January 1833 with the nationally renowned singers Mr and Mrs Joseph Wood, who lived at Woolley Moor[15] but there are no further records of licence applications to play in Barnsley until Joseph Smedley (1784-1863) brought his company later in 1833 and again in 1834.[16] Meanwhile, in 1819 and perhaps until 1825 when Salem Chapel was opened in Blucher Street, the theatre was used on Sundays for services led by theological students from the Independents' college at Rotherham. It is described as the 'Synagogue of Satan occupied as a Temple of God' in a pamphlet published in 1819 responding to an attack from Reverend Robert Ellis, minister of the Calvinistic chapel in Sheffield Road.[17]

Smedley, who had founded his own company by 1806 and who took over many of Huggins' and Clarke's venues, is recorded in 1833 as playing in more towns than any other provincial actor-manager, principally in Nottinghamshire, Lancashire and east Yorkshire, and in the mid 1830s he was looking to the growing industrial centres of the West Riding for his audiences, obtaining licences for Bradford, Huddersfield, Rotherham and Wakefield where he bought the theatre in 1836.[18] In 1835 a licence was granted to play in Barnsley to Daniel Grose, but Smedley returned in 1839 and 1840.[19] His Barnsley season, like that of earlier companies, would probably have been of only two or three weeks. An extensive collection of Smedley's bills for the Wakefield theatre[20] indicates that he would have sought the patronage of local organizations - including the Freemasons of which he, like very many actor-managers of his day, was a member. Again there would have been a different programme each evening with the customary two principal items. His fare regularly included plays by the two Colmans, Goldsmith, Mrs Inchbald, Rowe, Shakespeare and Sheridan as well as dramatised versions of Dickens' and Scotts' novels. A veteran in defending the theatre against evangelical, especially Methodist, opposition, Smedley frequently provided short homilies on his bills advising his audiences, for example, that:

The business of plays is to discountenance vices and to commend virtue, to show the uncertainty of human greatness, the sudden turns of fate and the unhappy conclusion of violence and injustice.

As one of the few places in Barnsley capable of holding a sizeable crowd the theatre was used at least once, and perhaps many times, for purposes other than entertainment. On 29 January, 1837, there was a meeting in the theatre regarding the state of sanitation in the town.[21]

From time to time Barnsley was visited in the mid-nineteenth century by a travelling theatre operated by the Wild family who brought their own booth with them. It was the stage of this that was used as a hustings at a mass gathering of Barnsley weavers on 23 August, 1829.[22]

Smedley retired from the stage in 1841. Provincial theatre almost everywhere was at a low ebb and the future for the Wellington Street theatre must have looked bleak. However, in 1849-50 it was leased by Barnsley Mechanics' Institute, the pit was covered over and the building was renamed and used as the Mechanics' Hall (Figure 3).[23] The Institute had been formed originally in 1837 but failed shortly afterwards, to be revived in 1848.[24] In 1850 it had 256 members including 37 women.[25] The theatre was acquired in 1852 by William James Dandison.[26] In 1855 the Institute reported a net loss of £33 15s, attributing this both to the increased rent for the Hall and to a drop in lettings but observing at the same time that 'the excellent qualifications of the hall for public purposes ought to command a more liberal patronage'. Attendance at lectures had been 'miserably meagre' and musical entertainments had evidently been especially disastrous.[27] There were at least some lettings. A public meeting was held in the Hall on 2 March, 1854, to assess the progress made by the Local Board of Health in carrying out the provisions of the *Public Health Act*, when it was resolved by an overwhelming majority that the Board should seek powers to buy the local Gas and Water Works. Barnsley's Temperance Fife and Drum Band made its first public appearance in the Hall at the soirée of the Franklin Institute on 9 April, 1855. A concert in support of the Lancashire Distress Relief Fund on 25 November, 1862, raised £41 and a recital, again in the Hall, by the Barnsley Musical Union on 7 January, 1863, brought in £40 for the Barnsley Relief Fund, following the explosion at Edmund's Main Colliery on 8 December, 1862, in which 59 people died.[28] In July 1863 Barnsley Choral Society gave a charitable concert in aid of the family of one Moses Garner who had died leaving a widow and six children 'unprovided for'.[29] The great Yorkshire vocalist Mrs Sunderland gave her last public appearance at

Figure 3.   Barnsley's first theatre, in Wellington Street, during its period as the Mechanics' Hall *John Goodchild Collection*

the Mechanics' Hall at a 'miscellaneous concert' on 15 September, 1863. On New Year's Day 1864 the Barnsley Heterogenous Society gave its 'first annual miscellaneous entertainment' at the Hall and on 9 January, 1872, 349 'aged poor' were entertained there.[30]

The Mechanics' Institute itself provided some entertainment of a relatively dramatic character at the Hall with, for example, George Grossmith's *Pickings from Pickwick* in 1859 and his *David Copperfield* in 1868. Again in 1868 Kate Hickson, of the Scarborough Theatre, gave a dramatic reading of *The Love Chase*.[31]

Meanwhile the Queen's Theatre, a building of a temporary character in Eldon Street, opened on 13 December, 1862, under the management of Matthew Wardhaugh. The first show there was *St.*

Clair of the Isles.[32] It was replaced in 1876 by a similar but rather larger building of wood, canvas and tarred felt named the Gaiety, catering principally for the working-classes and run by Ben Walker.[33]

The Hall, and the Institute's finances, fared better in the 1860s but in 1866 when the income from lettings was larger than in any previous period of their tenure, the costs of redecorating the Hall and of routine cleaning and repairs, together with the 'heavy' rent still meant that the balance of funds was very low and led the committee to recommend a serious review of the 'whole question of the Mechanics' Hall'. In 1874, however, the remarkably satisfactory financial position of the Institute, with a balance of £116 4s 2d, was attributed to the letting of the Hall 'which satisfies the committee of their wisdom in keeping that building in their own hands until another more suited to their requirements can be provided'.[34] Another was provided in 1878 when the Public Hall, designed by Hill and Swan of Leeds and Sheffield and with an auditorium capable of seating 2,000 (800 on benches and 1,200 on chairs) was opened on 25 January, 1878, by the Barnsley Public Hall and Mechanics' Institute Company.[35]

Provincial theatre had changed radically since the days when travelling players visited the Wellington Street building. The advent of railway travel meant that ready-made productions, usually of a single contemporary play but also with a repertory of Shakespearian or other classical drama, could tour the length and breadth of the country, occupying a theatre for a week before going on to the next engagement, perhaps more than a hundred miles away. There were also touring opera companies. The population, especially in industrial areas, had boomed (Barnsley grew from 3,606 in 1801 to 29,789 by 1881), but even small towns might expect to have theatrical entertainment available almost all the year round. New theatres were built and where no theatre existed companies played in other available halls. The old itinerant companies died out and the profession of theatre manager - overseeing the building, the permanent staff and the bookings - became entirely separate from that of actor. Shows were promptly booked for Barnsley's Public Hall which, for a time, under the management of G H Richardson, advertised as the Public Hall Theatre.[36] Two of the country's leading performers, Sarah Thorne and Charles Mathews, appeared there in May 1878 in Mathews' own play, *My Awful Dad*.[37] The Hall also housed concerts, bazaars and the predecessor of motion pictures, *dioramas*. In December 1879 the newly-formed Barnsley Amateur Dramatic Club presented its first productions there.[38] When the Carl

Rosa Opera Company paid its first visit to Barnsley, in February 1881, it too performed at the Public Hall[39]. An advertisement seeking bookings by 'first class companies only', published in 1886, refers to the building as the 'Opera House and Public Hall' and to the 'great success of the new gallery'; the general scale of admission was advertised as from 3s (15p) down to 6d (2.5p) and a full house was said to bring in £70.[40]

A new episode in Wellington Street theatre's history began a few months after the opening of the Public Hall when, now known as the Old Mechanics' Hall, from 27 May, 1878, it provided barracks for the Salvation Army Barnsley 45 Corps which was founded on the previous day with a hymn-singing in the Market Place in the morning and a procession and Sunday service at the Gaiety Theatre in the afternoon. The first Evangelists were Rosa Clapham and Jane Smith who lodged at 6 Racecommon Road.[41] General Booth reported that he had 'preached to over 800 people crammed into the old Theatre, occupied by the Mission for week night meetings' later that year.[42] The Army continued to hold week night services at the Mechanics' Hall until June 1882 when they moved into the much more spacious Barnsley Skating Rink in York Street.[43] This had been built in 1877 of stone to the design of Marcus Flockton of George Street at a cost of £2,000. It had an arched roof of wood and glass. The Army spent £150 on refurbishing the building and providing seating for 3,000 but on 8 December, 1882, after a particularly heavy snowfall, the building collapsed.[44] Subsequently the Army occupied the Temperance Hall in Pitt Street before moving into the purpose-built citadel in Wellington Street in 1896.[45]

Dandison, the theatre's owner, was a wine merchant with premises in Wellington Street. On his retirement he sold his business to George Horne, formerly landlord of the Coach and Horses, Market Hill[46], in 1876.[47] Perhaps spurred by the success of the dramatic entertainment at the Public Hall, Horne refurbished the Old Mechanics' Hall, uncovered the pit and reopened it as a theatre on 18 December, 1882.[48] Prior to 1843 the only theatres Royal were those for which an actor-manager held a royal patent but after the Act of Parliament of that year which introduced the licensing of theatres rather than of companies of players it became commonplace for theatres to be given the title Royal. For the first time the Wellington Street building was advertised as the Theatre Royal. It was said to seat 800; seat prices were 2s 6d (12.5p) for the Dress Circle, 1s (5p) for the Upper Side Boxes, 1s for the Pit and 6d (2.5p) for the Gallery. The first performances were given by Charles Percy

Emery's comic opera burlesque company. The bill changed each night and included a main piece and an after piece. The week saw the first night of Emery's own play, *Yorkshire Relish*. On 22 December the after piece was the 'popular burlesque', *Dick Whittington and his Cat* and on 23 December it was *Bluebeard the Barbarous*, or the *Woo-ed Widow*. We might regard these as the theatre's first Christmas pantomimes.

The theatre manager was initially Henry Cooper but W H Mitchell, who had originally come to Barnsley as Horne's commercial traveller and book-keeper, took over almost immediately.[49] There was a resident band conducted by Harry West and by February 1883 the theatre had a resident scenic artist, J Robinson.[50]

Each week saw a fresh touring production or productions, chiefly of popular plays such as Tom Taylor's *Ticket of Leave Man* or F A Scudamore's *Fighting Fortune* but there were also weeks when a company would provide a different classical play (including ones by Shakespeare) each night.

Horne's first season concluded on 6 June, 1883, when the theatre closed for the summer - initiating what was to become a tradition - and for alterations. It reopened on Feast Saturday, 18 August, with lower seat prices (ranging from 4d in the Gallery to 2s in the Dress Circle and no doubt reflecting the ongoing competition from the Public Hall) and with a production of *Uncle Tom's Cabin*.[51]

In 1888 Dandison's son, William James Fox Dandison, inherited the theatre[52] and the following year, with Charles Herbert Cobbold, Arthur Senior and Joseph Hewitt, he formed the Barnsley Theatre Royal Company to take over the building.[53] In August 1889 the *Barnsley Chronicle* proclaimed, 'As the property of a joint stock company (the theatre) now enters upon a new era in its history.' W H Mitchell stayed on as the manager and the policy remained much as it had done during Horne's proprietorship with a diet of touring productions each put on normally for a single week.

There was a fire at the Theatre Royal on 16 January, 1897, but the damage was confined to the box bar area where the counter and woodwork were blistered and charred and where the floor was burnt between the bar and the pit. Performances continued as normal.[54]

However, just over a year later the old theatre closed, on 26 February, 1898, after a production of *No Man's Land* by John Douglass. It had evidently failed to attract the 'cultured and the well-to-do' and 'patrons of the better sort' had preferred to find their entertainment at the Public Hall.[55] The Barnsley Theatre Royal

Company had decided to embark on a total rebuild to provide a much larger modern theatre.

Barnsley's new Theatre Royal and Opera House (as it was now designated) opened on 19 December, 1898,[56] with Morrell and Mouillet's no 1 company in *The Geisha*. The building was designed by Walter Emden but the detailed plans and specifications were prepared by the Barnsley architect, H Crawshaw. Seating some 1,200 and occupying approximately twice the space of its predecessor, it cost £16,000. Externally it was 55 feet wide and 106 feet long with a stage that was 30 feet 6inches deep and 50 feet 6 inches wide. The auditorium, divided into pit, circle and gallery, was 46' high. The contractors included Walter Dunk (masonry and bricklaying), Robinson and Son (carpentry), Hutchinson Bros (heating and lighting), T Lindley (plastering), Wright and Son of Hull (seating and upholstery) and Stephenson and Son (painting). The opening ceremony was performed by the Mayor, Councillor Wilkinson, who was himself a shareholder in the Barnsley Theatre Royal Company.

In the first few weeks some of the most popular entertainment of the time was brought to Barnsley including *The Sign of the Cross*. The first pantomime, *Cinderella* by Milton Bode's company, came to the theatre on 30 January, 1899. Hitherto opera had always been performed at the Public Hall but amongst the first companies to take advantage of the new theatre was the Moody Manners Opera Company.

W H Mitchell, who had been the manager of the theatre for more than eighteen years, died on 6 August, 1901, at his home at 26 Park Grove, Barnsley.[57] He was succeeded by one of his two sons, A C Mitchell who was then only twenty one but who had worked in the theatre from the age of thirteen when he joined the orchestra as a violinist.[58] He was to remain as manager into his sixties.

During the summer break of 1901 the theatre, until then lit by gas, was fitted with electricity.

Rival entertainment was provided from June 1908[59] at the New Empire Palace which, under the management of Will Smithson, offered a mixture of music hall/variety and films but did on occasions also host shows that might well have appeared at the Theatre Royal. By this time the Public Hall was screening films regularly.

In May 1913, after years of refusal by the West Riding County Council, the theatre was granted an excise licence at the first meeting of the General Purposes Committee of the newly-empowered and newly-designated Barnsley County Borough Council.[60]

By the time of the Great War the fare at provincial theatres was changing again, in part because of the increasing success of the cinema industry. There were fewer touring companies bringing high-quality productions and these were in part replaced by the more economical modestly-sized repertory companies who would remain for a season in residence at one theatre, producing a different play each week. These companies had no stars and the plays they chose usually required only commonplace scenery and unambitious costumes. The first repertory seasons at the Theatre Royal were provided by E Vivian Edmonds' company. Touring productions, visiting the theatre for the remainder of the year, were increasingly of revues rather than of straight plays.

A new rival in the form of the Alhambra, planned like the Empire as a variety theatre, opened on 1 October, 1915. The Alhambra went over to screening films on 8 June, 1925, after a last revue, *Scandals of 1925*.[61]

The 1920s and 1930s saw a wide range of shows at the theatre, including amateur performances by the Barnsley Co-operative Society Operatic Society and the Barnsley Amateur Operatic Society, plays, variety shows, revues, visits from the O'Mara Opera Company, seasons of repertory by Frank Fortescue's Players, musicals such as *No, No, Nanette* and *Lilac Time*, several weeks each year of bought-in pantomimes, and even an occasional circus or boxing-match!

The theatre, including the whole of the stage area, the 3-ton safety curtain and a part of the auditorium, was partially destroyed by fire in the early hours of 11 April, 1942, at the end of a week's run of the revue, *Always the Woman*. The roof collapsed but the façade was unscathed. At the time the theatre had a staff of 41, including the members of the permanent orchestra.[62] Despite wartime building restrictions it was reinstated and re-opened on Christmas Day 1944 with Charles Denville's pantomime *Cinderella*. Architects for the rebuilding were Dyson, Cawthorne and Coles.[63] A C Mitchell remained the manager until 1950-51 when he was succeeded by Angus McInnes (Figure 4).[64]

In 1954 there was a £10,000 renovation. However by this time both live theatres and cinemas were losing audiences rapidly to domestic television. By June 1956, when it closed ostensibly for the summer, the future of the theatre was uncertain. Notices outside said 'closed until further notice'. However, the theatre re-opened on 30 July after Charles Denville leased it and brought together a repertory company with 31-year old Patrick Johns as its producer.[65] Denville was the son of Alfred Denville, one-time proprietor of a portable

GOWNS, BLOUSES   **HOSIERY SPECIALIST**   **UNDERWEAR**

Telephone—4248

TOTTY & BRAMHAM

23 THE ARCADE, BARNSLEY

Proprietors : CHALMERS   WOOD   THEATRES   **LTD.**

General Manager : ANGUS   MacINNES

PHONE : 2103

THEATRE ROYAL BARNSLEY

PROGRAMME

We have a Good Word for Everybody "MELBOURNE"

Figure 4. The Theatre Royal programme for week commencing 9 July 1951, shortly after Angus MacInnes took over as General Manager *Brian Elliott Collection*

wooden theatre which had toured Yorkshire mining villages, who later founded the Denville repertory companies. One of these had provided summer seasons at Barnsley Theatre Royal in 1935-39. The theatre closed again on 12 January when, it was said, Charles Denville had been advised to rest and the theatre's heating system and fireproof curtain needed overhauling. It reopened on 18 March under Denville's management but with a touring show, *Disc Doubles* and, in the following week, a revue, *Godiva Rides Again*. Denville began a new season of repertory on 8 April but brought it to an end on 18 May when the theatre finally closed after the production of *Peg o' my Heart*. Denville observed that 'Barnsley people just don't seem interested in the live theatre any more.[66]

Four years later, on 23 October 1961, the building re-opened - as the Gaumont and Globe had already done - as a bingo and social club.[67]

For amateur groups in particular the loss of the Theatre Royal was a serious blow but in 1981 the opportunity was seized to adapt the former Globe Cinema, opened in 1912 but converted for bingo in 1961, for amateur use. This had been acquired by South Yorkshire County Council under a compulsory purchase order so that it could be demolished to make way for the proposed western relief road and was leased at a peppercorn rent. Participants in the scheme, which

was masterminded by Roger Walton and administered by Barnsley Theatre Trust, included Barnsley Playgoers (founded in 1924), Barnsley Children's Theatre Group (founded in 1968), and the Barnsley Junior Operatic Society (founded in 1922). After repair and adaptation, including the provision of dressing-rooms, it opened on 12 March, 1983, with the Playgoers' production of *Filumena*.[68] The implementation of the relief road brought the closure of the Globe Theatre on 7 April, 1990, after the Playgoers' had put on *The Boy Friend*.[69]

Hopes of reviving the Theatre Royal for live performances were raised when the social club closed and in the autumn of 1992 the Barnsley Theatre Trust was formed aiming to raise £400,000 to buy and refurbish the building. Leading members included John Kelly, Arts Editor of the *Barnsley Chronicle*, Iain Sutcliffe, Roger Walton, Nigel Wilkinson, Duncan Wood and Julian Wroe. On Sunday 24 January 1993 the Steering Committee held a public launch of their scheme at the theatre outlining plans to seek funding from the Arts Council and English Heritage as well as the local authority. However by June 1994 the Trust had to report that fund-raising had proved 'disappointingly slow'[70] and in May 1995 its work came to a halt when it accepted that the price agreed with the building's owners, the NB and DC Pension Fund (Barry Smith and Philip England), was unrealistic.[71]

Today the theatre is 'alive and kicking' as a live entertainment centre).

Notes and References

1. The marriages of Thomas Thorpe, and of John Chambers to actress Harriet Taplin.
2. West Yorkshire Archives: West Riding Magistrates' Quarter Sessions Order Book, 10/32
3. *Ibid*. 10/34.
4. *Ibid*. 10/35.
5. *Ibid*. 10/41.
6. J H Burland, *Annals of Barnsley*.
7. *Leeds Mercury* 22.7.1815.
8. *Barnsley Chronicle* 17.8.1889.
9. White, *Directory of the West Riding* (1837); West Riding Registry of Deeds, 1818 Vol.GU p 145.
10. Burland, *op. cit.*
11. *Barnsley Chronicle* 17.8.1889.
12. Eli Hoyle, *History of Barnsley and the Surrounding Districts*.
13. West Riding Magistrates' Quarter Sessions Order Books, 10/44.
14. B J Parker, *The Theatres of Gainsborough* from 1772 until 1850, referring to the *Rockingham and Hull Advertiser* of 24.11.1821.
15. Hoyle, *op cit.*
16. West Riding Magistrates' Quarter Sessions Order Books, 10/51

17. Burland, *op. cit.*
18. C M P Taylor, *Right Royal: Wakefield Theatre* 1776-1994 (1995).
19. West Riding Magistrates 'Quarter Sessions Order Books, 10/53.
20. Wakefield MDC Library Headquarters, Cryer Collection.
21. Hoyle, *op. cit.*
22. *Ibid.*
23. Yorkshire Union of Mechanics Institutes Reports 1851.
24. Rowland Jackson, *The History of the Town and Township of Barnsley*, 1878.
25. *Bairnsley Foaks Annual* ,1851.
26. West Riding Registry of Deeds, 1852, Vol RM p324.
27. Yorkshire Union of Mechanics Institutes Reports, 1855.
28. *Bairnsley Foaks Annuals*, 1855-64.
29. Bill, the John Goodchild Collection (JGC).
30. *Events and Occurrences of Interest In Barnsley* (1922).
31 Yorkshire Union of Mechanics' Institutes Reports 1859 and 1868.
32. Bill, (JGC).
33. *Barnsley Chronicle*, 21.9.1878; 6.3.1880.
34. Yorkshire Union of Mechanics' Institute Reports, 1866 and 1874.
35. *Barnsley Chronicle*, 26.1.1878 and 2.2.1878.
36. *Barnsley Chronicle*, 4.1.1879.
37. The Theatre Museum, London, volume of Barnsley ephemera 1878-1891.
38. *Barnsley Chronicle*, 4.12.1879.
39. *Ibid.*5.2.1881.
40. The Theatre Museum, volume of Barnsley ephemera 1878-1891.
41. *The Christian Mission Magazine* 1878.
42. *Ibid.*
43. *The War Cry* ,15.6.1882.
44. *Ibid.* 14.12.1882.
45. *Ibid.* 1.2.1896.
46. Obituary of William Horne, Barnsley Local Studies and Archives.
47. West Riding Registry of Deeds, Vol. 750 (1876), p.615.
48. *Barnsley Chronicle*, 9.12.1882.
49. *Ibid.* 24.12.1898.
50. *Ibid.* 24.2.1883.
51. *Ibid.* 18.8.1883.
52. West Riding Registry of Deeds, 1888 Vol 4, p346.
53. *Ibid.*1889 Vol. 27, p834.
54. *Barnsley Chronicle*, 23.1.1897.
55. *Ibid.* 24.12.1898.
56. *Ibid.* 17.12.1898 and 24.12.1898.
57. *Ibid.* 10.8.1901.
58. *Ibid.* 18.4.1942.
59. *Ibid.* 27.6.1908.
60. *Ibid.* 24.5.1913.
61. *Ibid.* 6.6.1925.
62. *Ibid.* 18.4.1942.
63. *Ibid.* 18.12.1944
64. Mary Fairhurst, *The Theatre Royal, Barnsley: its climb and decline*, (ms Barnsley Local Studies and Archives).
65. *Barnsley Chronicle*, 21.7.1956.
66. *Ibid.* 18.5.1957.
67. *Ibid.* 23.10.1961.
68. *Ibid.* 11.3.1983.
69. *Ibid.* 13.4.1990.
70. *Ibid.* 17.6.1994.
71. *Ibid.* 19.5.1995.

12. 'Open all Hours...': Grandmother's Corner Shop

by Eileen Umpleby

MY GRANDPARENTS, Mr and Mrs E C Larcombe bought the corner shop at 19/21 Wellington Street, Barnsley during the First World War. My grandfather, Charles Edward, had been employed as a glass-blower but was advised to give up for health reasons. They were going to run the business together. However, grandfather did not take to serving behind the counter and soon gave up and got a job taking him into the fresh air. Grandmother (Figure 1) took it on with no previous experience and became a formidable business woman, looking after the ordering and financial side personally.

Figure 1. Grandmother, aged 50

The family of seven lived over the shop, which was a strange accumulation of buildings. The centre was the kitchen with a room above and a cellar. It had originally been a 'one-up, one-down' single house. It still had a beamed ceiling, flagged floor and stone steps upstairs. On to this was added at a later date, the front room facing Wellington Street, with bedrooms above, and joining back and front, the shop. It was quite large for those days, with one huge window facing Wellington Street and the other facing Castlereagh Street. Inside, were two long counters at right angles to each other, with shelves on the walls behind reaching from floor to ceiling.

All the family were called upon to help, since it was such a busy shop - a bit like Asian family shops today. The two sons never married; I always felt they were married to the shop, the youngest most reluctantly. The three daughters, even after they married and had homes of their own, were called upon to help. My own Mother went there five days a week - hence my involvement, particularly during school holidays (Figure 2). By the early 1930s I was attending Barnsley Girls' High School, and we had longer holidays than other schools. I was born in the front room

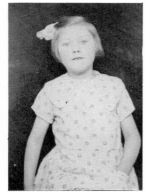

Figure 2. Me at the age of 8

in 1922, and being older than the other grandchildren by several years, always felt part of the older generation. They all seemed to take part in taking care of me until I went to school.

The shop never closed until the 'second house' had started at the *Theatre Royal* further along Wellington Street (Figure 3). It also opened on Sunday mornings until the *Shop Act* of 1937, and had Tuesday afternoons for closing. There were two sides to the business, the sweets and cigarettes on one hand, and the grocery trade serving the needs of the terrace houses around, the various theatre lodgings and the several public houses.

The window in Wellington Street was given over entirely to chocolates and sweets to tempt the theatre trade. There were no individual boxes or tubes or packets of sweets, and apart from wrapped bars of chocolate, all had to be weighed out. Starting on the right of the window, there were displayed the expensive chocolates such as *Terry's, Cadbury's* and *Rowntrees* mixed

Figure 3. The Theatre Royal (to the right of 'Morton's, Wellington Street, photographed in June 1960 *Tasker Photographic Trust*

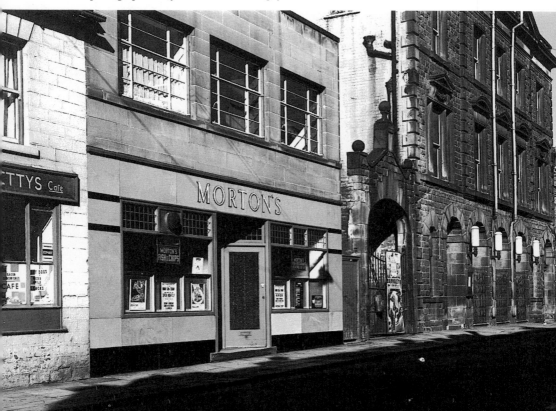

chocolates, neopolitans and liqueurs. At the opposite end of the window were the cheaper children's sweets, such as love-hearts, wine gums and liquorice alsorts. In the middle were the medium range, like sugared almonds, cherry lips, chocolate beans (the forerunner of *Smarties*). On a shelf above were glass bottles containing humbugs, buttered walnuts and brazils, chocolate eclairs and mint rock. The sweets window was always kept in immaculate condition and it was a boast that 'rubbishy' sweets were not sold.

I can remember the suppressed excitement of children coming to the shop to buy sweets on their way to the theatre matinee during Pantomime season. This was the greatest of treats in the days of no television and few radios.

As soon as I was tall enough to see the scales to be able to weigh, I was allowed to serve the children. I was also allowed to help myself to a sweet (but not a chocolate) if I wanted one - perhaps I was entrusted because I did not. I much preferred, if I had a halfpenny to spend, to go up Castlereagh Street to one of the terraced houses, where the occupier advertised that it was a 'halfpenny to look in t' drawer'.

The drawer in question was a very small one in her kitchen table and one could choose something from it - things like sherbert dabs and small trinkets, like those contained in crackers today. She had hit upon a scheme which was fascinating to children, but the few pence of profit must have been very meagre and perhaps it is indicative of the importance of even a few pence extra at that time.

On this side of the shop were also kept the cigarettes - *Woodbine, Park Drive, Players* and *Capstan* and also *St Bruno* tobacco, sold loose. On the floor were the soaps: *Persil, Rinso, Lux Flakes, Sunlight* and *Lifebuoy*. Most people who came to the shop could not afford the patent washing powders and washed with a rubbing board and bar soap. There were also the blue bags and starch, all very necessary to wash day. The blue bag was for adding to the final rinse of white clothes and linen to counteract the yellow soap. Lots of things were starched, like men's shirt collars and table linen. I remember that starch was tricky to make, a bit like making custard.

On the other side of the shop were kept the groceries and like supermarkets today, all culinary needs were catered for. A few things were delivered ready packed, like sugar in blue bags, some margarine and packets of tea: *Hornimans, Typhoo* and *P.G. Tips*. However, most things had to be weighed, hence the several sets of scales, regularly checked by Avery. These ranged from the large potato scales to a small one with a marble tray for weighing small amounts like yeast for making bread. This was always called 'barm'. As this was the age before Baby Clinics I remember mothers asking to have their babies weighed to see if they were thriving. This took place on the potato scales. The large scoop was lined with tissue paper before putting the baby in.

White flour was delivered by Ranks in ten-stone sacks and had to be weighed into half-stone bags in the store room above the kitchen and then carried down to the shop. I always hated 'flour weighing' because everyone was bad-tempered, perhaps it was the persistence of flour dust which irritated. Most families baked bread every day, for this was the staple diet of a community who were mostly unemployed and lived on Public Assistance. I was astounded to hear on a recent television programme about the fiftieth anniversary of the end of the Second World War, that people were still complaining about evacuees from poor families not being used to sitting down for a meal. The truth was that some homes did not have a table, as I witnessed. Either the table had been burned for firewood, or they had never had one. Anyway, it was not necessary to sit down to eat a piece of bread. Our family always baked brown bread made with Turog flour. This came packed in cotton bags, which were carefully washed after the flour had been used.

There was butter, lard and cheese in solid blocks which sat on marble slabs, a dish of pork dripping (most popular) and bacon to be sliced to desired thickness on the new bacon machine and cooked meats such as brawn, polony, corned beef and potted beef. But on Wednesdays and Saturdays (market days) boiled ham was available and was popular with a wider clientele. This was gammon ham 'on the bone', and one ham was sold on Wednesdays and two on Saturdays. There was never any left at the end of the day. The three hams were boiled on Mondays in the 'set pot' next to the kitchen range. This was stoked by its fire, and never used for boiling clothes, its original use. I can still remember the smell of Monday afternoons, when the hams were lifted out after boiling and the race to peel off the the outer skin before they cooled - at the risk of burnt fingers.

On Wednesdays the 'Egg Woman' came from a farm at Haigh. The rest of the family would be selling their produce on a stall in the market. She was a very elderly lady and would laboriously count out ten dozen eggs, and woe betide anyone who interrupted her counting. She would sometimes bring a half pound of her pale farm butter and a chicken, but these would be for the family.

On Thursdays, a pork butcher delivered sausages, black pudding, pig's fry (offal) and 'penny ducks'. These looked like squares of very solid stuffing. I never tried them but they smelled very savoury.

There were only a few canned goods stocked - mainly tinned peas, but also tinned salmon and tinned fruit for Sunday tea - for those who could afford these luxuries. There was an absence of baked beans in the early days, for I can well remember the first time I tasted baked beans on toast, at about the age of ten. I thought they were delicious. There were no packets of cereals except *Quaker Oats*. A cereal called 'Grapenut' was tried out, but was not a success. The only coffee available was in a concentrated liquid form, a brand called *Camp*.

There was a row of cuboid tins of biscuits along the Castlereagh Street window; the varieties were very much the same as they are today. The broken biscuits were kept in the 'Sweets' side of the shop, for the customers for these were mostly children from the Roman Catholic school at the top of Castlereagh Street. Many of these Catholic children came from outside of the local catchment area and could not get home midday. There were no school dinners then and the halfpenny they were given to spend would buy a halfpenny bag of chips, if the chip shop was open or a halfpenny worth of broken biscuits. I often served these and was horrified when told that this was their dinner and tried to find nice pieces.

Figure 4. Buildings opposite Grandmother's Corner Shop in Wellington Street: from right to left, The Friends' Adult School, Barnsley and District Grocers' Company and The Salvation Army Citadel *Tasker Photographic Trust*

There must have been some regular customers who were Irish Catholic, for on St Patrick's Day, the congregation were given a bunch of Shamrock if they attended church on that day. A piece of Shamrock was always brought for my Grandmother – for luck. She wore it for the day, although she herself was staunchly C of E and attended St George's Church to the end of her days.

There were a number of chapels in the area and directly opposite the shop in Wellington Street was the Salvation Army Citadel (Figure 4). Since it closed for the day, the shop took delivery of parcels for them. One of the weekly deliveries was a huge stack of the *War Cry*. I was always given a copy of this, which I read assiduously, as I did any printed matter that came to hand.

The items which intrigued me most as a child were on a high shelf, where were kept medicines and pills. This was long before the National Health Service and most people never saw a doctor. It was all a matter of self-help and advice, which would be readily given by all and sundry. There were large bottles containing cough medicine, *Fenning's Fever Cure*, *Violet Squills* (an expectorant), Liquid Paraffin, Syrup of Figs, and so on. There were also pills and powders for a bewildering variety of ailments. If a liquid medicine was to be purchased, a suitable container was brought, which was first weighed and then the required mixture was measured into it.

There were large sacks of potatoes standing on the floor, upon which customers often sat when awaiting their turn to be served. It seemed to me that some customers came to sit there for the purpose of the gossip. There were also carrots, turnips and fresh fruit available.

Figure 5. My grandparents at the entrance to the shop in 1944. They were both in their late sixties and everyone wanted my Grandmother to retire

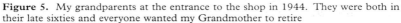

The majority of these goods came from the Barnsley District Grocers' Company just across the road in Wellington Street, which was very convenient for ordering and delivering. I often had to run across to order things which had been forgotten.

Of course, my Grandmother's shop was competing with the BBCS Grocery store which used to be on Wellington Street at the top of the Co-op Arcade. I suppose one of the ways of combating the competition was that many customers bought 'on tick'. the bill to be settled when their Public Assistance money was paid. Paying for the food was most important. The rent collector, if he could not be avoided by being 'out', was mollified with money from the 'Pop Shop' - the pawn shop in New Street/Baker Street. There was a regular trek there on Monday mornings to pawn suits and shawls.

The Barnsley District Grocers' Company also had a Drapery Department and clothes were often ordered from there for customers, also to be paid 'on tick'. This was particularly so at Whitsuntide, when it was the custom for everyone to wear at least one item of new clothing. The new clothes were mainly for the benefit of the children, who would be taking part in the Whit Monday Walk. This was a very important date in the Calendar when congregations of nonconformist chapels, including large contingents of the Children's Sunday Schools, would walk in procession to Market Hill to sing hymns. Having taken part in the 'walk-round', the children would be given tea back at the chapel.

I often felt that many local people survived the Depression of the 1920s and 1930s because of my grandmother's help. She was invariably kind and considerate to all customers, listened to their worries and gave good advice as well as practical help. People always shopped on a daily basis, and it seemed from a child's point of view, that they just came for a gossip. Of course, there were no refrigerators to store food, and the majority were living 'hand-to-mouth'. In spite of the long hours the shop remained open, customers would often come to the back door after closing time, for things which had been forgotten. Security was a problem and the shop was the target for burglaries. The family felt that no one should be served at the back door and that it was a way of assessing how to break in. There were heavy iron gates put up at the front of the shop and iron bars at the back, but this did not stop the break-ins.

By 1950, my Grandmother was in her seventies and becoming very tired. She was persuaded - albeit reluctantly - to leave the shop in the hands of her eldest son. She had carried on through the rationing of the two World Wars (Figure 5) and the Depression between. By now, many of the local people were being re-housed as the streets of terraced houses were demolished. Many families went to Council estates at Kendray, and for a time they still came to do their weekly shop. The sweet rationing during and after the Second World War had killed off much of that lucrative trade and the Theatre Royal was finding it difficult to attract much support.

After I had started work in 1939, I walked from the Town Hall to the shop at lunch-time and was usually called upon to write some 'new-fangled' cheques for my Grandmother's signature and take others to the Bank. She never got used to new business methods.

The shop was sold in 1953 and then was made into two shops (Figure 6). The building always looked very isolated in the new planning system.

Acknowledgements

Barnsley Local Studies & Archives
Mr R Walker and the Tasker Trust

Figure 6. The Corner Shop in June, 1960. Most of the houses in Castlereagh Street had been demolished *Tasker Photographic Trust*

13. SHEPHERDS, SHEEP AND GENTLEMEN: PENISTONE MOORLAND AGRICULTURE IN THE EARLY NINETEENTH CENTURY

by Sam Sykes

ON MONDAY 27 FEBRUARY, 1804, a group of local farmers met at the *Rose and Crown Inn*, Penistone, under the patronage of Mr James Stuart Wortley Esq., of Wortley Hall. They were united with a wish to promote 'the improvement of the district extending along the moor edges', and determined to form the *Wortley Farmers' Club*, which would offer a number of prizes to those farmers and agricultural workers who seemed to best achieve these objectives.[1] These were the aims of a new age of scientific farming that was in the process of irreversibly changing the nature of agriculture. Like its industrial stablemate, the Agricultural Revolution depended upon the investment of large amounts of capital and it was therefore pioneered not by the lower echelons of tenant farmers, but by the landed gentry and dilettante country gentlemen. Up and down the country these enlightened and fashion conscious souls were establishing Agricultural Societies and Farmers' Clubs. The Wortley farmers were among the vanguard, Breckonshire being the first society to be formed just fifty years earlier, the 'Bath and West' had established a show in 1777 and *Smithfield Cattle Club* was founded in 1798 under the patronage of the Duke of Richmond. Under the aegis of Earl Spencer the *Yorkshire Show* was not started until 1837, nor the *Royal Agricultural Society of England* until 1838. By this time around one hundred local societies were in existence and the number was growing. It has been argued that those organisations styled as 'clubs' were somewhat less pretentious than the 'societies', more practical, parochial and more likely to reach the ordinary tenant farmer.[2] However, they all held a common desire to promote and explain the best of modern practices. In this article I wish to concentrate on just one specific aspect of their varied interests, the local sheep and associated shepherding practices, for as much as

Figure 1. *The Penistone* is a large, strong-boned sheep with a white face and medium length fleece. It is horned in both sexes, but the ram has magnificent horns
Barnsley Chronicle

anything, these were at the economic root of upland South Yorkshire and the Penistone district.

The Wortley Farmers' Club has seen many changes over the last two centuries, not least in its name, but its legacy is still known to us today as the *Penistone Show*, one of the largest one day shows in the north of England. It promotes the agricultural characteristics of an area more generally noted for its industry and, at the beginning, it vigorously promoted one aspect of its agriculture thought to be particularly important - the local breed of sheep, known as *The Penistone* whose meat and fleece contributed greatly to the local economy. The *Penistone* (Figures 1-2) was a large horned sheep, said to produce the sweetest mutton and a medium length wool that was finer than the wool of other moorland sheep. Its wool contributed to both the local 'broad cloth' industry and to felt making for milliners.[3] It had a distinctive white face which marked it out from its black and speckled-faced cousins, like the *Derbyshire Gritstone*, the *Swaledale* and the *Lancashire Lonk*. Actually the *Penistone* breed is still in existence but is now more commonly known as *Whitefaced Woodland* and is officially categorised as **critically endangered** by the Rare Breeds Survival Trust.

Penistone Market

As a town on the moorland fringe Penistone stood at the meeting point of several important Pennine routes, notably the Cheshire salt trail via Woodhead, the Cut Gate into Derbyshire via the Woodlands Valley, a route via Thurlstone Towngate, Holmfirth and Meltham to

Figure 2. *Penistone* ewe and lamb in their native country at Dunford Bridge. Taken shortly after shearing *The author.*

Marsden and Huddersfield and finally the main road south from Halifax which came via Penistone. All of these routes linked up to the easier going south and eastwards thereby joining the moorlands and heavy woollen districts to Sheffield, Rotherham, Wakefield, Doncaster and Barnsley. Penistone was thus a natural trading centre where the uplands met the lowlands. It also marks the southern end of the Yorkshire clothing district and in its vicinity were a number of small cloth works that utilised the wool of the moor sheep. Some of these early buildings of domestic industry can still be recognised, particularly around Thurlstone. *Baines' Directory* for 1822 shows Thurlstone to have had fourteen woollen manufacturers and a fulling and scribbling mill. Penistone had three cloth manufacturers, a cloth dresser, scribbling mill and a flax dresser. *Baines* also shows that a coach linked Penistone to Halifax and Sheffield and a wagon to Huddersfield. Fifteen years later *White's* Directory described Penistone as

> *a place of trade, through the linen and woollen manufacturers extend into some of the out-townships of its extensive parish... the market is of small importance except for the sale of cows, calves moor sheep and butter.*

Writing in 1831, Joseph Hunter considered the cloth market as 'never considerable'. It is true that the industry never really took off here, but it had been of sufficient promise to cause Jonathan Wordsworth to invest £800 in the erection of a Cloth Hall in 1763. Penistone did in fact serve a vital function for the agricultural trade of the region, not least in providing a market for the 'moor sheep' which came to be known as *Penistones,* named after the town in which they could be bought and sold. For a while, too, the broadcloth manufactured from their wool took the Penistone name and was so referred to in at least three acts of parliament (1551, 1596 and 1606).

In its early days the market occupied the centre of town, spreading out from the open area in front of the church and extending as far as was necessary into the adjacent streets. The trading was not focused around an auctioneer's ring as we are accustomed today, but took the form of a number of private bargains struck up in the streets and, not infrequently, along the roads to the market. Gordon Knowles of Ingbirchworth can recall his father telling tales of this practice continuing into modern memory. [4] As he drove the cattle along the road to Penistone he would be met by dealers anxious to strike the first bargain. Sometimes a tentative price would be agreed which both parties could return to if they had failed to procure a better deal at the market. In 1903 Public Health legislation forced the authorities to define a specific livestock market place, away from the public streets.

The Age of the Gentleman Farmer

The late eighteenth and early nineteenth centuries was the age of the gentleman farmer. This was the great period of Parliamentary Enclosure, whereby large tracts of previously open, communal land were privatised and enclosed by Acts of Parliament. The numerous stone walls that march across the Pennine moorlands are visual symbols of this passage from old feudalistic to new capitalistic agriculture. Scarcely a township escaped without some impact of enclosure. Between 1760 and 1800 Parliament passed over 2,000 Acts allowing for what were inevitably the wealthier individuals to privatise and enclose the open arable fields and commons, as the poet John Clare put it, 'In little parcels, little minds to please'. Barnsley, for example, enclosed its Church Field, Far Field and most of its Common Fields between 1777-79. In 1801 the *General Enclosure Act* virtually gave *carte blanche* for large landowners to mop up whatever bits of common remained. The rhyme is well known but worth repeating:

> *The law's severe on man and woman,*
> *Who steals the goose from off the common,*
> *But lets the greater villain loose,*
> *Who steals the common from the goose.*

In most lowland townships the area of commons had already been reduced to just a few acres, but in the moorland districts vast tracts remained, all ripe for private ownership. The table below gives some local examples from which the lowland/upland divide can be clearly seen:

Some Local Enclosure Acts and Awards

Year	Township	Acreage	Type
1806	Dodworth	90	Fields, commons, wastes
1809	Cawthorne	216	Commons, wastes
1809	Hoyland Swaine	652	Fields,commons, waste
1810-13	Hunshelf	700	Moors, commons, wastes
1800-13	Ingbirchworth	580	Moors, commons, wastes
1811-20	Langsett	3014	Moors, commons, wastes
1818-31	Oxspring	250	Commons, wastes
1819-26	Penistone	420	Fields, commons, wastes
1809	Silkstone	154	Commons, wastes
1813-15	Thurgoland	400	Moors, commons, wastes
1812-16	Thurlstone	5001	Moors, commons, wastes
1817-26	Worsbrough	300	Commons, wastes

By and large the moorland enclosures proved to be unsuitable for any form of farming other than extensive grazing and the mile upon mile of walls that were erected to define ownership were rendered useless as livestock barriers. Consequently, they have been allowed to fall into disrepair just as the rationale that spawned them has become obsolete. These vast areas, however, soon assumed a new importance and the sheep had now to contend with their new landlords' growing interest in grouse shooting. Writing in 1906,

Figure 3. Cannon Hall and Park

about a century after the enclosures, John Ness Dransfield, the Penistone solicitor, hunter and antiquary nevertheless wrote:

> *Now moorland sheep as a general rule have had to give place to grouse…the enclosure Acts…and consequent extinction of commoners rights may have tended in a great measure to the decrease of the sheep on our moors and commons.*[5]

We are indebted to Dransfield, for although his *History of Penistone* is more a *pastiche* of opinion rather than fact, he displayed a passion about the area which caused him to record much information that would otherwise have disappeared. He was an improving and conserving spirit in the true mould of the Victorian *dilettante* gentleman and played a leading role in promoting the Penistone Show for over fifty years. He was a devotee of the *Penistone* sheep and without him the breed's destiny would have been poorer.

Another gentleman worthy of note was John Spencer-Stanhope

(1787-1873) of Cannon Hall. His country house and park show him to have been a follower of fashion in both architecture and landscape design (Figure 3) and it is no surprise therefore to find him dabbling in matters agricultural. His interest was such that he wrote two instructional works for schools: *A Catechism on Agriculture* and *A Catechism on Cattle* and married Elizabeth, daughter of the great agricultural pioneer, Thomas Coke of Norfolk.[6] In 1830 Spencer-Stanhope purchased about 1,000 acres of recently enclosed moorland near Dunford Bridge to which his son, Walter, was later (1871) to add another 250 acres.[7] The moor was managed for grouse and with the coming of the railway to Dunford (the last station before the Woodhead Tunnel) in 1845 the Spencer-Stanhopes also built a shooting lodge (now the *Stanhope Arms*) from which to indulge their sport. According to Dransfield, in 1836 John Spencer-Stanhope's moors supported eight separate flocks of the local *Penistone* sheep, all managed by his tenants. Dransfield implies that the good gentleman was deliberately conserving the local sheep breed. I can see no evidence to either prove or disprove this, although his relationship with Coke may well have encouraged such interest. However when Walter-Spencer Stanhope's gamekeeper (Metcalf Sedgewick) sold off a flock of sheep in 1920 it was of the *Lancashire Lonk* breed, not Penistones.[8]

The Wortley Farmers' Club

In 1804 the Club already had more than thirty members paying a subscription 'of not less than half a guinea'. We have already noted that its aim was to promote good agricultural practice in the 'district along the moorland edges'. In fact this membership was spread over an extensive area, well beyond what we would now call the moorland fringe: Wortley, Pilley, Thurgoland, Penistone, Hoylandswaine, Cawthorne, Thurlstone, Bradfield, Langsett, Hunshelf, Oxspring, Longendale, Gunthwaite, Ingbirchworth, Woodland, Denby, Silkstone, Dodworth, Stainborough, Shepley and Ecclesfield. This is basically the whole of upland South Yorkshire plus its lowland fringe and the adjacent portions of Cheshire and Derbyshire. This boundary is almost co-terminous with that of the Penistone breed. The Club decided that from the money raised from subscriptions it would award the following *premiums* (each worth one guinea):

> For the best Penistone Wether Sheep...
> For the best Penistone ewe above two years old ...
> For the best Two-shear Penistone Ram...
> For the best Shearling Penistone Ram Sheep...

> For the best Cross-bred Shearling Wether out of a Penistone Ewe...
> For the best Two-shear Wether of the same sort as the last...
> For the best Two-shear Ewe of the same sort as last...
> For the best Two-shear Sheep of any Polled sort...
> For the best Shearling of any Polled sort...
> For the best Two-Shear Ram of any Polled sort...

In addition, there were to be prizes for 'horned cattle', pigs, horses, servants and labourers. The juxtaposition is mine but the sentiment is theirs: farm workers are spoken of in similar terms to stock. The following categories go some way to displaying the paternalistic mentality of these gentlemen farmers:

> To the best Sheep Shearer....two pair of shears
> To the shepherd having raised most lambs from a flock of Penistone ewes...one guinea
> To the Shepherd having raised most lambs from a flock of Polled ewes ...one guinea
> To the Male servant in Husbandry, who had lived the longest time in his place with a good character....one guinea
> To the Female Servant, who has lived the longest time in a farmer's place with a good character...one guinea

In 1804 the above prizes were won respectively by: Benjamin Thorpe, James Haigh of Blackmoor (61 lambs from 67 ewes), John Sampson (131 lambs from 110 ewes), John Beevor (27 years for John Greaves of Alderman's Head) and Martha Wordsworth (53 years for the Crossley family of Handbank). Martha was given a special citation with a certificate signed by John Crossley.

The Wortley Farmers' Club had a short life. In 1853 Dransfield was involved in relaunching it as the *Penistone Agricultural Society*, at which time he commented that it had been 'for many years discontinued at Penistone'. Sir Walter Spencer-Stanhope acted as President of the new society which, according to Dransfield, had more cattle entries than the Great Yorkshire Show in 1879.[9] The Penistone Show (Figures 4-5) has continued to be held regularly since that date although it has now moved to a Saturday rather than the original Thursday, the traditional market day. Agricultural classes are still held, though thankfully the old paternalistic servants prizes are no longer on offer.

The Shepherds' Society

The shepherds and tenant farmers came into their own with a parallel organisation known as the Shepherds' Society. Only a handful of farmers were members of both organisations. Dransfield

Figure 4. Penistone Show in 1949

Figure 5. Line up of *Penistone* sheep and owners with the Penistone Viaduct in the background, just after the Penistone Show had been restarted in 1959. It was then held in the meadows by the waterside at Water Hall.

Figure 6. Sheepwash at Dunford Bridge: the man in the water, far left, is Thomas Smith. The sheep behind him appears to be a *Penistone*, but the next one in is a Lonk. The man in the straw boater may have been John Spencer-Stanhope *Annie Knott*

believed that the Shepherds' Society had existed 'from time immemorial', but was only able to show evidence of its formal existence from 1807. It has been claimed that a membership book for 1790 was previously extant, but its whereabouts is not now known.[10] All three versions may be correct, the old pre-enclosure free- ranging grazing system that operated upon the high moorlands necessitated its own management techniques depending upon co-operation between the various shepherds. 'Shepherds Meeting Stones', might well commemorate a traditional site where the shepherds gathered to sort their own sheep from those of their neighbours. To this end the shepherd needed identifiable marks and each of these marks needed to be recognised. This meant that the shepherds had to meet and agree marks. The meetings also provided an opportunity for the gathering together of the sheep to perform the appropriate tasks like washing, shearing and dipping, all of which

Figure 7. *The Millers Arms*, Saltersbrook, kept by Annie Knott's grandmother, Mary-Anne Taylor Armitage *Annie Knott*

Figure 8. The Millers Arms, Saltersbrook, venue for the shepherds' meetings, pulled down in 1913 *Annie Knott*.

were labour intensive (Figure 6). Such a system demanded co-operation and as such was intrinsically a part of the old communal pre-enclosure system of agriculture.

The rules of the Shepherds' Society in 1807 were remarkably simple. Any person bringing stray sheep to the meeting was entitled to reasonable expenses from the rightful owner. Unclaimed sheep were sold and the profits put into the Society's funds. The Society was to meet twice a year, on 20 July and 5 November, except when those days fell upon a Sunday, when it should meet the following day. These dates correspond with, firstly, shearing time and, secondly, the start of the breeding season. Nowadays shearing is often much earlier, but 'Tupping Time' is still widely adhered to on these high moors. Although many lowland farmers will begin the mating season in July and August, that would be considered foolhardy in these parts where winter lingers long and most ewes are still left outside, not brought indoors. Here, the natural cycle is observed and a ewe that is tupped on 5 November should lamb on 1 April, when the worst of the weather has passed and the grass has a little spring growth.

The 1807 meeting referred to above was held at the 'house of Thomas Taylor of Saltersbrook'. This was a public house, later to be known as the *Millers Arms*, on the side of the important cross-Pennine turnpike (see Figures 7-8). The Taylor family were publicans and farmers who also held Windleden Farm, just over the hill from Saltersbrook. A photograph survives (Figure 9) of a Shepherds' meeting held just over one hundred years later at the *Millers*, by which time the pub was run by Thomas's descendant, Mary Jane Taylor, a widow. She was shortly to retire to Windleden, which is still held by Mary's descendants and still home to a flock of Penistone-type sheep.

The membership was divided into areas or 'Liberties' , as shown below, each with the number of members indicated:

	1807	1836
Penistone	28	32
Woodlands	33	28
Holmfirth	50	25
Bradfield	30	22
Longendale	19	26
Glossop	18	13
Saddleworth	6	7
Kinder	2	
Armfield		4
Hollingworth		6
Meltham		4
Marsden		12

Figure 9. Shepherds' Meeting at the *Millers Arms*, Saltersbrook, 1907. This pub was kept by the Taylor family who also farmed at Windleden, just half a mile away and it was to here that Mary Jane Taylor Armitage went in 1913 when the pub was pulled down at the Water Board's behest. The photograph shows that the whitefaced *Penistone* sheep was already in decline by 1907. There is just one *Penistone* in the photograph, a lamb being held by the young lady in the second row. Next to her is Jimmy Crossland who was farmhand to Metcalf Sedgwick, the man holding the dog in the front row. Sedwick was gamekeeper to the Spencer-Stanhopes, as his father had been before him, but he was a keeper of *Lonk* sheep, like the one being held by Jimmy Crossland. Mary Jane Taylor Armitage is the small lady behind Metcalf Sedgwick *Old Barnsley*

From this we can see that the Wortley Farmers' Club and the Shepherds' Society covered very similar areas, but whereas the Club extended into the Pennine foothills, the Society restricted itself to the high tops. It is this geographic restriction that links the Shepherds' Society strongly to *Penistones*, for the natural boundaries of that breed are precisely co-terminous with those of the society. Many of the members and farms listed in 1807 have been known as Penistone breeders into modern times. The Wortley Farmers' Club prize list also confirms that at least some of the Shepherds' Society members were *Penistone* breeders: Thomas Eyre of Woodlands, Mr Ronksley of Hollow Meadows and John Hague of Blackmoor were all Shepherds' Society members who won prizes at the Wortley Club. Mr Ellis of Midhope, who had the best *Penistone* tup lamb and Mr Bedford of Pond, who had the best two-shear *Penistone* ewe, do not however appear to have been Shepherds' Society members. This raises the possibility that *Penistones* were farmed beyond the upland limits of the Shepherds' Society boundary. Pond Farm is known to have continued to breed *Penistones* into the present century, Mr Bowman of Thorpe Hesley bought his foundation stock from here in the 1890s and took them over to Thorpe, only to then return with them later, when he bought the farm![11]

The members of the Penistone Liberty in 1807 are listed below, most of the farms being on the western side of Penistone, adjacent to the high moors:

Edward Taylor, Windleden, 2 flocks
Samuel Hadfield, Townend
Josh Hinchcliffe, Dickroyd
Joshua Hinchcliffe, Dickroyd House
Thomas Wainwright, Townhead
George Hall, Carlecoates
Joseph Kenworthy, Carlecoates
William Booth, Carlecoates
John Martin, Carlecoates
George Hirst, Softley
James Hirst, Softley
Joseph Goldthorpe, Saville House
John Greaves, Ranah
Wm Charlesworth, Hazlehead
Edward Milnes, Flash House
Joseph Shaw, Smallshaw
Daniel Wainwright, Shore Hall
William Lockwood, Penistone
John Haigh, Blackmoor
John Crossley, Langsett
Joseph Brownhill, Bruck House

Jonathan Bramhall, Swinden
Elizabeth Bramall, Swinden
Daniel Charlesworth, Swinden
Benjamin Crossley, Swindin Walls
William Bagshaw, Horden, 2 flocks
Joseph Clark, Middlecliff

The Shepherds' Society still meets today, although the *Millers Arms* has long since disappeared from Saltersbrook, the Society has only moved a mile down the road, to the *Stanhope Arms* at Dunford Bridge. Its functions are now as much social as practical, but perhaps they always have been. 'The Shepherds' was known until very recently to locals at the *Stanhope Arms* as as an occasion of much drinking, tale-telling and singing. The late Arthur Howard in particular was noted for his singing recitals of local classics such as *Pratty Flowers, Gossip John* and *Mrs Holroyd* as well as some less than salubrious verses 12. The loss of such charismatic individuals who carried the old customs with them has led to current meetings seeming rather more restrained, but this may be a passing phase.

The Sheep

By 1800 the British Isles had around forty breeds of sheep, each with their own distinctive appearance and qualities.[13] These breeds were in the main regionally determined, having evolved to meet the specific demands of local conditions. The hill sheep tend to be hardier than the lowland sheep, better able to survive harsh climates and to thrive on poorer grasses, but the lowland sheep are generally larger and more prolific, that is, they bear more lambs. The latter point can be observed from the Wortley Farmers Club prize list, the champion *Penistone* ewe flock raised only 61 lambs from 67 ewes, whereas the champion polled flock raised 131 lambs from 110 ewes.

The most common hill types are now black or speckled face, like the *Swaledale* or *Lonk*, but all up the western side of the country several different types of whitefaced horned sheep have evolved. It is to this group that the *Penistone* belongs. Some of the group, *The Dorset Horn, Welsh Mountain and Herdwick* (Figure 10) are quite numerous, though very localised.[14] Others, however, like the *Lancashire Silverdale* and its North Yorkshire cousin, became extinct earlier this century. The *Penistone* was perilously close to joining them.[15]

The *Penistone* breed must have been subject to some infusion of 'improved blood', for it is not only much bigger than primitive sheep but is now one of the largest of the British hill breeds.

Figure 10. *Dorset Horn* (1), *Welsh Mountain* (2) and *Herdwick* (3, Laked District) breeds.

I have found no definite references to Penistone-type sheep before 1804. This is not, however, surprising. We have seen that 'scientific breeding' only emerged as a gentry pastime in the mid to late eighteenth century. For most ordinary farmers of this period and before, a sheep was a sheep and a cow a cow. Where we have examples of local farmers who kept diaries, like John Hobson of Dodworth Green (1730s), Arthur Jessop of Holmfirth (1740s) or the cattle dealer Ralph Ward of North Yorkshire (1750s), without exception they never mention breed type. As we know that regional variation must have existed at this time, we must presume that either these writers were uninterested in variations, or they never came across them because in any given area the animals mostly conformed to a normal type. The truth probably lies somewhere between. The likelihood is that the local type of sheep was widespread and therefore unremarkable, but does that mean that Penistone-type sheep were around in Hobson's time? Youatt, writing in 1840, thought that they had been around 'from time immemorial', a suggestion easily accepted by others, but difficult to prove.[16] Some light may be thrown on this by Adam Eyre, who wrote almost a century before Hobson, in the 1640s. Like the other diarists, he gives us little to go on, with no specific references to a Penistone-type, but he does offer a couple of glimpses of light that we shall now explore.

The area usually defined as the natural home of the *Penistone* stretches westwards from that town across the moors to Glossop, northwards to Marsden and southwards to Edale in Derbyshire. The area is, as we have seen, criss-crossed with ancient routeways leading to Penistone, the most famous being the ancient salt route via Woodhead (cutting right through the heart of the territory) and the Cut Gate, linking Penistone to North Derbyshire via Langsett and Derwent. This latter route emerges into the bottom end of the Woodlands valley, better known today as the Snake Pass. It is this valley that has given rise to the Penistone's alternative name of *Whitefaced Woodland*, a confusing name for moorland sheep!

The Cut Gate was a route used extensively by Adam Eyre, whose family originated in North Derbyshire and who still lived there at the time of the diaries. The *Eyre Arms* at Hassop records this family to the present day. On 17 October, 1684, Eyre went over Cut gate and upon reaching Hassop at his southern end he met his cousin:

> *There to see some sheepe which Thos Eyre was driving towards Tidwall* [sic] *fayre, and offered him 7s. a piece for 100 ewes, but he would not take it.*

The bartering was obviously tough but on the following day, 18 October, 1648,

> *Bought 101 ewes for 7s. a piece, and 5 tuppes at 11s, a piece, of Thos Eyre of Alport, and gave him 1s, in ernest, and promised to pay the residue within a month.*

As an indication of relative value, Eyre had recently sold a mare for £8.10s, or twenty-five times as much as a ewe - this is not inconsistent with modern values. The important point here, however, is that Eyre was trading in sheep within the acknowledged boundaries of the *Penistone* breed. This might well suggest that although no specific breed standards were established at that time, the breed would be reasonably consistent, simply because all of the breeding stock were being traded within a confined area. The boundaries are important, for they correspond closely to those established as the logical boundaries of both the Shepherds' Society and the Wortley Farmers' Club, one hundred and fifty years later, the latter being a body philosophically devoted to the promotion of the *Penistone* sheep, and the former being one practically committed to the same end.

Adam Eyre gives us one other reference which may indicate that the moorland sheep were distinguishable from their lowland cousins. On 26 June, 1647, he tells us:

> *After dinner I went to the wash pitt, where Wm Wordsworth and Geo*

Morton washing Winleden sheep.

The interest here is *Winleden*. This is doubtless a reference to Windleden, a farm situated three miles west of Haslehead, currently the highest, most isolated farm in these parts, it stands in a small valley just below the summit of the old salt road. 'Winleden' sheep might simply indicate possession, the sheep of Winleden, but it could just be that Eyre is using the term generically to describe a type of sheep, as we would today talk of *Penistones* or *Suffolks*. If true, this could be the earliest reference to Penistone-type sheep.

Livestock historians acknowledge the geographical limits of the *Penistone/Woodland* but there is some dispute as to whether this was (or is) a single breed. So little evidence survives to adequately confirm the point that we are inevitably left with a great deal of conjecture. One accepted view is that the *Woodland* took its characteristic white face from Spanish *Merino* rams introduced by the Duke of Devonshire. The *Merino* is an exceptionally fine-wooled sheep that was undoubtedly used on the *Penistones,* and on almost every other English breed, to improve the quality of the wool, but it was probably not used on ordinary flocks until well into the nineteenth century.[17] The Spanish government were so well aware of its attributes that, in order to protect their wool trade, they fiercely prevented the export of *Merino* stock until Sir Joseph Banks eventually managed to obtain a pair in 1785. Following this, a trickle of Merinos seeped through to the British nobility. George III had some *Merinos* in 1789 and about this time so did Coke of Norfolk, future father-in-law of John Spencer-Stanhope. The Duke of Devonshire did not obtain stock until 1814. The connection between Coke and Spencer-Stanhope has been overlooked by livestock historians who, perhaps influenced by the *Woodlands* name, have concentrated on Devonshire's role.[18] It is entirely possible, however, that Spencer-Stanhope used his father-in-law's Merinos upon the Penistone stock that roamed his grouse moors around Dunford Bridge and thus influenced the breed as much as his more famous contemporary.

Other local landowners also claimed to have stocked their parks with 'Spanish' sheep, including the Marquis of Rockingham (Wentworth) and the Earl of Strafford (Stainborough), but in these two cases they were almost certainly the multi-horned Piebald Jacob type which became a fashionable park attraction.[19] One of these *Jacob* sheep can be clearly seen in a picture of Stainborough Park by Richard Catton (c1780), now hanging in Cannon Hall. The picture also shows some whitefaced sheep but distance makes it impossible to tell whether they are supposed to be horned or not.

Clearly, the *Merino* could not have put a white face on the Penistone by 1804, ten years before Devonshire imported them. By 1804, however, the Wortley Farmers' Club had a clear idea of what constituted the breed. Unfortunately they forgot to tell us. Their schedules never define the breed's characteristics, although they do insist (in rule three) that *Penistone* sheep entered for prizes, 'must have been kept according to the customs of the country [sic]'. [20] For a description of the breed we have to wait until the agricultural scientists had begun to catalogue breeds a little later in the century. Foremost amongst these was Professor David Low of Edinburgh, whose work was quoted in Spooner's *History of Sheep* (1844). Low included illustrations of a Penistone lamb and ewe, shown here as Figure 11, which he said were respectively the property of Mr Kenworthy and Mr Booth, both of Carlecoates:

> *The Penistone is a breed of sheep found on the borders of Yorkshire, Lancashire, and Derbyshire, on a healthy tract of land about twenty six miles in length by twenty in breadth, and they call the 'Penistone' from the market town of that name, where they are sold. They are described by Low as having wool of a medium length, of a silky appearance, but harsh and wirey, and weighing from 4lbs to 5lbs the*

Figure 11. Probably the earliest representation of the Penistone breed: 'A five year old ram, property of Mr Booth, Carlcoates and a four year old ewe, property of Mr Booth of Carlecotes'. The painting was part of Professor David Low's collection at Edinburgh University and was probably commissioned between 1830-42 *Courtesy of the Trustees of the National Museum of Scotland*

fleece. They have white faces and legs. The rams exceed the ewes and wethers in a universal degree, a peculiarity which is ascribed to their being taken to the lower country to be reared. The rams alone have horns, which are very large, lying close to the head and projecting forward. A distinguishing character of this breed is an extreme coarseness of form, and especially of the extremities. The feet are large, the limbs long, the shoulders heavy, the sides flat, but the most singular characteristic is the length and muscularity of the tail, in which respect the Penistone sheep differ from all others in this country. This enlargement of the tail is merely muscular and long, and not analogous to the growth of fat which takes place in the tails of certain sheep of eastern countries. The mutton of these sheep is highly valued for its juiciness and flavour.

In all but one respect this could still describe the modern *Penistone*, but the reference to only the rams being horned is disturbing, for in the modern breed both sexes are most definitely horned. Spooner may simply have made a transcription error here, but that would be surprising when the rest of the text is so detailed. He could otherwise have been confused, for amongst the Penistone's relatives, the *Herdwick* and the *Welsh Mountain* are only horned in the ram. So too is the primitive *Shetland* and the resemblance between a *Penistone* ram and a *Shetland* is striking in many ways. The Wortley Farmers imply that a *Penistone* is horned by distinguishing the two categories as *Penistone* and *Polled*. Other commentators, including Dransfield, the nearest we have to a local contemporary, believe that Spooner is simply wrong on this point, but the conclusion is unsatisfactory. This must remain an open question, pending further evidence.

Amongst today's breeders there is still some debate as to whether the *Penistone* and the *Woodland* were once, and are still, separate breeds. Most informed opinion that I have canvassed seems to believe that if there was a difference, and there probably was, it was in the fleece, with the *Penistone* having a coarser, more weather-resistant fleece than its *Woodland* neighbour. Beware how you phrase this quality however, for a fleece that serves the sheep well is not necessarily the one most valued by clothiers. To one breeder, the *Penistone* coat was poorer, because he didn't get as good a price for it from the Wool Board, whilst to another it was better, because it shed the rain and the ewes thrived better.[21] If this fleece difference is true it could again refer to the *Merino* having more influence in Derbyshire than in Yorkshire, for the finer *Merino* wool would achieve a better price without offering greater protection.

The only other noticeable difference today is the skin colouring, some breeders preferring a pure pink nose and others liking the pink nose to be speckled with black. This latter is seen as a sign of the old pure lines, with the pink nose being attributed to out-crossings to the near relative *Dorset Horn* sheep.[22]   One breeder was sure that the black speckled ones were hardier and suffered from less footrot, although he conceded that these were probably as much a point of fashion than serious breeding considerations.[23]   For the purpose of registration the Rare Breeds Survival Trust now accepts the two as one breed and prefers to refer to it as the *Whitefaced Woodland*.

Despite its vigorous promotion by the old Wortley Farmers' Club, the *Penistone/Woodland* was already in decline by the end of the nineteenth century.   Dransfield, a lover and advocate of the breed, thought that the decline had set in earlier, and in 1906 noted wistfully:

> *The enclosure and sale of the commons after 1807...greatly reduced number of keepers of Penistone sheep...[the Agricultural Show] entries gradually became less and prizes ceased to be offered. The black faced Scotch sheep appear to be now kept by many in preference to the old breed.*[24]

Ever inventive, he suggested a remedy:

> *It is to be trusted that the owners of the moorlands in this district will not let the old breed of white-faced moorland sheep - which were formerly kept on the moors of the locality in their thousands — be lost, but will either keep flocks themselves or otherwise stipulate that they shall be kept by their tenants.*

Sadly, neither measure became common.   It is generally reckoned that one of the other factors leading to the *Penistone's* decline was, perversely, the quality and quantity of its mutton, for during and after the First World War many of the moorland breeding sheep were slaughtered to combat the problems of food shortage.   By the 1920s the *Penistone* had become a rarity.   Frank Roberts of Midhope, born in 1905, was a young man at the foot of the farming ladder in those days, he was to become one of the foremost farmers in Midhope, an area previously renowned for its *Penistones*, but talking to me in 1988 he had only vague, if fond, recollections of the old breed.[25]   His most outstanding memory being of one tup lamb that used to like cigarettes, which it would take from his pocket:

> *It got into churchyard one day and this chap says, 'I can't get it out*

*of the churchyard,' I says 'You would have done if you'd given it a
cigarette'. It would eat cigarettes by the hundred.* This tale looses
something in the writing down, for Frank's dialect was as old as
the Penistone breed!

Since the heyday of the Shepherds' Society the number of *Penistone*
breeders has fallen dramatically. One of the last of the old guard was
Arthur Howard of *Saville House*, Haslehead, whose ancestor, Joshua
Howard of Holme was recorded in the Shepherds book of 1807
(Figure 12). He was a stalwart of the Society and ardent believer in
the *Penistone*. I do mean here the *Penistone*, for Arthur was convinced
that the *Penistone* and *Woodland* were different sheep.[26] Today, only
three farmers locally keep *Penistones* on a large scale, two of these are

Figure 12. Seven shepherds and four sheep c.1950-55. Possibly taken at Pikenaze
Farm, Woodhead, home of the Howard family. The young lad is Ryder Howard, standing to the right of his father, Arthur. The tall man, back centre, is Thomas Edward
Smith. All three noted *Penistone* breeders. The sheep, however, have too many black
speckles on their faces to be pure-bred *Penistones*.

Arthur 's descendants, his son, Ryder at Pikenaze, Woodhead and his nephew Jimmy Howard, at Holme. The other breeder, Harold Smith of Carlecoates, is a direct descendant of Thomas Taylor, keeper of the *Millers Arms* at Saltersbrook. Harold's family also own Windleden, which is occupied by his greatest asset, his shepherd, James Gill. Just a little north of Marsden, at that famous farmhouse in the gap of the M62, near Ripponden, lives Ken Wild, the remaining large scale *Penistone/Woodland* breeder in this region (Figure 13).

Figure 13. Penistone tups on show at the Annual Show and Sale. The judge is Ken Wild, who runs a large moorland flock above Marsden. This photograph was taken in September, 1989 when the show was held at the Dog and Partridge, Bordhill.

Many of the sheep owned by the above four farmers are unregistered for breeding purposes. It is difficult therefore to place a precise figure on the number of true *Penistone/Woodlands* that still exist. Only the best ewes and rams are registered with the Rare Breeds Survival Trust (it costs money to register them) and at the time of writing there are only about 300 registered ewes, placing this breed on the Trust's **critically endangered** list (category 1). The actual situation is, however, not quite as serious, as there are possibly a thousand or so unregistered in the moorland flocks. Many of the registered ewes are in small flocks dispersed throughout the country, ironically the Breeders' Group Secretary lives in Northamptonshire! Such a small number of breeders inevitably means that there are a restricted number of breeding lines and therefore dangers of inbreeding. At least one of the large flock owners believes that their genetic base is dangerously close to becoming too narrow. The future of the *Penistone* breed is therefore in the hands of the many small flock owners, most of whom have never been near Penistone and who prefer to call their sheep *Whitefaced Woodlands*. Whilst this article was in preparation James left Harold's employment but still lives in the area and is trying to establish his own small flock of *Penistones*.

Conclusion

I have tried to show the inter-relationship between sheep, shepherds and gentlemen farmers and their importance to the local economy of the Penistone area in the early nineteenth century. The Penistone Burial Board recognised the significance of the sheep by choosing a *Penistone* ram's head as the symbol upon its seal. When the railway came through Penistone in the middle years of the century, the town followed the rest of south Yorkshire and its economic base shifted to steel and engineering. Today, it is a straggling town, suffering many of the signs of post-industrial decay, but at its heart lies the visible signs of a much older culture. The Cloth Hall, the Livestock Market and the Penistone Show are all extant, all part of the old shepherding traditions. Naturally, they have changed over the years, but have retained an essential link with Penistone's heritage, whilst newer fads have come and gone. Today, however, we still need to be wary that the modernisers are not about to eliminate these remaining tenuous strands. There are current proposals to remove the livestock market from the town centre. The Shepherds' Society continues to meet, but functions now mainly as a social organisation and has recently opted to change its meeting into a formal dinner date. Local farmers are deserting the *Penistone* in favour of current, more fashionable breeds. Even the Rare Breeds Survival Trust have opted to give the sheep a name that does no credit to its past importance in this region, however they have recognised that the annual show and sale held at Hade Edge, near Dunford Bridge every September, should be known as the national show and sale. This is an important recognition of the breed's origins. Even more importantly, this year after a long absence and much lobbying by the author, the Penistone Show Committee have agreed to put a class for *Penistone Sheep*. The sheep is coming home!

There are those that argue, 'We have to change with the times', but our culture is such that we spend a great deal of our national resources preserving 'heritage', landscapes, buildings and traditions. Perhaps Penistone's people, farmers and policy makers could bear that in mind before allowing any of the above items to pass into oblivion.[27]

We should, however, finish on a positive note. Some traditions continue and some individuals continue to uphold the best of them. Way up there at Windleden, the farm known to Adam Eyre, we are fortunate to have in residence one of the county's and country's finest shepherds. Still in his twenties, James Gill has represented England at sheepdog trialling, he has won the *One Man and His Dog* event and in 1994 proved victorious in his sheep shearing class at the Great Yorkshire Show. To watch James at work (Figure 14) is to be able to share in the skills of a millennium, appreciate the fine tuning of generations and marvel at the traditional wisdom of the shepherd's art. And he does it with *Penistone* sheep. Long may he, the sheep and shepherds continue.

Figure 14. James Gill *The Author*

Notes and References

1. Dransfield J N, *History of Penistone* (1906), pp 270-75.
2. Goddard N, 'Agricultural Societies', Victorian Countryside (1981),pp 245-52.
3. Henson E, *Rare Breeds in History* (1982), p 29.
4. Gordon Knowles was interviewed privately by the writer, in March,1988.
5. Dransfield, *op cit*, p130.
6. Jackson, B, *Cawthorne,1790-1990*, (1991), pp 37-38.
7. Dransfield, *op cit* , p 130.
8. Robinson G, 'The Sedgewicks', Old West Riding, v.12 (1992).
9. Dransfield, *op cit*, p 130.
10. Jimmy Howard of Lane Farm, Holm, in a personal conversation, March 1995.
11. Mary Knight, now of High Green, but daughter of gamekeeper from Thorpe Hesley, personal conversation with Sam Sykes, 1995.
12. Arthur Howard of Saville House, Carlecoates, as remembered by his daughter-in-law,Rocky Howard of Townhead,Dunford Bridge, in a personal conversation,March 1995.
13. Ryder M, *Sheep and Man* (1980) p 487.
14. Hall S G & Clutton-Brock J, *Two Hundred Years of British Farm Livestock* (1989), p 129 estimated that out of about 14 million breeding ewes in Britain, about 2.5 million were *Welsh Mountain*, making it the most numerous of all our breeds. In contrast *Herdwicks* only number about 25,000.
15. Ryder *op cit*, p 460.
16. William Youat was a veterinary surgeon who died in 1846, after publishing several books that became standards for the profession. His popularity and influence was paralleled by David Low, Professor of Agriculture at Edinburgh University. Low's *The Breeds of the Domestic Animals of the British Islands 1842*, contained engravings from specially commissioned paintings by William Sheils. These are often the earliest illustrations of a particular breed.
17. Hall & Clutton-Brock, *op cit*, p 149.
18. I have made use of all the standard texts on livestock history and the modern variations by authors perusing the rare breeds theme, but none of the sources quoted here attribute any role to Spencer-Stanhope, whilst all accept Devonshire's contribution.
19. Ryder, *op cit*, p 458.
20. The word 'country' was often used in a much more parochial sense than now, implying a much more local area. Frank Roberts of Midhope, interviewed by the author in April 1988, uses the term in the way 'We've been all over the country,Hawksworth,Stannington, Bradfield, up top end, you know.'
(21) Dr Ross Harrison of Beckermonds and Harold Smith of Carlecoates respectively, both in personal conversations, March 1995.
22. Tony Hirst of Dunford Bridge (married Arthur Howard's granddaughter) in a personal conversation,March 1995.
23. Ross Harrison, *op cit.*
24. Dransfield, *op cit*, p 279.
25. Frank Roberts, *op cit.*
26. Rocky Howard and Tony Hirst, *op cit*; Richard Beard of Penistone collected similar comments in an unpublished dissertation for Asham Bryan College of Agriculture in 1968 - these were reported in an article by Jill Rose, 'History and appraisal of the Woodlands Whitefaced Sheep', *The Ark* (Journal of the Rare Breeds Survival Trust (June,1982): copy provided to me by Mr George Punt of Penistone.
27. Councillor Nora Collet, quoted in the *Barnsley Chronicle*, March 1995, during discussions on the future development of Penistone's town centre and livestock market.

My thanks are due to all those people quoted above for their comments and advice but none of them are responsible for any errors of judgement or interpretation.

14. THE CONCEPTION AND CONSTRUCTION OF THE BARNSLEY CANAL

by Roger Glister

IN JULY 1792 THE AIRE AND CALDER Navigation Company instructed its manager, William Martin, to obtain a plan and estimate for the building of a canal from Barnsley to Wakefield. This scheme was to facilitate the exploitation of the vast coal reserves beneath the environs of these two towns. Thus on 7 August the Aire and Calder Navigation shareholders meeting asked William Jessop, the company's consulting engineer (Figure 1), to survey a route to be presented at a public meeting. Jessop at this time was heavily committed to other canal projects and was too busy to survey either the Barnsley or Dearne and Dove Canal that had also been offered to him. Once again the job fell to William Martin and his assistants, John Gott and Elias Wright, who promptly surveyed several routes between the Aire and Calder and Barnsley.

Figure 1. William Jessop (1745-1814), Consulting Engineer for the Barnsley Canal *Barnsley Canal Group*

They did not waste a lot of time, for on 20 September the shareholders were told by Jessop that he had perused the various routes surveyed and in his opinion one line in particular, from Wakefield to Barnsley, with a branch to Silkstone, 'Will be Practicable, be a very eligible Line to be Adopted and that the Expense upon a cursory View wou'd not exceed the Sum of Fifty Thousand Pounds'.

A public subscription meeting was held at the *White Bear Hotel* in Barnsley, now known as *The Royal Hotel*, on 15 October, 1792, with a leading A & C N proprietor, John Smyth of Heath, in the chair. The route and estimate, now revised to £60,000, was presented to those in attendance and no fewer than 86 investors quickly subscribed the capital sum.

The principal shareholder, who invested £1,600, was Walter Spencer-Stanhope of Cannon Hall. He stood to gain vast sums with the building of the Barnsley Canal due to his ownership of the land around Silkstone beneath which lay the rich Silkstone coal seams.

Born plain Walter Stanhope in 1749, the son of a Leeds cloth merchant, he added Spencer to his name upon succession to the Cannon Hall estates from his uncle, ironmaster John Spencer. Already a trustee of the A & C N due to stock he gained by his marriage in 1783, he was made chairman of the Barnsley Canal Company, a position he enjoyed throughout the building of the waterway. There can be little doubt that it was he who lobbied for the five tramroads linking points on the coalfield with the canal at Barnby that were included in the Parliamentary Bill that was now prepared.

The Barnsley Canal duly received its Royal assent on 3 June, 1793, at a cost of £2,000 to the promoters, with confirmed capital of £80,000 to cover the latest estimate of £72,000. On the same day the Dearne and Dove Bill also gained assent.

The first sod was cut on Heath Common by William Martin, who was appointed as company treasurer, on 27 September, 1793. The contractor was John Pinkerton, well known for his work on a number of canals and closely associated with William Jessop. Pinkerton's weakness was a well developed ability to miscalculate estimates which resulted in skimped works and disputes with his employers. The Barnsley commission was to be no different and Samuel Hartley, the company surveyor, was soon at odds with the contractor.

By the summer of 1794 Pinkerton was experiencing great difficulty in the Cold Hiendley cutting and needed large amounts of gunpowder for blasting that had not been anticipated which meant very slow progress being made in this area. The making of the whole line, excluding locks, had been expected to cost about 6d [2.5p] per yard in the main and no-where more than 1s.4d. [6.66p]. However, no less than 5,000 yards had cost almost 2s [10p] and one stretch at Cold Hiendley over 4s. [20p] per yard, therefore way over budget.

Despite the bickerings, specification changes and construction setbacks, most of the earthworks were complete by the middle of 1793 and Hartley was able to report that the canal was in water from the top of the Walton flight to Barnsley. He also had to report that the top five locks on the flight may have to be demolished and rebuilt as the puddle had not been carried under the foundations properly.

The completion of the works resulted in the opening of the Barnsley Canal on 8 June, 1799, from the Calder at Heath to Barnsley Basin. The remaining length to the terminus of the Barnby Basin was opened in the early part of 1802. The total expenditure by the company from the canal's inception to completion was £95,000. The litigation between the Canal Company and John Pinkerton was

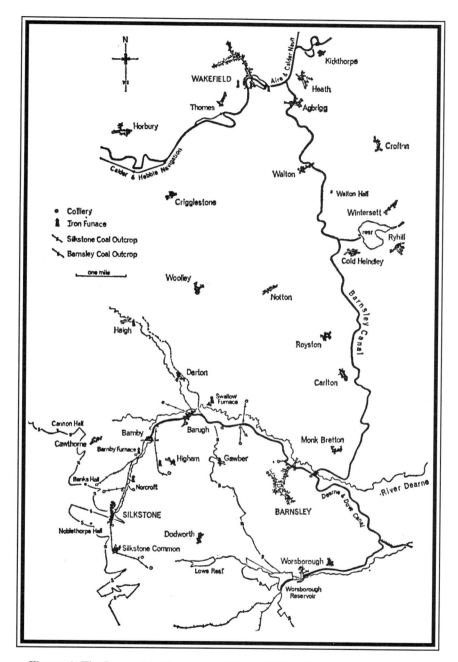

Figure 2. The Route of the Barnsley and Dearne & Dove Canals

not resolved until 1812 when the contractor paid £3,137 to the Company as compensation for unfinished and remedial work.

The waterway was sixteen miles in length (see Figure 2) with a navigable depth of five feet. There were fifteen locks between the Calder and the summit level with three at Agbrigg and twelve at Walton which were built originally to accommodate craft of 58 feet long by 14 feet 10 inches wide. These were increased in size to 79 feet by 14 feet 10 inches wide in 1881 and the depth of the channel increased to six feet. The water supply was taken from a reservoir built at Cold Hiendley which was inadequate from the start. Enlarged in 1839, the reservoir still proved too small and another, Wintersett, was constructed adjacent to Cold Hiendley in 1854. There was insufficient capacity even then and the final attempt to keep pace with water usage was made in 1874 when the area of the two reservoirs was increased by 55 acres.

The other locks on the canal were a flight of five which lifted the canal to its terminus at Barnby Basin. The water for these locks was obtained by back-pumping up the flight and using the same water again. This was done using a steam-powered beam engine pump built by the Low Moor Iron company at a cost of £1,630.

Knowing that an adequate supply of water would be crucial to the smooth running of the canal, William Jessop designed the lock chambers of each flight to have equal falls. Eight feet on the Barnby locks and seven feet six inches on the Agbrigg/Walton flight. This, coupled with identical dimensions, ensured that when one lock emptied, its contents exactly filled the chamber below without wasting any water. This feature also meant that lock gates were interchangeable.

The Dearne and Dove Canal and the Don Navigation were protected by a stipulation in the Barnsley Bill calling for a stop lock at the junction of the two canals. This lock, situated at Hoyle Mill, prevented loss of water in both directions and was jointly managed. The Barnsley Company was also forbidden to extract any water from the River Dearne.

The most handsome structure on the waterway was the aqueduct over the River Dearne at Hoyle Mill (Figure 3). Originally an embankment with one 30 foot arch for the river had been intended but the Woolley Edge Rock was found to outcrop on both sides of the valley and Jessop decided to construct a masonry aqueduct of five 30 foot arches. This monument to the canal builder's art cost £1,547 and was used as the company logo on toll tickets and other paperwork.

Figure 3. The Barnsley Aqueduct at Hoyle Mill. This fine engineering structure was demolished in 1954 *Barnsley Canal Group*

In 1799 the first lock at Agbrigg was located at the end of a long cutting some way from the River Calder. This proved troublesome as when the river level rose in times of flood the cut became choked with debris and the entrance tended to silt up. In 1816 this was remedied by making a new cut slightly to the west and moving the lock closer to the river.

It was very much in this form that the Barnsley Canal carried on its life. Subsidence and lack of trade took their toll and following two disastrous breaches, in 1945-46, abandonment was sought. The warrant was granted in 1953 and the canal was officially closed.

However, its spirit still lingers and by the tireless efforts of the Barnsley Canal Group new life is being breathed into the derelict and sorry waterway. The Group has published a report, *The Barnsley Canal - a Forgotten Waterway?* which outlines the plans for rescuing the canal and returning it, along with the Dearne and Dove, to full navigation.

The photographs shown at the end of this study (Figures 4-11) are further examples taken from a large collection in the care of the Barnsley Canal Group, selected by Alan Hall and Brian Elliott.

Further Reading

Copies of *The Barnsley Canal - a Forgotten Waterway?* at £2.50p (including postage) can be had from Roger Glister, 2 Moorside Court, Cowpasture Road, Ilkley LS29 8UF.
Rodolph de Salis Henry,   *Bradshaws Canals and Navigable Rivers of England and Wales,* 1904
Slatcher W N, 'The Barnsley Canal and its first Twenty Years', *Transport History*, 1968
Hadfield C,   *The Canals of Yorkshire and North East England* , 1973

Figure 4.   Heath (No.1) Lock , River Calder, near Wakefield. The Lock-keeper's cottage can be seen on the right. Note the loaded barge about to enter the lock and therefore start its journey on the Barnsley Canal   *Barnsley Canal Group*

Figure 5. A closer view of the Heath Lock and Keeper's Cottage at Heath
Barnsley Canal Group

Figure 6. High Town Bridge and Lock Number 11 at Walton, looking South, 27 October, 1953 *Barnsley Canal Group*

Figure 7 (a). Looking up Cold Hiendley Reservoir, from Cold Hiendley Sluices, 24 April, 1955. The Pumping Station can be seen in the distance   *Barnsley Canal Group*

Figure 7 (b). Cold Hiendley Pumping Station. The engine is believed to have been built by Harvey & Co of Hayle, in 1864, working at the Tremenheer tin mine in Cornwall for ten years before being sold to the Aire & Calder Company and shipped round the coast on board *Lizzie Hawke*. It worked until 1947 when the canal burst and was scrapped in about 1960. Boiler coal was delivered by boat, one of which can be seen in this photograph, having just been unloaded by wheelbarrow *Barnsley Canal Grou*

Figure 8. 'Upstream' side of Church Hill Bridge, Royston, 15 February, 1951

Figure 9. Old Mill Locks, Stop Lock and Junction House where The Barnsley Canal met the Dearne & Dove Canal   *Barnsley Canal Group*

Figure 10. (above) Barnsley Basin at Old Mill. This photograph shows a barge unloading oil to the petroleum depot (out of picture), an event that was viewed with interest, judging by the number of spectators on Old Mill Bridge, c 1925   *Barnsley Canal Group*

Figure 11. The old Warehouse at Barnby Basin, Cawthorne. The upper storey appears to have been used as a pigeon loft or dovecote   *Barnsley Canal Group*

15. A Midland Railway Branch in South Yorkshire

by Trevor Lodge

Introduction

A HUNDRED YEARS AGO the rich South Yorkshire coalfield between Sheffield and Barnsley was reaching its commercial zenith. At the time most of the area's coal was produced from some twenty or so major collieries, with transport largely provided by the Manchester, Sheffield & Lincolnshire Railway (MSLR) as successor to the South Yorkshire Railway, which had tapped the area from 1855 onwards.

The traffic potential of the coalfield did not go unnoticed by the Midland Railway, which came no closer than its Sheffield-Leeds main line running east of the area via Rotherham, Swinton, Wath and Darfield. In an attempt to break the MSLR monopoly on this lucrative traffic, the Midland drew up proposals for a direct line through the coalfield from Sheffield to Barnsley, seeking approval for the first stage in the 1890 Session of Parliament. The Bill for a 41/2 mile branch from Wincobank (Sheffield) to Chapeltown received the Royal Assent on 25 July, 1890.

A number of interesting developments and 'behind-the-scenes' struggles occurred during the promotion and construction of this branch. These largely involved Newton, Chambers & Co Ltd, whose coal and iron complex dominated the area and so are of interest to both students of industry and railways. In addition to covering this aspect of the line, the article provides some details of the contractors' work, sources of industrial traffic on the branch, and a résumé of the passenger services. Paradoxically, though the latter were never financially important in the line's earlier decades they now constitute its only traffic.

Since most of the industrial concerns which would be served by the proposed branch were already connected with the MSLR's Sheffield-Barnsley line (which it closely paralleled for two lengthy stretches) the Midland's scheme not unnaturally met with considerable opposition from the MSLR and its allies, principally the Great Northern Railway (GNR). The interests of the GNR were quite straightforward. It enjoyed a virtual monopoly of supplying London with South Yorkshire coal originating on the MSLR, and it was not anxious to enter into competition for it with the Midland! The MSLR was not the only concern to object to the Midland's plans. Newton, Chambers & Co Ltd, which owned Thorncliffe Ironworks at Chapeltown, and its associated collieries, coking and chemical works, was a particularly vociferous opponent. At first sight this action seems to have been totally contrary to Thorncliffe's traffic requirements; however, Newton Chambers was a company with a strong sense of business acumen and knew almost instinctively how to get the best out of a situation. On the face of it the opposition was natural enough, for the Vice Chairman of Newton Chambers was the first Lord Wharncliffe, who also just happened to be Chairman of the MSLR at the time! However, then as now, 'business is business', and by opposing the Midland's new line (partially tongue-in-cheek) Newton Chambers was able to lever attractive concessions from the Midland in return for eventually withdrawing its opposition, as will become clear later.

Needless to say, once Newton Chambers and the Midland reached agreement, and the former withdrew its objections, the Thorncliffe company was literally bombarded in April 1890 with letters from Sir Edward Watkin and William Pollitt, Chairman and General Manager of the MSLR, complaining of its change of allegiance! It is doubtful if Newton Chambers paid too much heed to these letters, for the Thorncliffe company's pre-occupation was to put its own interests paramount, a feature of management demonstrated time after time through its 150 years of independent existence as a coal and iron empire. Indeed, later differences of opinion between Newton Chambers and the London North Eastern Railway (LNER) over coal carriage charges from the former's various collieries to a central coking and by-products plant at Smithywood, Ecclesfield, caused it to build a transport system totally independent of railways - an aerial flight - but that's another story.

Construction

The tender of local contractors Dransfield and Smith was accepted for the building of the Chapeltown Branch, which was to commence at Wincobank, on the Midland's Sheffield and Rotherham line, and run roughly due north to Chapeltown, with a short extension to Thorncliffe Ironworks. The Midland Directors' Report for the half year ending 31 December, 1890, stated that the branch was actually then in course of construction, but it is almost certain that this referred to the initial work of surveying and levelling: the order for ironwork for the bridges on the branch was not placed with Newton Chambers until 19 January, 1891. It is quite likely that Dransfield and Smith were instructed by the Midland to place this order with the Thorncliffe company, as one of the concessions mentioned earlier, but I have not been able to confirm this. According to the Midland's *List of Sidings* for 1892, Dransfield and Smith, as 'contractors for the new Chapeltown Branch', had a siding at Meadow Hall in connection with the work. This was only regarded as a temporary feature, the list stating that the 'siding will be taken out when work completed'. The exact location of the siding is not known, but is thought to be very near to the area now occupied by British Rail's Meadowhall Interchange Station.

Construction of the line proceeded from the Wincobank end only, despite the fact that Dransfield and Smith could have gained rail access to the Chapeltown end via the MSLR and Newton Chambers' sidings at Thorncliffe. Not until 4 December, 1892, could George Dawson, Manager of the Thorncliffe Ironworks, record that 'Dransfield and Smith, contractors for the new Midland Railway through Chapeltown, have now got their railway connected with our sidings in the works'. Dawson's report presumably refers to the contractor's overland (temporary) line, though the MR Directors' Report for half year ending 31 December, 1891, claimed that a portion of the branch was ready to receive the permanent way.

The course of the line from Wincobank to Chapeltown ran up the valley of the Blackburn Brook and in consequence required few earthworks, other than minor embankments and the odd shallow cutting to maintain an evenly graded trackbed. The only civil engineering feature of any note occurred at Chapeltown, where two steel girder bridges and five intervening stone arches carried the line over two major roads in the town centre. The original contract was for a single line branch only, essentially to serve Thorncliffe Ironworks and its associated collieries, but *Engineering* in its issue of 12 May, 1893, stated that 'the line has since been doubled', and that stations 'are to be built for passenger traffic'. This intention to upgrade the line and its facilities is understandable since Parliamentary powers had just been granted for extending the branch to Barnsley, on completion of which it would offer the MR an alternative route between Sheffield and Leeds, compared with that through Rotherham and Swinton.

What of the locomotives employed by Dransfield and Smith? The Yorkshire Engine Company Ltd, Meadow Hall Works, Sheffield, recorded that spares were supplied to Dransfield and Smith between 1891 and 1894 for a total of five locomotives - AIRE, LIZZIE, LORD COLVILLE, NAVVY and SYDNEY, Figure 1. The use of five locomotives on such a short line may seem excessive but the following tantalising entry in George Dawson's diary for 4 September, 1894, offers an explanation, 'Midland Railway commenced working goods traffic on the new Chapeltown branch by their own engines on the 1st. The traffic up to this time has been worked by engines of the contractors, Dransfield and Smith'. Since the line had been opened to mineral traffic in the summer of 1893*, the contractors would certainly need more than the one or two locomotives normally required for the building of a branch of this size. The fact that the contractors obtained spares from the Yorkshire

Figure 1. LIZZIE (Hunslet 164 of 1876) was a typical example of the maker's inside cylinder six-coupled saddle tank type. The locomotive is seen here on Dransfield and Smith's LYR Bank Hall - Bootle - Seaforth contract of the 1880s. By 1890 it was being used by the partners on the MR Chapeltown Branch *Collection F Jones*

Engine Company is further substantiation, because the latter's Meadowhall Works was only 600 yards from Wincobank Junction and the contractors' siding. Thus, even though none of the Dransfield and Smith locomotives were Yorkshire Engine products, it would not have been difficult for fitters from Yorkshire Engine to measure up any of them in need of attention and produce spares on a tailor-made basis.

Dransfield & Smith locomotives used on Wincobank Junction-Chapeltown Contract

Name	Type	Builder	Works No	Date	Notes
LIZZIE	0-6-OST IC	Hunslet Engine	164	1876	1
LORD COLVILLE	0-6-OST IC	Hunslet Engine	257	1881	2
SYDNEY	0-6-OST IC	Manning Wardle	598	1876	3
AIRE	?	?	?	?	4
NAVVY	?	?	?	?	5

Notes

1.   *Built by the Hunslet Engine Company of Leeds. Previously used by Dransfield & Co at Pontefract and by Dransfield & Smith on the Lancashire & Yorkshire Railway Bank Hall - Bootle - Seaforth contract. Sold to contractors Walter Scott & Co.*
2.   *Formerly with contractors Baker & Firbank where it carried the name DUNSTON. Sold to Walter Scott & Co by April 1895.*
3.   *Delivered new from the maker's Boyne Engine Works, Leeds, to contractors Logan & Hemingway. Sold to Walter Scott & Co.*
4.   *No further details known.*
5.   *Origin uncertain. Possibly ex-St Helens Railway or built (or rebuilt) by Cross of St Helens.*

The Thorncliffe complex was the largest industrial concern linked with the new railway. As built, the branch proper deviated slightly from the original plan, terminating just north of the site chosen for Chapeltown Station. At this point an extension of 90 chains was constructed which encircled the western and northern edges of Thorncliffe Ironworks, crossing the Blackburn Brook valley on a 25ft high five-arch stone viaduct north of the works in the process, and making an end on connection with the ironworks' existing High Level sidings. This extension, known officially as the MR's Thorncliffe High Level branch, was without doubt the largest single concession that the Midland gave the Thorncliffe company; indeed it was reported in the *Sheffield Daily Telegraph* for 22 February, 1890, that the construction of the branch from Chapeltown to Thorncliffe had been approved by the MR Board at an estimated cost of £16,601. Within very little time the Midland connection to Thorncliffe was proving its worth. By 1898 iron ore and limestone

---

* Contemporary sources vary. Engineering (issue of 12th May 1893) claimed 8th May 1893; others state 30th August 1893.

- raw materials for charging the blast furnaces via the High Level sidings - were entering Thorncliffe at the rate of 60,000 tons annually and expansion was such that this figure had doubled within 15 years.

We are overstepping our story, however, for only six months before the connection was put in to Thorncliffe, Newton Chambers was still playing a game of cat and mouse with the Midland to secure the best possible terms. On 18 May, 1892, a petition signed by two Newton Chambers directors and its Company Secretary was deposited with the House of Lords specifically opposing the MR Bill for extending the Chapeltown Branch to Barnsley. Again, on the face of it, the matter was straightforward enough, for the branch extension would involve construction of a tunnel under land on which Newton Chambers held mining leases. The presence of such a tunnel would effectively sterilise several acres of coal which would have to be left as an unworked pillar below the tunnel for support. There must have followed some fairly hectic correspondence on the subject for on 29 August, 1892, Newton Chambers was able to affix its seal to an agreement with the Midland in which the Thorncliffe company withdrew its opposition to the extension. In return, the Midland (at its own expense) had to construct a line connecting its Chapeltown branch to Newton Chambers' Smithy Wood Colliery (at Ecclesfield) and a short spur off the High Level branch to link into Thorncliffe Ironworks yard and the associated Thorncliffe Drift Colliery. Newton Chambers was to provide the land (already in its possession) for these connections, without charge. In addition, the Midland undertook to connect the High Level Branch at Thorncliffe with Newton Chambers' Silkstone Colliery, near Westwood. The quarter mile extension from the High Level sidings at Thorncliffe to Silkstone Colliery was purely Newton Chambers' property and was never regarded as part of the Midland, although it was presumably built by Dransfield and Smith. And having got the Midland to assist it in this way, the Thorncliffe company then employed a contractor named Trippett to extend the line beyond Silkstone Colliery to link with its coke ovens adjacent to Westwood Station on the MSLR. True to form, Newton Chambers suggested that the Midland might like to contribute financially to this final half mile extension by Trippett - estimated to cost £500 - when it approved the conveyance to the Midland of land required for the Chapeltown Branch extension to Barnsley! Despite this display of almost petty penny-pinching by Newton Chambers, the Midland subsequently gave much good business to Thorncliffe in the form of orders for fabricated steel bridge sections, Figure 2.

Figure 2. The cordial relationship which evolved between the Midland Railway and Newton Chambers & Co Ltd brought much new business to Thorncliffe. This view of the ironworks yard, about 1897, shows a train of rivetted bridge sections for the MR's 'Marple contract' (sic) standing on 'Derby curve'. The background is taken up by rows of beehive-type coking ovens, with the screening plant for Thorncliffe Drift Colliery to the left *Author's collection*

The contract for the Chapeltown Branch extension, announced as already 'let' in the MR Directors' half year report dated 30 June, 1894, was awarded to Walter Scott & Company of Newcastle. *Engineering*, in its issue dated 6 July, 1894, reported that the estimated cost of the new railway was put at about £420,000, and it would consume some 144 acres of land, acquired at a cost of £60,000. The total estimate for tunnelling along the route was £103,308, of which £81,000 would be incurred on the four miles between Chapeltown and Wombwell. This latter sum was largely for the construction of one lengthy tunnel immediately north of Chapeltown.   Some   £12,000   was   allowed   for   station accommodation.   Little further time was wasted by the various interested parties.   The Midland already had possession of a large proportion of the land needed and, on 2 July, 1894, George Dawson of Newton Chambers recorded the following in his diary: 'Went to Rugby to see Mr Middleton and arrange with him for us to supply Walter Scott and Middleton with bridges for the Midland Railway extension to Barnsley'.   This was put on a formal footing by an indenture of 31 December, 1894, in which Newton Chambers undertook to supply iron and steel work and girders for 'bridges etc' on the line between Chapeltown and Wombwell Main Colliery.   By August 1894, Scott & Middleton had at least one steam navvy on site to help with excavations, and a month later ironwork had been delivered for the bridge which was to carry the line over Black Lane, some 200 yards north of the point where Tankersley Tunnel was being driven**.

Built over more difficult terrain than the original branch to Chapeltown, the extension required three major items of civil engineering - the boring of the 1498 yards long Tankersley Tunnel immediately north of Chapeltown; the construction of a 200 yard long viaduct to carry the railway over a cleft in the land between Elsecar and the oddly named village of Jump; and a lengthy viaduct north of Wombwell taking the railway over Worsbrough Dale. Scott & Middleton established a temporary plant depot at Elsecar in connection with building the extension, and had equipment and material consigned to the existing MSLR railhead at Elsecar. From here the supplies were conveyed to the construction site by haulage up a rope-worked incline on an existing standard gauge mineral line which connected Lidgett Colliery at Skiers Spring with the canal and MSLR at Elsecar.

A contemporary diary, kept by G Johnson, a deputy at Lidgett Colliery, recorded that on 15 August, 1894, Scott & Middleton's steam navvy, during the course of negotiating the mineral railway from Elsecar, got fast under the colliery screens! Johnson's diary makes several other interesting references to the construction of the branch extension, as follows:

9th July 1894 (Monday) 'Commenced New Mid. Railway at Spring brick yard' [refers to Skiers Spring]. *14th August 1894 'Started tail end of Tunnel. Length of Tunnel 1496 yards'.* [This was Tankersley Tunnel, presumed to have been driven initially from the Chapeltown end]. *4th September 1894 'First MS&L wagon taken up to Black Lane with Bridge for Crossing'. 6th September 1894 'First Loco came for New Line; Steam got up and run same day'. A later, undated entry records 'First Loco (Saltburn)'.*

** Black Lane is a minor road connecting Wentworth village with Tankersley, and it crossed the course of the line approximately equidistant from the northern portal of Tankersley Tunnel and Wentworth & Hoyland Common Station.

27th September 1894 'Steam Navvy taken up to Black Lane; Steam got up on Friday'.
1st October 1894 'Steam Navvy began to work'. 8th October 1894 'Boiler and engine for
[2nd] Steam Navvy arrived at Milton'. 17th October 1894 'Loco arrived at Milton'
[This is presumably referring to the second contractor's locomotive to arrive]. *18th*
October 1894 '[2nd] Steam Navvy began to work'. 17th December 1894 'First coping
stones put on the Bridge at Corner pin (Mary Cooper). The loco ran over the Bridge first
time' [This bridge was immediately east of Wentworth & Hoyland Common
Station]. *19th December 1894 'Steam Navvy got over the bridge to fill up dirt from*
Lidgett pit hill'. [The inference is that spoil from the pit heap was used as
embankment 'fill' on the new line]. *2nd January 1895 'No 3 Steam Navvy started at*
[Skiers Spring] *Brick yard'. 23rd May 1895 'Steam Navvy finished near to footrill*
hole'. [The Footrill Hole was a small drift coal mine located south of the trackbed
at grid reference SK 371995]. *9th July 1985 'First girder put across Moodyfield for*
Bridge'.

Construction of Tankersley Tunnel presented the contractors with
no peculiar problems, but it did form an effective barrier which
prevented the main operations for the branch extensions from being
based at Chapeltown. Photographic evidence, however, suggests
that the contractors used at least one locomotive, LORD
COLVILLE, on excavations based at the Chapeltown end of
Tankersley Tunnel, Figure 3. To expedite the boring of the tunnel,

Figure 3. LORD COLVILLE (Hunslet 257 of 1881) was used by Dransfield and
Smith on the original MR branch to Chapeltown, then from 1894 by Scott and
Middleton on the branch extension towards Barnsley. On the reverse of the original
print of this picture was written 'Sheffield Line Construction' and 'Near Railway Inn
at Chapeltown, Brightside, in 1895.' Ignoring 'Brightside'-an obvious error - allows us
to deduce that the picture was taken on the branch extension immediately north of
Chapeltown MR station, for the Railway Inn was located on Station Road,
Chapeltown *Collection R N Redman*

Scott & Middleton entered into an agreement with Newton Chambers, details of which were recorded in a Thorncliffe Board Meeting of 31 December, 1894. Newton Chambers leased a siding and an area of land at Thorncliffe and certain fields at Warren 'for two years certain from 1st July, 1894, and thereafter until determined by six months in writing at a yearly rental of £150'. This enabled the contractors to lay a temporary overland line through Warren Bridge (near the entrance to Thorncliffe Drift Pit), alongside the road to Warren and over adjacent fields to the site of one of the tunnel air shafts, Figure 4. Here Scott & Middleton established a temporary smithy and a reversal at the end of the line enabled a second air shaft site to be reached. The siding and land leased to the contractor - also near Warren Bridge - were used by Scott & Middleton as a storage area. Their Manning Wardle locomotive GERTRUDE collected wagons of material as needed for the excavation and lining of the tunnel ventilation shafts. To dispose of surplus spoil from the tunnel shaft excavations, two tipping banks were established; one near the most southern of the ventilation shafts and the other to the west of it. A further part of the agreement between Scott & Middleton and Newton Chambers covered the supply by the latter of between six million and eight million common red bricks from its Thorncliffe brickworks 'at 21/- (£1.05) per thousand' in connection with the building of the railway. (These were mostly used in connection with station and bridge building. The lining and ventilation shafts of Tankersley Tunnel, however, were essentially in Staffordshire blue bricks). Newton Chambers also supplied from its Chapeltown Foundry literally hundreds of tons of cast iron chairs for track on the extension.

The itinerant navvies working for Scott & Middleton seem to have been reasonably well behaved, unlike earlier generations of their ilk responsible for building Britain's trunk railways in the 1840s and 1850s. According to the *Tankersley Parish Magazine* for July 1894, about 500 navvies were expected to be used on the extension between Chapeltown and Barnsley, and it was intended to establish a Navvy Mission at Warren to cater for their spiritual needs. In August 1896 the magazine reported further, 'Now that the tunnel under Hound Hill [i.e, Tankersley Tunnel] is practically finished a large number of the navvies who occupied the huts at Warren have left for other fields of labour'.

Scott & Middleton's locomotive fleet on the branch is less well defined than that of Dransfield & Smith. Various records show that Scott & Middleton had SALTBURN and SYDNEY based at Elsecar

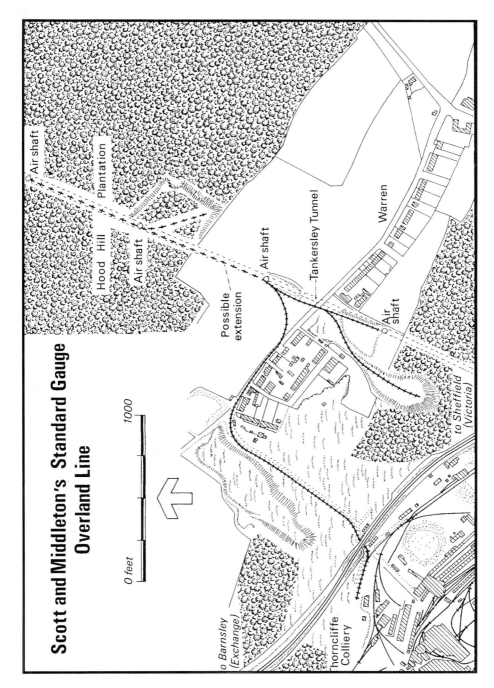

Figure 4. Scott and Middleton's overland line, used in the construction of Tankersley Tunnel *Ian Lloyd*

at this time. The construction of the viaduct here must have been somewhat hampered, for it had to be built over an existing standard gauge mineral railway incline which ran down the cleft between Elsecar and Jump from Hoyland Silkstone Colliery at Platts Common to the canal at Elsecar.

Scott & Middleton locomotives used on Chapletown Branch Extension

Name	Type	Builder	Works No	Date	Notes
LORD COLVILLE	0-6-OST IC	Hunslet Engine	257	1881	1
LIZZIE	0-6-OST IC	Hunslet Engine	164	1876	1
SYDNEY	0-6-OST IC	Manning Wardle	598	1876	2
BEAUCLERC	0-6-OST IC	Manning Wardle	1293	1895	3
SALTBURN	0-6-0(ST?)	Black Hawthorn	511	1882	5
GERTUDE	0-6-OST IC	Manning Wardle	1121	1889	5

Notes

1. *Ex Dransfield & Smith.*
2. *Ex Dransfield & Smith; later with contractors Whittaker Bros at Hull.*
3. *New from Manning Wardle; later with contractors Whittaker Bros at Hull.*
4. *Built by Black, Hawthorn & Company of Gateshead. Further details not known.*
5. *Originally with contractors J D Nowell at Belle Vue, Manchester; to Newton Chambers 1897, renamed TANKERSLEY.*

By inference, Scott & Middleton also worked from the northern end of the line, via Wombwell, to meet up with their workings at Elsecar, for they are known to have used BEAUCLERC based at Stairfoot. Indeed, this locomotive was delivered new from Manning Wardle to Stairfoot for Scott & Middleton. It was almost as if Scott & Middleton regarded their operations based at Stairfoot as totally independent of their Elsecar base, an inference further substantiated by the fact that a supplier of bridges and girderwork other than Newton Chambers was used for the section north from Wombwell Colliery to Barnsley, and also from Stairfoot to Cudworth. The MR's Chapletown Branch extension to Barnsley officially ended at Mount Osborne, one mile east of Barnsley's Court House Station, where it made a junction with the existing MR line from Court House to Cudworth.

BEAUCLERC was in all probability used by Scott & Middleton on the Stairfoot-Cudworth link to the branch, which did not receive final Parliamentary authorization until 6 August, 1897. This section, from Wombwell (Monk Spring Junction) to Cudworth was also built over terrain which was far from ideal. It involved constructing a high 323 yards long skew viaduct at Ardsley to carry the line over the Great Central Railway and two roads; boring the 209 yards long Ardsley tunnel; and finally crossing the River Dearne and a stretch of marshy land just to the south of Cudworth. By 4 November, 1898, *Engineering* was able to report that this final link, just over 2¼ miles in length, was 'making good progress' and it was eventually opened on 11 September, 1899.

The final act in the mutual co-operation between Newton Chambers and Scott & Middleton took place following completion of Tankersley Tunnel in 1896. A board meeting at Thorncliffe on 26 July, 1897, authorised the purchase of GERTRUDE from the contractors. The locomotive, fittingly renamed TANKERSLEY, became part of Thorncliffe's colliery locomotive fleet and served its new owners in this capacity a further 59 years until closure of the drift pit at Thorncliffe in 1955 rendered it surplus to requirements, Figure 5.

The least documented section of the railway, in terms of its construction, was the 3¼ mile long single line goods only

Figure 5. Contractors Scott and Middleton used Manning Wardle 1121 of 1889 on the building of Tankersley Tunnel. The locomotive carried the name GERTRUDE at this stage, but following its purchase by Newton Chambers was soon renamed TANKERSLEY in honour of its former exploits. Photographed at Thorncliffe in the early 1950s *Author's collection*

Wharncliffe Branch to Birdwell and Pilley, which left the branch proper just north of Wombwell. Authorised by Parliamentary Act of 9 June, 1893, this line passed close by several large collieries and coking plants, and in the event was responsible for providing much of the mineral traffic which ran over the line. *The Midland Railway - A Chronology* by John Gough (Railway & Canal Historical Society, 1989) records that the Wharncliffe Branch was opened to goods traffic on 1 September, 1897. It was not, however, until June 1898 that Newton Chambers sealed an agreement with the Midland for the free use of land by the latter in connection with sidings (not built at this stage) to connect Newton Chambers' Rockingham Colliery at Birdwell with the Wharncliffe Branch. Why this delay of almost a year after the branch opened, or is the date quoted by Gough erroneous? I have been unable to confirm which contractor built the Wharncliffe Branch, but have a note that Logan & Hemingway did some work on the MR Chapeltown Branch in 1897, and wonder whether this is relevant.

Mineral Traffic

Nine sizable collieries (three of which were part of the Thorncliffe empire) were linked with the railway on its opening, inclusive of the Wharncliffe Branch, Figure 6. Over the next twenty years or so the traffic generated by these collieries and Thorncliffe Ironworks was supplemented by that from several coke/chemical works, together with the occasional brickworks, quarry and foundry. Most of the mineral movements were achieved using private owner rolling stock carrying the owning companies' distinctive liveries, Figures 7, 8. Appendix 1 lists the undertakings served by the branch.

The first major change in mineral movements on the line occurred in the 1920s. Prior to this time nearly all the collieries served by the line operated 'beehive' coke ovens to manufacture foundry coke from an otherwise unsaleable product, namely small coal (or duff) produced during screening. Consequently coke traffic (from oven batteries at eight distinct sites connected to the branch) was responsible for a sizable proportion of its income. The introduction of large modern batteries of vertical coke ovens in the 1920s enabled a greater proportion of lucrative by-products (tar, benzol and ammonia) to be recovered during carbonization but also had the effect of concentrating coke production at three main sites locally - Wharncliffe Silkstone, Barrow and Smithy Wood Collieries, Figure 9. The first two of these new batteries drew coal from their adjoining

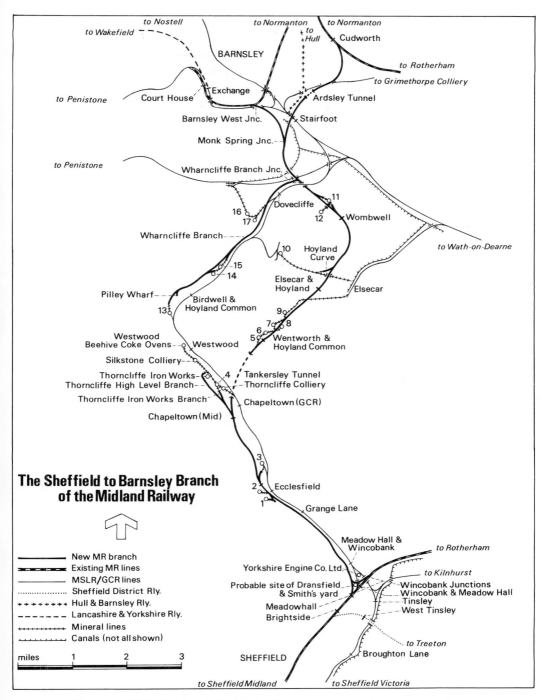

Figure 6. Midland Railway's Sheffield to Barnsley Branch and neighbouring lines.
See Appendix 1 for details of numbered locations *Ian Lloyd*

Figure 7. Barrow Colliery was originally developed by the Barrow Haematite Steel Co Ltd as a source of prime metallurgical coke for the company's iron smelting operations at Barrow in Furness. Once the Midland branch to Barrow Colliery was completed, this coke traffic could travel over MR all the way to Carnforth, whereas previously the first leg of the journey to interchange sidings south of Cudworth had been over rival lines. Some 200 such wagons were supplied to Barrow Steelworks by Roberts in the 1930s to work this coke traffic. This particular example, in yellow and black livery, was built by Charles Roberts in 1937 *Author's collection*

collieries and continued to provide traffic on the branch; additionally the Barrow By-product Ovens coked coal from nearby Barnsley Main and Wombwell Collieries, Figures 10, 11.

Newton Chambers' Smithy Wood Coking Plant, on the other hand, was not connected to the ex-Midland branch. It received its coal feedstock from Thorncliffe and Rockingham Collieries by aerial flight, and despatched its product (principally coke) via the ex-MSLR Sheffield - Barnsley line. Consequently, when the plant came on stream in 1929 the London, Midland & Scottish Railway (LMS), as successor to the Midland, lost significant coke traffic as a result of the closure of Newton Chambers' coke oven sites at Thorncliffe and Rockingham, both effectively superseded by the Smith Wood Plant.

Coke traffic was also lost from Hoyland Silkstone Colliery at the same time, and for a related reason. Newton Chambers had acquired this colliery property, and its associated activities at Platts Common,

Figure 8. Tank wagons were once commonplace on the MR branch for transporting benzol and similar products from the various coking by-products plants. Here we see a rake of such stock, which includes six cylindrical tank wagons for Barrow Colliery newly completed about 1913, in the yard of builders Charles Roberts & Co Ltd, Horbury Junction Wagon Works, Wakefield. The livery was Indian Red for the tank and frames, with plain white lettering. A Lancashire & Yorkshire Railway Aspinall 0-6-0, No 212, is visible on the main line *Author's collection*

Figure 9. Three identical outside cylinder ogee 0-4-0 saddle tank locomotives built by Yorkshire Engine of Sheffield were the shunting mainstay at Wharncliffe Silkstone Colliery for many years. This view shows No 4 (Yorkshire 483 of 1895) in the pit yard about 1910 *Author's collection*

Figure 10. The Barnsley & District Coking and By Products plant adjacent to Barrow Colliery was typical of several such units established in South Yorkshire in the 1920s and 1930s *Author's collection*

Figure 11. Edwardian view of Wombwell Main Colliery, with the MR line prominent on the embankment. The bridge to the left permits the colliery branch to pass under the MR to a small landsale yard and wagon repair area just off the picture. This branch also served Wombwell Quarry, located behind the photographer *Collection J M Ryan*

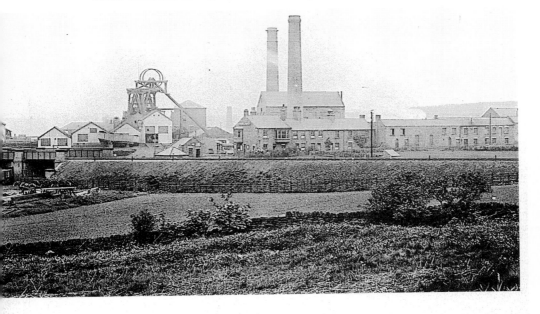

in 1925 from the Hoyland Silkstone Coal & Coke Co Ltd, and very soon merged its underground workings with those of the neighbouring Rockingham Colliery. The Hoyland Silkstone shafts were retained for ventilation purposes and winding men and materials, with coal raising being concentrated at Rockingham. The relatively new Semet Solvay coking and by-products plant at Platts Common was closed as part of Newton Chambers' plan to concentrate coal carbonization activities at Smithy Wood.

World War Two was indirectly responsible for the cessation of iron ore and limestone traffic over the branch into Thorncliffe Ironworks; the former mainly from Northamptonshire quarries and the latter from Topley Pike Quarry near Buxton. Taking Thorncliffe's last blast furnace off wind (stopping the blow) to reduce glare during air raid warnings over a period of months caused premature collapse of the lining, and the furnace was blown out (shut down) for the very last time in October 1942. After a period of 150 years, the almost sacred Thorncliffe tradition of iron smelting had come to an end. The High Level Branch connected to the ex-Midland line was retained for general traffic, but by about 1960 was used mainly to store *Izal* pallet vans. It had been lifted by the mid 1960s and suffered the ultimate ignominy when part of the trackbed which ran behind Newton Chambers' Headquarters Building (*The White House*) was asphalted and used as a car park! A shortened spur - the lower level Ironworks Branch, continued in use until 1971, serving the engineering shops, foundry and chemical works at Thorncliffe, Figure 12.

The serious loss of the Thorncliffe blast furnace traffic was to some

Figure 12. Plate steel for fabrication purposes formed the last regular rail-borne traffic into the Thorncliffe complex. The view shows Newton Chambers No 1 (built by Hudswell Clarke of Leeds, work number D963 of 1956) after it has just coupled up to a short rake of six plate wagons in the 'Midland' low level exchange sidings. 9 March, 1971 *Author*

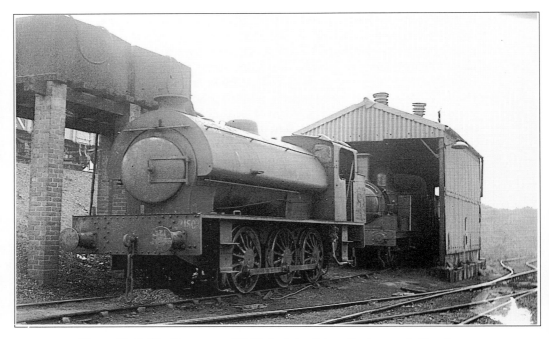

Figure 13. Ex War Department 71507 (built by Robert Stephenson & Hawthorns, works number 7161 of 1944) at the NCB Opencast Executive's Skiers Spring South Disposal Point on 4 September, 1954. The occupant of the shed was ex-LNER class J77 No 8416 (built by the North Eastern Railway at Gateshead in 1877). Both these locomotives moved quite extensively under NCBOE ownership *B Roberts, copyright J A Peden*

extent made good by the upsurge in opencast coal production which occurred locally from the mid-1940s. A number of railhead screens were established alongside the branch, the principle ones being at Skiers Spring, and over the next ten years literally millions of tonnes of opencast coal were despatched by rail, much to electricity generating stations, Figure 13. The majority of the deep mines originally connected with the branch on its opening were still producing coal on Vesting Day (1 January 1947) but most were closed during the 1950s and 1960s by the National Coal Board, following exhaustion of economically workable reserves.

Colliery closures and traffic rationalisation through the 1950s and 1960s drastically reduced the number of loose fitted coal and coke trains originating on the line, which had become part of the nationalised British Railways network in 1948. In particular, the two-stage closure of the Wharncliffe Branch (Pilley to Birdwell in 1954, Birdwell to the Wharncliffe Branch Sidings near Wombwell in

1958) resulted in all the traffic from Barrow Colliery and Coking Plant and Rockingham Colliery being re-routed over ex-MSLR metals into Wath marshalling yard for forward transit. Similar elimination of duplicate railhead facilities at Wombwell Main Colliery about the same time also took its coal traffic off the ex-Midland line and into Wath.

Thus, by the time that Merry-go-round (MGR) hoppers began replacing British Railways' standard sixteen ton mineral wagons for conveying coal to power stations in the 1970s, only one colliery, Skiers Spring, was still served by the ex-Midland line, Figure 14. MGR workings from Skiers Spring were short-lived, however, for rail traffic at the colliery - worked latterly as part of the Rockingham Colliery unit - ceased about September 1975.

The ex-Midland line saw little replacement freight traffic to compensate for the loss of its coal and coke trains. There were two

Figure 14. Skiers Spring Colliery had the distinction of operating some of the last steam locomotives to be built for the Yorkshire Coalfield. Here we see 1962 Leeds-built Hudswell Clarke locomotives (works numbers 1891 and 1892) by the colliery engine shed on 31 August, 1970 *Author*

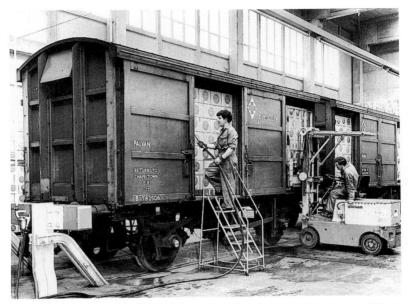

Figure 15. Customised *Izal Palvans* being loaded at the Thorncliffe Chemical Works in the 1960s. The worker to the left is operating a compressed air line which will inflate an air 'cushion' around the bottled goods to protect them from shunting shocks. The vans were finished in *Izal* green, with a white diamond containing a cross. The distinctive red *Izal* logo is located above the word 'products' but is barely discernible in this black & white photograph *Author's collection*

notable but brief exceptions, chemicals and bulk oil products. In the 1950s, Newton Chambers adopted the *Palvan* scheme to allow for safe transit of relatively fragile goods (boxed bottles of *Izal* disinfectants, tins of *Zalpon* liquid soap etc) from its Thorncliffe chemical complex. The goods, stacked on pallets, were dock loaded by fork lift trucks into specially modified vans, Figure 15. Air bags fitted to the interior walls of the vans were inflated once the vans were loaded, thus cushioning the goods against shunting shocks in transit. The *Izal Palvan* fleet carried a distinctive house livery of Izal green with a 'first-aid' cross motif and the *Izal* logo, and formed regular block trains running to various distribution centres.

In the late 1950s the creation of a number of new rail-served fuel distribution centres throughout the UK brought an upsurge of bulk movement of oil products by train from coastal refineries. One such distribution centre was established by Esso on the down (west) side of the line immediately south of Ecclesfield passenger station in the former goods yard, Figure 16. Serving the whole of the northern Sheffield region, the centre was later jointly administered by Shell

Figure 16. Discharging 100 ton oil tank wagons at the Ecclesfield West Depot of Shell Mex and BP. This was the last installation to provide regular freight traffic on the ex-MR branch *Author's collection*

Mex and BP. Block trains to the centre normally originated at Stanlow Refinery in Cheshire and all shunting at the Ecclesfield end was carried out by the BR train locomotive. Regrettably, the terminal was short-lived. Its closure about 1980 was particularly significant, since it marked the end of regular freight traffic over the line.

Passenger Trains

The provision of a passenger service on the line was initially very much a secondary consideration, with the movement of minerals, principally coal, paramount.

Through passenger trains from Sheffield to Barnsley began on 1 July, 1897, a few months after the extension had been officially opened to goods traffic. According to a Mr A H Waters, one time signalman on the line, immediately prior to the passenger service commencing the whole of the employees of the new branch were brought on a special one coach train with workmen at one end and officials at the other. At each station, names were called out and the men were then allotted to their jobs. Before this they had no idea at which location they were to work. On the opening day Elsecar Station was packed and hundreds travelled on the 7.30 am to Wombwell and back for the novelty of the first ride at a return fare of 3d (1.25p), Figure 17.

To work passenger trains on the Barnsley branch, a batch of ten inside cylinder 0-4-4 side tanks, Midland numbers 2238-2247, were allocated to Sheffield. They also worked the Barnsley - Cudworth passenger service, previously worked by a Normanton based engine. Built in 1895 by Dübbs & Co of Glasgow to the designs of S W Johnson, the Midland's Chief Mechanical Engineer, these locomotives had 17 inch diameter by 24 inch stroke cylinders, 5 feet 4′ inches diameter driving wheels, and weighed 53 tons 4cwt in working order, Figure 18.

I have not been able to locate an early timetable for the line, but the 1944 *Bradshaw's Guide to British Railways* showed the basic service to consist of nine weekday and four Sunday trains each way between Sheffield and Barnsley. In addition, on Saturdays and Sundays only there was an extra train from Barnsley to Sheffield. The highest frequency occurred in the mornings and evenings, and during the day trains ran approximately every two hours.

By the post war period, passenger trains were being worked by relatively new LMS Ivatt-designed outside cylinder 2-6-2 side tank

Figure 17. Elsecar and Hoyland Common Station, seen here shortly after completion, was typical of the standard station design employed on the branch
Authors' collection

Figure 18. The inside-cylinder 0-4-4 side tank type was a favourite of the Midland Railway for working passenger trains in secondary lines. Between 1895 and 1900 Dübbs & Co of Glasgow supplied forty such locomotives to Johnson's final 0-4-4T design, ten of which (M R numbers 2238-2247) were allocated to duties in South Yorkshire. The example illustrated, M R number 2625, was from the final (1900) batch *Author's Collection*

locomotives, supplemented from 1952 by ageing ex-LNER (former GCR) Robinson - designed inside cylinder 4-4-2 side tanks.

Major changes to the established routine occurred in 1960, following rationalisation of BR's local passenger services. All local trains on the 'rival' ex-MSLR line from Sheffield (Victoria) to Barnsley (Exchange) had been withdrawn in 1953, services thereafter being concentrated on the former Midland line. Initially these continued to run to Barnsley (Court House) from Sheffield (Midland) but in April 1960, following the construction of a new link at Quarry Junction, east of the town, they began running into Barnsley (Exchange). This development, coupled with the contemporary replacement of the steam hauled trains by diesel railcars, allowed the introduction of a through service from Sheffield to Leeds via Barnsley and Wakefield.

The line has never been regarded as part of a north-south trunk route, though for a period in the 1950s the short-lived 'Thames-Forth Express' (London St Pancras to Edinburgh Princes Street) was routed over it, using the link from Monk Spring Junction to Cudworth to by-pass Barnsley and regain the ex-Midland main line. The opportunity to use this link for such trains, including diversions off the main line, ceased in 1964 when it was abandoned, largely due to the deterioration of Ardsley Tunnel. The section between Cudworth and Ardsley Tunnel was reopened for freight trains after a newly constructed spur connected it in 1967 via the former Hull & Barnsley line to Stairfoot (ex MSLR), but even this arrangement succumbed to full closure, about 1979.

In 1977 the South Yorkshire Passenger Transport Executive began providing financial support for passenger services between Sheffield and Barnsley, and in 1982 Chapeltown Station was re-sited slightly to the south of the original location, putting it closer to the town centre, and improving the town's rail/bus interchange facilities. All the other ex-Midland passenger stations on the branch remain open except Wentworth (originally Wentworth & Hoyland Common), which closed in 1959, and Ecclesfield (1967).

Since 1983 passenger services have been modified several times following the re-opening of the Barnsley - Penistone line (ex MSLR). This has resulted in a markedly improved regional service, and currently on weekdays the Sheffield - Barnsley line offers a basic service of three trains each way every hour. North of Barnsley the service splits, and each hourly trio comprises trains which travel to Leeds, to Wakefield, or to Huddersfield (via Penistone), with equivalent return workings.

Modern developments

Today few traces remain of the Wharncliffe Branch. The whole former mining area from Rockingham Colliery through Barrow to Worsbrough is currently (1996) being opencast and landscaped, a development which is sweeping away traces of the branch trackbed in the process. Some signs of earthworks and bridge remains/abutments are visible between Rockingham and Pilley, then the trackbed is lost once again as it enters the Wharncliffe Silkstone Colliery site, which in recent years has been redeveloped into a light industrial estate.

When the Sheffield-Barnsley line was originally promoted by the Midland Railway, it provided a classic example of needless duplication of the sort for which rival railway companies became notorious. However, the Midland's route served more important centres of population than the earlier MSLR (ex South Yorkshire Railway) rival line and this aspect of its geography has fortuitously kept it in business.

So, although coal, iron and associated heavy industries provided the line's life blood for over 80 years, from about 1980 the movement of passengers has become its sole function. However, without the South Yorkshire PTE grants, this passenger service would face an uncertain future. Despite these problems, which are common to many secondary lines on the British Rail network, one hopes the line will survive privatisation to celebrate its centenary in 1997.

Acknowledgements and Sources

This article is based on one which was first published in the official journal of the Industrial Railway Society, the *Industrial Railway Record* (issue No 136, 1994). I am grateful to *Record* editor Cliff Shepherd and the IRS for permission to reproduce it here and thus make it more widely available. The section on passenger trains has been added to the present version to give a more balanced treatment for the general reader.

Thanks are due to my former employer, Newton Chambers & Co Ltd, for allowing me access in 1970-71 to its archives, which form the basis for much of the early part of this account. The periodical *Engineering* proved a useful contemporary source of information, and individual references are cited in the main text. I have also consulted various editions of *Bradshaw's Railway Manual and Shareholders' Guide* and the Railway Clearing House *Handbook of Stations including Junctions, Sidings, Collieries, Works etc.* Much of the information on the contractors and their locomotives was kindly provided by Ken Plant and Jim Peden, and the maps were specially prepared by Ian Lloyd. I also acknowledge the help of Roy Etherington, Gordon Green, Frank Jones, Ron Redman, John Ryan and the late Mrs Stenton of Elsecar (for access to the diaries of her grandfather, Mr G Johnson). Information relating to the post British Railways period, especially 1955 onwards, is based heavily on personal observations.

Appendix 1

Industrial Undertakings Served by the Wincobank (Sheffield) to Barnsley Branch

This list covers the sidings connected to the line cumulatively from 1892 to 1980. The siding numbers are not official railway nomenclature but have been adopted to simplify site locations on the accompanying map. Undertakings shown in bold type are known to have employed industrial locomotives for shunting. At the remainder, shunting was carried out by the railway company, or gravity (or, in the case of Rockingham Colliery, by gravity and horses).

Siding No	Installation	Period Served	Notes
1	John Robinson Ltd, Royds Foundry	c1920-1929	
	Brightside Foundry & Engineering Co.Ltd	1929-1968	
2	Esso Oil Terminal (later Shell Mex &BP)	c1960-c1980	
3	**Smithy Wood Colliery**	c1893-1961	a, b
	(incl. beehive ovens to c1910)		
4	**Newton Chambers & Co Ltd, Thorncliffe**		
	A large industrial complex including the following rail-served installations:-		
	Thorncliffe blast furnaces	1892-1942	a
	Thorncliffe foundry	1892-1971	a
	Thorncliffe colliery	1892-1955	a
	Thorncliffe coke ovens	1892-1929	a
	Norfolk tar works	1892-1900	a
	Izal chemical works	1900-1971	
	Thorncliffe brickworks	1892-c1920	a
	Chapeltown foundry	c1905-1920	
	A Newton Chambers' private standard gauge mineral line also gave connection to Silkstone Colliery and Westwood beehive ovens.		
5	**Ministry of Fuel and Power, Harley opencast coal dock**	c1944-c1947	
6	**Lidgett Colliery**	1897-1911	a
7	Skiers Spring Brickworks (J Smith & partners)	1900-1910	
	Earl Fitzwilliam's Skiers Spring pottery and brickworks	1910-c1919	
	NCB Opencast Executive Wentworth North coal disposal point	c1948-1954	
	NCB Skiers Spring Colliery	1955-c1975	
8	**NCB Opencast Executive Wentworth coal disposal point**	c1948-1954	
9	Adamson's Siding (A Adamson)	1921-c1925	
	Skiers Spring Drift (Earl Fitzwilliam)	c1925-c1931	
10	**Hoyland Silkstone Colliery** and coke ovens	1897-1929	a
11	**Wombwell Main Colliery**, including coke ovens and brickworks	1897-c1960	a, b
12	Wombwell Wood Quarry	1897-c1936	a, d

13	**Wharncliffe Silkstone Colliery**, including coke ovens, brickworks and Knoll Drift Pit (latter c1912-c1930)	c1897-1954	a, b
14	**Ministry of Fuel and Power, Rockingham Opencast Coal Stocking Ground**	c1946-1949	
15	Rockingham Colliery, including coke ovens (latter until 1929)	1898-c1959	a, e
16	**Barrow Colliery**, including beehive ovens (latter until c1925)	c1897-c1959	a, b
17	**Barrow Coking and By-products Plant** (Barnsley District Coking Co Ltd)	c1925-c1959	b

Notes

a   *Prior to the earliest date shown, the installation was already being served by a connection to MSLR lines.*

b   *After the last date shown, the site continued to be served by an alternative main line connection, over former MSLR lines.*

c   *Developed initially as service pit for Rockingham Colliery by Newton Chambers c1913. No known industrial locomotives here prior to NCB Opencast Executive use of sidings. Rail traffic ceased 1975; full closure of colliery took place in 1979.*

d   *Thought to have been shunted by Wombwell Main Colliery locomotives.*

e   *After c1959, served by former MSLR lines. Colliery ultimately (from 1974) shunted by industrial diesel locomotive.*

16. MEDIEVAL AND RENAISSANCE STAINED GLASS IN THE VICINITY OF BARNSLEY

by Brian Sprakes

THE OLDEST STAINED GLASS in the vicinity of Barnsley is the excavated glass from the ruins of Monk Bretton Priory which was dedicated to St Mary Magdalene. The priory was founded c1154 as a Cluniac house and colonised from La-Charitie-sur-Loire, but from 1281 the order changed to Benedictine until it was dissolved in 1538.

There were two excavations during which fragments of glass were discovered (Figure 1). The results of the first were published in 1926 and showed that most of the glass came from a dump outside the north wall of the Infirmary kitchen and a few fragments from the east end of the church which had been extended eastwards in the fifteenth century.[1] The second excavation took place in 1937 when over thirty pieces were recovered from an unrecorded location. All of this glass was heavily pitted and decayed. After conservation work in London the glass was eventually returned in the late 1950s and is now in store in the Weston Park Museum, Sheffield.

Most of the glass is of the type commonly called *grisaille* - from the French meaning to paint grey, and consists of acanthus patterns boldly painted in black on white or clear glass, and against a cross-hatched background. The patterns found on the fragments are similar to the geometric grisaille glass at Lincoln Cathedral and would therefore appear to be of a similar date - 1265-85.[2] Two fifteenth century 'strapwork' border quarries were also found executed in black paint and yellow stain on white glass. Similar quarries of this type and date (c1485) can still be seen in the windows of the north chapel at St Peter's, Woolley, the advowson of which was held by the Prior and Convent of Monk Bretton.

The rest of the surviving glass in the area belongs to the Tudor period, namely the reigns of Henry VII (1485-1509) and Henry VIII (1509-1547), when so much glass was painted for the churches of South and West Yorkshire including Darton, Royston and Woolley. Though much of this glass has either disappeared or is in a fragmentary condition, there are two sets of records which stand out from the others which give invaluable information by means of heraldry and Latin inscriptions placed in the windows by the donors. The first, Roger Dodsworth's Yorkshire *Church Notes,* made between 1619-31, were eventually published in 1904.[3] The importance of these notes is that they were made before the Civil War and the iconoclasm of the Commonwealth era which followed. Dodsworth (1585-1654) was the son of Matthew Dodsworth, Registrar of York Minster, and had access to the records there. He also possessed notes relating to Robert Glover's heraldic *Visitation of Yorkshire* which took place in 1584-85. Dodsworth later studied in the library of Sir Robert Cotton in London, and had access to the records in the Tower of London. The second major source is the Reverend Joseph Hunter's South Yorkshire: *The History and Topography of the Deanery of Doncaster,* published in two volumes, in 1828 and 1831. Hunter (1783-1861) was born in Sheffield and is buried in

Figure 1. Excavated glass from Monk Bretton Priory

Ecclesfield churchyard. In 1833 he was appointed sub-commissioner of the Records Commission in London, becoming Assistant Keeper in 1838 when the Public Record Office was established.[4] Hunter repeated Dodsworth's notes but with several additions and corrections. Again, the value of this work is that it was written before the 'Victorian Revival' when much fragmentary medieval glass was swept away or was crowded into one window irrespective of age or iconographical content, as is the case at Ecclesfield.

The advowson of the church at Darton (All Saints) was anciently in the hands of the Lacis, the earls of Lancaster, and afterwards the Lancastrian kings Henry IV and Henry V as dukes of Lancaster until the reign of Richard III when a great change took place. In the first year of his reign (1483) Richard granted the advowson to the Prior and Convent of Monk Bretton. They presented Richard Hunter to the archbishop as vicar, not rector as it had been previously, and he was duly instituted on 29 June 1484. But when Henry VII deposed Richard in 1485 he tried to remove Hunter and presented Thomas Ridley as rector on 14 December 1486, so Darton had both a vicar and a rector vying for control of the parish. It seems that Hunter prevailed and continued as vicar, though Ridley retained some interest in the parish. Hunter died in 1522 when William Harrison succeeded him. So Hunter was the vicar during the time when Thomas Tykyll, prior of Monk Bretton, was altering the chancel at Darton and the parishioners were rebuilding the nave.

John Heathfield, vicar of Darton, 1642-54, was in the habit of writing notes in the margin of the parish register. One note refers to the almost complete rebuilding of the church: 'The church and quire of Darton were built in 1517. The steeple [tower] was built by a vicar before that time.' This appears to be Hunter's work, for there was once in the belfry window a shield bearing three stags' heads - an obvious illusion to Hunter. To this day the wallplate of the chancel has this inscription cut into it:

> Ad laudem Dei Omnium Sanctorum istum cancellum de novo
> consruxit Thomas Tykyll prior monaserii Monk Britanniae,
> et hujus ecclesiae patronis: et eundem complete finivit
> anno Domini millesimo quingentissimo decimo septimo.[5]

Dodsworth, in September 1623, recorded the following inscription in the east window of the chancel beneath the figure of St Mary Magdalene and a shield of the arms of Monk Bretton :

> Orate pro bono statu Thome [Tykyll,Prioris] de Monkbretton
> et hujus ecclesiae patroni qui hanc fenestram [fieri fecit]
> anno Domini MCCCCCXXVI.[6]

The inscription and coat of arms have gone, but the figure of St Mary Magdalene is now in a window (nIV) in the north aisle of the nave, Figure 2. The saint is portrayed full length with a halo and holding a long tress of her hair with which she dried Christ's feet after washing them with her tears, and in the other hand is a jar of ointment with which she then anointed the feet (Luke 7:37). Beneath this figure and on two separate pieces of glass is written Sca [sancta] Magdalena. The window has a thin border of collected medieval fragments, and in the base of the window appears: 'This window was restored at the expense of the women of the church

1959'. The restorer was A G Mills.

The church at Royston (St John's) was given to the Priory of Monk Bretton by Adam Fitz-swein before his death in 1158 and remained in their hands until the dissolution, 21 November 1539. The remaining glass is a disappointing display of late fifteenth century fragments leaded into the tracery lights of the vestry and the windows on the south side of the church. The fragments are of architectural canopies; brocaded backcloths against which figures once stood; parts of a rayed mandorla from a depiction of the ascension of Christ or the Virgin Mary; and parts of at least three golden eagles. There is also part of a man's face in the east window of the south chapel. This arrangement was devised in 1980. [7]

Dodsworth, on 11 July 1621, records the donors of some of the windows: the east window of the chapel contained the arms of Stangeways together with an inscription telling us that he was the donor, but no date. Also in this window were the arms of Lord Darcy, complete with supporters as befitted his rank. In the south window of the chapel was a shield bearing the arms of Oxspring and Wortley set above donor figures showing a man in armour together with his wife and three daughters. The inscription asked for prayers for William Oxspring and Elizabeth, his wife, but no date. In a window in the north chapel was a shield of Bosvile (of Chevet) quartering Tempest and the inscription asked for prayers for John Bosvile and his wife and children, again no date given. In another window in the north chapel was a picture of *An angell holding a plough drawn by four Oxen, and another angel driving. Above written: God speed the plough. And send us corn enow* [enough]. Of all these, only four coats of arms remained in 1831 when Hunter made his notes: *In the south chapel the arms of Oxspring and Wortley. In the north chapel the arms of Bosvile and Mounteney*, not Tempest as Dodsworth said. The arms have identical charges but differed in tinctures, so Dodsworth was mistaken. Of these nothing remains.

Figure 2. St Mary Magdalene, nIV, Darton *RCHME (Crown Copyright)*

Externally, All Saints Church at Silkstone appears to be wholly Perpendicular. The western tower was built by the Cluniac priory of Pontefract after 1479, and the rest altered before the beginning of the sixteenth century when it seems that a complete reglazing scheme was begun. Dodsworth's notes of 1629 show that two of the windows were given by the townships of Thurgoland and Hoylandswain, the other windows contained the shields of arms, donor figures and inscriptions of local families:

'North Quyer' (chapel). The arms of Everingham and Wadisley together with kneeling figures of Henry Everingham and his wife Margory Wadisley accompanied by their six sons and three daughters. Usual inscription but no date.

'Great East Window'. The arms of Lord Darcy together with shields of Dransfield and Clarell.

'In the South Window' (of the south chapel) was an inscription to Nicholas Nicols and Elizabeth his wife. The date broken out. 'South Ile of the church:Pray for the sawles [souls] of John Denton and Julyane his wife who made this window in the yere of Our Lord MoCCCCoXVIJ', and 'Pray for the good statys of ye township of Thurgoland the founders hereof.' This may have referred to a guild chapel within the church. These are the only inscriptions in English, all the others were in Latin as was usually the case.

'In the belhouse window' the arms of Everingham and Keresforth.

'North window' - given by the people of Hoylandswain, and other north windows given by John Galber and Agnes his wife, and Richard Thurgoland and Joan his wife. No dates given.

The only window to retain any stained glass is the east window of the south chapel where there are two shields which Dodsworth saw, one now fragmentary, the other virtually intact. The fragmentary shield to the left is almost unrecognisable but once displayed the arms of England impaling Castile and Leon. It is of fourteenth century date but has been heavily patched - one intruded piece is part of a seventeenth century sundial[8] and the shape of the shield has also been altered to match the one in the next light to the right. This is the shield of Charles Brandon, Duke of Suffolk (d 1545), second husband of Mary, daughter of Henry VII and widow of Louis XII of France. The shield is typical of the Tudor era with flaunched sides, and dates from about 1540. It has been suggested that two heraldic crests of the Wentworth family, dated c1800, and removed from the redundant church in the grounds of Wentworth Castle, be inserted into this window, close to the Wentworth tombs.

St Peter's Church at Woolley was originally a chapelry of Royston parish and so was also in the gift of the prior and convent of Monk Bretton. The church was almost completely rebuilt at the end of the fifteenth and the beginning of the sixteenth centuries - the nave and chapels first, and then the chancel under the direction of prior Thomas Tickhill,1504-1523.[9] A lost portrait panel from the east window had an inscription asking for prayers for the soul of the prior who died whilst still in office. This was flanked by portraits of Richard Woodrove (d1522) and Beatrix Fitzwilliam his second wife, and it seems that all three were joint donors of the window.

Four windows still have some ancient glass in them - the east window of the south chapel, and three in the north chapel. All of this glass is so heavily restored that it almost amounts to a complete reconstruction of the windows by the firm of Clayton & Bell under the famous architect John Loughborough Pearson during his restoration of the church, 1869-71. And it is clear that some heraldry was introduced into the glass that had not previously been seen. Most of the remaining medieval glass has been moved around and so is not in its original position.

The east window of the north chapel (nII) shows a Crucifiction scene, *Ecce Mater Tua*, Figure 3.[10] In the centre is the Crucified Christ set between the Virgin Mary and John the Evangelist. Of the Virgin, only the head and left hand are original, Christ's head, the upper part of the cross bearing INR, and a few sections of canopy are also old, as is the head of St John with his 'corkscrew' hairstyle. The rest is from the1871 restoration.[11]

Two of the three windows in the north wall of this chapel also hold some ancient glass. In the centre of the middle window (nIV) is the large figure of St George and the Dragon with shields of arms to either side and two small donor figures with fragments of inscriptions below. The figure of St George is Victorian. In the left-hand light the shields of Wheatley impaling Dransfield and Woodrove belong to the early sixteenth century. Beneath these is the heavily restored donor figure of John Woodrove (d1487), which was formerly in the east window together with his inscription. In the right-hand light is another shield of Wheatley set above the arms of Hammerton with its three hammers on the shield, and below this the figure of Elizabeth Hammerton, the wife of John Woodrove and again removed from the east window. Only the prayer desk is original, the figure is a reconstruction.

To the left of this, the next window (nV) displays the figure of the Risen Christ in the centre, with more shields of arms in the outer lights. The Risen Christ stands facing the beholder, holding a Banner of Victory, his right hand raised in benediction, thus revealing the wound in his side and the holes in his hands. The head is really the head of God the Father taken from another window and although parts of the robe are old the rest is a nineteenth century conjectural reconstruction. Beneath the figure is the inscription *Ego*

Figure 3.   Ecce Mater Tua, nII, Woolley
RCHME (Crown Copyright)

sum resurrectio et vita. In the left-hand light are sixteenth century shields of Wheatley with an unidentified impalement (heavily restored); Woodrove impaling Hammerton; and Wheatley again. Fragments of inscriptions below. The right-hand light shows the arms of Popley with its three eagles displayed; Frost with a chevron between three trefoils; and Mirfield with restored passant lions. Beneath these are more fragments of inscriptions.

The east window of the south chapel (sII) is another composite window showing the Holy Trinity flanked by the Virgin and Child; and St Catherine (Figure 4). The crowned Virgin cradles Christ in her left arm and offers him a pear-shaped fruit. The figures are early sixteenth century but her dress, and the background and canopy are Victorian.

In the central light God the Father is seated supporting the Risen Christ on his knee. The Holy Spirit is portrayed as a winged dove just above Christ's head. The figures, lower canopy arch, and floor tiles are original. The rest, date from 1871. St Catherine is also crowned. She holds a book and the wheel of her martyrdom. A descending scroll bears the inscription Sancta Catherina. The figure, scroll and some of the floor tiles are original. In 1661 Dr Nathanial Johnston of Pontefract saw this figure with one of St Margaret in another window.

Dodsworth visited the church in 1627. He recorded many of the inscriptions and shields noted above. One north aisle window that has completely disappeared was given by Edward Haygh, chaplain of the chantry in the church,

Donors have always played an important part in the glazing of churches but two in particular stand out above the others. The first is obvious - prior Thomas Tickhill was the driving force in the renovations not only at Monk Bretton, but also Darfield, Royston and Woolley. The second is not immediately apparent. The arms of Robert Frost appear in window nV in the north chapel at Woolley, and Dodsworth tells us that this shield, together with the following inscription appeared in a window in the north aisle of the church: *Orate pro anima Magistri Roberti Frost, sacerdotes.* Robert Frost was rector of Thornhill, 1482-98; rector of Tankersley,1486;prebendary of York, 1490-1507;archdeacon of Stow (Lincoln), 1497-1506 and prebendary of Lichfield, 1500-1507. After holding all of these offices he retired to the vicarage of Sandal Magna (Wakefield) in 1511 where he died and is buried in the chapel. His will directs that his arms be placed in the churches of Tankersley, Thornhill, Warmfield and Woolley.

Figure 4. Virgin and Child, Holy Trinity and St Catherine, sII, Woolley *RCHME (Crown Copyright)*

Notes and References

1. Barker W R 'Notes on the Medieval Window Glass found at Monk Bretton Priory', *Yorkshire Archaeological Society*, extra volume V, pp103-5
2. Morgan N J *The Medieval Stained Glass of of Lincoln Cathedral*, The British Academy. O.U.P. (Figure C. 12:15;17)
3. *Yorkshire Archaeological Society*, Record Series, volume XXIV, 1904
4. Hunter was the editor of the first *Pipe Roll*, and of the first volume of the *Fleet o f Fines*. He also wrote the introduction to the *Valor Ecclesiasticus*.
5. Thomas Tickhill, prior of Monk Bretton,1504-23
6. Sable, three covered cups argent. The covered cups are an allusion to St Mary Magdalene's ointment jar.
7. By the Modern Art Glass Company of Leeds and Pudsey.
8. The sundial was very probably the work of Henry Gyles of York who did much work for the Wentworth family in the second half of the sixteenth century, and in whose chapel the window stands.
9. Walker J W 'The Manor and Church of Woolley', *Yorkshire Archaeological Journal*, volume XXVII, 1924,pp296-311
10. Following the *Corpus Vitrearum Medii Aevi* international window numbering system.
11. Letters and papers deposited in the vestry safe. The restoration was ordered by the vicar, the Rev Frederick Fawkes, together with G H Wentworth, Esquire.

THE CONTRIBUTORS

1. LIFE IN SERVICE AT WENTWORTH CASTLE

Phyllis Crossland (née Bramall) was born at Oxspring. She attended the village school until the age of eleven, when her education continued at Penistone Grammar School for the next five years. After two years spent in commercial work she took a two year course at Darlington Training College to qualify for the teaching profession. Her career was interrupted after marriage in order to bring up three children but she resumed teaching later on, her last school before retiring being Oxspring which she first attended as a five year old. Being married to a farmer, Phyllis has, over the years, also helped with work on the land. She has three published books: *Years of Grace*, *Echoing Hills* and *On Active Service 1939-45*, and several magazine articles. Other articles have appeared in previous *Aspects* volumes. She lives with her husband Charles at Trunce Farm, Greenmoor. They have three daughters and four grand-children.

2. MAPPLEWELL BETHEL

Joan Hartley (neé Birkinshaw), born in Mapplewell and a member of Mapplewell Bethel Methodist Church until its closure, was educated at local schools and in Barnsley. Later she trained as a teacher at Avery Hill College, specialising in English and History. Most of her teaching life was for the West Riding Education Authority. Her last post before early retirement was Head of English at the Cathedral CE School in Wakefield. She has lived in Great Cliffe, Crigglestone, for about thirty-eight years but still takes an interest in Mapplewell affairs. She and her husband Ken are active in church work and they are also involved in fund raising for the RNLI Her leisure activities are reading, writing, music, nature watching, gardening with Ken, getting together with friends and a little light crochet and tatting.

3. JOSEPH WILKINSON OF BARNSLEY

John Goodchild is a native of Wakefield and was educated at the Grammar school there. He has been active in local historical research since about the age of thirteen, and is the author of 140 books and published essays on aspects of the history of the West Riding. He was founder-Curator of Cusworth Hall Museum and subsequently Archivist to Wakefield MDC; in his retirement he runs a Local History Study Centre at Wakefield which houses his immense collection of manuscripts and research materials, and which is open to use, free of charge, by appointment. Mr Goodchild holds an honorary M Univ from the Open University, awarded for academic and scholarly distinction and for public services. Outside historical research, his interests lie in Freemasonry and in Unitarianism - and his dog.

4. Barnsley, Becketts and Big Ben

Gerald Alliott was born in Crewe but came to Barnsley in 1934 where he has spent most of his life. He began his career at Barclays Bank in Barnsley staying there for five years, interrupted by almost three years in the RAF. The following five years were spent in a local law office where he was also assistant secretary to the Barnsley Chamber of Commerce. In his late twenties he married Gloria and together they went into business at Townend with two shops and a wholesale confectionery business. This carried on for twenty five years when all the properties were demolished to make way for the new Westway. His last six years were spent back in Cheshire as Estate Director at Great Moreton Hall near Congleton. He retired in 1988 and decided to come back to Barnsley where he became a member of various local history groups, researching and writing local history. He is the author of *Vanishing Relics of Barnsley*, also published by Wharncliffe Publishing Ltd. He has two sons, Simon, a solicitor practising in Barnsley and Nicholas who is an officer with the Woodland Trust in North Yorkshire.

5. Joseph Beaumont, Mining Steward

Geoffrey Hall is a married man with a son and daughter, and two grandchildren. Born in Hoyland, where he has lived all his life, he was educated at the village schools before gaining a scholarship to Ecclesfield Grammar where he matriculated in seven subjects. After leaving school he worked for a few months at Newton, Chambers and Co Ltd prior to beginning a career in mining at Rockingham Colliery. Having found his vocation he attended Barnsley Mining and Technical College part time, obtaining his Colliery Manager Certificate in 1955. His first managerial post was at Rockingham Colliery in 1958. History has always been his favourite subject and meeting local historian Arthur Clayton, whilst working underground at Rockingham Colliery, resulted in a friendship which has encouraged him to research the ironstone mining industry of the locality and the history of Messrs W H and G Dawes at the Milton and Elsecar Ironworks. *Mining Verses* was the subject of his previous contribution in *Aspects of Barnsley* (1993).

6. Child Labour in Mines in the Barnsley Area in the Early Victorian Period

Melvyn Jones, who is editor of *Aspects of Rotherham 1* and *2*, was born in Barnsley and educated at the Holgate Grammar School and the universities of Nottingham and Leeds. He taught for seven years at Myers Grove, Sheffield's first comprehensive school, and then for nine years at Sheffield City College of Education before its amalgamation into Sheffield City Polytechnic in 1976. He is now Head of Academic Resources in the School of Leisure and Food Management at Sheffield Hallam University. He has written extensively on the economic and social history of South Yorkshire. Recent publications include *A Most Enterprising Thing* (an illustrated history of Newton Chambers) and a revised edition of the widely acclaimed *Sheffield's Woodland Heritage*. A new book on *Rotherham's Woodland Heritage* was published by Rotherham Libraries, Museum and Arts in 1995. He is co-editor of *Chapeltown and High Green*, a new title in Chalford Publishing's Archive Photographs series.

6. Child Labour in Mines in the Barnsley Area in the Early Victorian Period

Joan Jones (née Gregory) was brought up in Charlton Brook near Chapeltown and was educated at Ecclesfield Grammar School, Matlock College of Education and what is now Sheffield Hallam University. She has taught in primary schools in the West Riding, Nottingham and Sheffield, latterly as Deputy Head at Bankwood School. She is currently on secondment to Sheffield Hallam University where she is a Senior Lecturer in the School of Education. She is Honorary Secretary of the Chapeltown and High Green Archive which was founded in 1987. The Archive is noted for its wide range of publications and Joan has most recently co-edited *A Most Enterprising Thing* (a history of Newton Chambers at Thorncliffe) and *Ecclesfield Parish: People and Places*. Between 1983-86 Joan acted as adviser to the award-winning BBC TV's schools history series *Now and Then*. She is co-editor of *Chapeltown and High Green*, a new title in Chalford Publishing's Archive Photographs series.

7. Uncle Ben in America

Philip Hansen has spent most of his life in Southampton, but came to Sheffield in 1990. He has always had a strong interest in the past and trained as a historian at Southampton and the Open Universities, before moving to Sheffield University, where he began postgraduate work on British political history. He was awarded a PhD in 1995 for his thesis on the attitude of British radicals to Eastern Europe between 1900 and 1914. While writing his dissertation, he worked as a research assistant for Geoffrey Tweedale on a Leverhulme project on Sheffield's steel industry. More recently, he has been writing a commissioned history of William Cook Plc, the largest manufacturer of steel castings in Europe.

7. Uncle Ben in America

Geoffrey Tweedale has been studying industrial history for nearly twenty years, first at the London School of Economics (where he was awarded an MSc and PhD in American economic history), then later at Manchester and Sheffield University. He has written a number of books and articles on the history of computers, pharmaceuticals and British businessmen, but his main field of interest has been the Sheffield steel industry. He has recently completed a detailed history of the subject - *Steel City: Entrepreneurship, Strategy and Technology in Sheffield, 1743-1993* (Oxford University Press, 1995) - and another study, *The Sheffield Knife Book*, was published by Hallamshire Press in 1996. He is currently Senior Wellcome Fellow at Manchester Metropolitan University, where he is writing a book on the history of occupational health in the asbestos industry.

8. Barnsley Comes of Age

Harold Taylor was born in Staincross. After attending Barnsley Grammar School, he studied Geography at Cambridge University before entering a career in schoolteaching. Since retiring he has followed his interest in local history. Membership of the South Yorkshire Industrial History Society (Sheffield Trades Historical Society) involved him in the study of the former linen industry of Barnsley and district, in particular with the handloom weavers' cottages and the bleachworks. Tracing his own family history in Staincross-Mapplewell led him to make a study of the hand-made nail industry of the village. He has followed this with research into the influence of the Non-Conformist chapels on the musical, social and educational activities.

9. The Superlative Professor Best

James Walker was born in Rotherham, the youngest of four children. His father, a steelworks blast furnaceman, was from a mining background and his grandmother's family were of Penistone origin. He studied medicine at the University of Sheffield, graduating in 1983 and furthered his post-graduate training in Barnsley. Since 1990 he has been a full-time GP in Worsbrough. He gives talks on old remedies and related topics, and takes a keen interest in local history. He has written for maedical journals and is a regular contributor to *Aspects of Barnsley*. In 1994 he was appointed as a Trainer in General Practice by the University of Sheffield, and now combines his clinical work with teaching post-graduate doctors. He lives in Chapeltown, Sheffield with his wife Vicky and children Kate, Rebecca and Lucy.

10. Barnsley's Photographic Pioneers

Brian Elliott was born in the Barnsley area, the son of a miner. He left Edward Sheerian Secondary Modern school at the age of fifteen and had several jobs until part-time study enabled entry to Matlock College of Education where he obtained a B Ed(Hons) degree. Whilst teaching at Royston Comprehensive School Brian tutored a series of local history courses for the WEA and University of Sheffield and published short histories of Royston parish. He continued his interest in local history, researching his home town for an MPhil, completed at the University of Sheffield in 1990. His book, *The Making of Barnsley* (1988) was the first published history of the town since Victorian times. He initiated the *Aspects* series, edits the Barnsley and forthcoming Doncaster volumes and advises Wharncliffe Publishing Ltd on matters relating to local books. Since 1984 he has worked at Rother Valley College, Dinnington, where he is now Head of the School of General Education.

11. BARNSLEY'S WELLINGTON STREET THEATRE

Coral M P ('Kate') Taylor was born in Wakefield in 1933 and educated at the Girls' High School before going on to St Anne's College, Oxford, where she read English Language and Literature. After teaching in Leeds, at West Park C S School and the City of Leeds and Carnegie College of Education, she took up a post as Principal Lecturer in English at Wentworth Castle College of Education at Stainborough. Following the closure of the College she became Vice-Principal (Community) at the Barnsley Sixth Form College when it opened in 1979. Since her retirement in 1990 she has spent her time researching local history, in particular in the field of entertainment. Her book *Right Royal: Wakefield Theatre 1776-1994* was published in 1995. She works part-time as a tutor for the Open University and is the Hon Managing Editor of Wakefield Historical Publications, President of Wakefield Historical Society and Chairman of the Mercia Cinema Society.

12. OPEN ALL HOURS

Eileen Umpleby was born in Barnsley and educated at Barnsley Girls' High School and Barnsley Technical College. Her early employment, from 1939-46, was at the Education Department, Town Hall, for the most part as secretary to the Director of Education. She married Tom Umpleby (also an *Aspects* contributor) and had three children. Later, she qualified as a primary school teacher at Wentworth Castle Training College; thereafter teaching at schools in Barnsley, London and Sheffield. After retirement she studied for a BA (Hons) with the Open University.

13. SHEPHERDS, SHEEP AND GENTLEMEN

Sam Sykes is a regular contributor to *Aspects of Barnsley*. His interest in agricultural history and traditional local livestock is reflected in the present contribution. Sam is a native of Dodworth and began his working life as an apprentice at Dodworth Colliery. He left to take a BA (Hons) in Fine Art and Art History, followed by an MA in Local History at the University of Sheffield. He now lectures in the Adult Education section of Sheffield College. Sam lives at Dunford Bridge where, with his wife, Sue, he keeps a smallholding. Needless to say, rare breeds, especially *Penistone* sheep are a great interest.

14. CONCEPTION AND CONSTRUCTION OF THE BARNSLEY CANAL

Roger Glister was born a stone's throw away from the Sheffield and South Yorkshire Navigation at Sprotbrough. This close association with the 'cut' has resulted in a life-long interest in inland waterways about which he writes extensively. He is a long-standing member of the Waterway Recovery Group, the national body for the organisation of voluntary labour for canal restoration. Lately his efforts have concentrated on the two Barnsley Canals. Educated at Mexborough Grammar School and the Doncaster College of Technology, he is an engineer by profession and a specialist in church heating. His other interests include fell-walking and vintage cars. This is Roger's second contribution to *Aspects of Barnsley*.

15. A MIDLAND RAILWAY BRANCH IN SOUTH YORKSHIRE

Trevor Lodge, Sheffield born and bred, was educated in the city's Abbeydale Grammar School and Manchester and Sheffield Universities. An industrial chemist by training, he had an earlier career which comprised spells of teaching interspersed by a memorable (but all too brief!) period as a research chemist with Newton, Chambers & Co Ltd at Chapeltown. He eventually 'found his feet' in South Yorkshire's special steels industry, retraining as a metallurgist in the early 1970s and currently works as an Information Officer. He was editor of *Industrial Railway Record*, the journal of the Industrial Railway Society, between 1971 and 1979, and is still a regular contributor. His most notable published works - the histories of Park Gate Iron & Steel Co. Ltd; Steel, Peech & Tozer Ltd and Samuel Fox & Co Ltd - appeared in British Steel's *Steel News* and United Engineering Steels *Stocksbridge Gazette*, between 1981 and 1993. He is a regular contributor to Wharncliffe's *Aspects* series.

16. MEDIEVAL STAINED GLASS

Brian Sprakes was born in Doncaster in 1937. He studied European Architecture and Stained Glass & Heraldry as a mature student in Sheffield and has been a part-time lecturer for the WEA and Sheffield University since 1973. He is author of several articles for art journals and learned societies. In 1987 has was appointed author for the international *Corpus Vitrearum Medii Aevi*, charged with the task of cataloguing medieval stained glass. South Yorkshire awaits publication, and work is in progress on Nottinghamshire. He is also Stained Glass adviser to the Diocese of Sheffield.

272